MEN IN BLACK

MEN IN BLACK

HOW THE SUPREME COURT
IS DESTROYING AMERICA

Mark R. Levin

Since 1947
REGNERY
PUBLISHING, INC.
An Eagle Publishing Company • Washington, DC

Library of Congress Cataloging-in-Publication Data
Levin, Mark (Mark Reed), 1957–
Men in black : how the Supreme Court is destroying America / Mark Levin.
    p. cm.
Includes bibliographical references and index.
ISBN 0-89526-050-6 (hardcover)
ISBN 1-59698-009-5 (paperback)
1. Judges—United States—Popular works. 2. Judge-made law—United States—Popular works. 3. Justice, Administration of—United States—Popular works. I. Title.
KF8775.Z9L48 2004
347.73'14—dc22
2004026156

First paperback edition published in 2006

Published in the United States by
Regnery Publishing, Inc.
One Massachusetts Avenue, NW
Washington, DC 20001
www.regnery.com

Distributed to the trade by
National Book Network
Lanham, MD 20706

Manufactured in the United States of America

10 9 8 7 6 5 4 3 2 1
Books are available in quantity for promotional or premium use. Write to Director of Special Sales, Regnery Publishing, Inc., One Massachusetts Avenue NW, Washington, DC 20001, for information on discounts and terms or call (202) 216-0600.

For the Levin family: my wife, Kendall; our children, Lauren and Chase; my parents, Norma and Jack; and my brothers, Doug and Rob.

Contents

Foreword to the Paperback Edition

I wrote *Men in Black* to warn you, my fellow citizens, that our freedoms are at risk from judges who usurp the Constitution. I wanted to help spur a national debate—as I do on my radio show—over the Supreme Court's role, the judicial oligarchy that increasingly rules over us, and the sort of justices who should be appointed to the Court.

Since the hardcover edition of this book appeared, President George W. Bush has successfully appointed two outstanding individuals to the Court—Chief Justice John Roberts and Associate Justice Samuel Alito. And I believe the public is now more aware of the dangers of liberal judicial activism—and they want something done about it.

The problem, however, remains: judges still routinely usurp power from the other branches of government and act as though they are unconstrained by the Constitution. One recent case in particular underscores the spectacular arrogance and lawlessness of the Supreme Court.

Judicial Land Grab

Wilhelmina Dery had lived her entire life in a house in New London, Connecticut, that her family had owned for more than one hundred years. She was born in the house in 1918. Her husband, Charles Dery, moved in after they were married in 1946. Their son and his family lived next door (in a house that was the Derys' wedding present). Then, a few years ago, the Derys were told that the city of New London had taken title to their homes by eminent domain and that they had to leave. Eminent domain involves the government condemning and taking private property for a public use.

One of the Derys' neighbors, Susette Kelo, a registered nurse, found a notice of eviction on her house the day before Thanksgiving in 2000. Why was New London trying to evict them? Well, the city wanted to take their homes (claiming the neighborhood was blighted) and transfer them to private developers, purportedly to improve the area and generate more tax revenue. The Derys, Kelos, and other homeowners challenged the city's plan and placed their hopes in the Supreme Court—often said to be our great guardian of civil liberties.

The case has become famous for what the Supreme Court failed to do. In *Kelo v. City of New London*, the Court gutted a part of the Bill of Rights called the takings clause of the Fifth Amendment.[1] The Bill of Rights recognizes certain (albeit not all) important natural rights that we possess as human beings and seeks to ensure their protection. One of these rights is the right to own property. The takings clause provides that private property may not be "taken for public use, without just compensation."[2] Therefore, if the government takes your land to build a road or military base, it must properly compensate you.

In *Kelo* the issue became the meaning of "public use." As has happened in so many areas of the law, the Supreme Court made seemingly small, subtle changes to the clear meaning of the words. Over time, this led to dramatic departures from the Constitution's original meaning. According to the Court's activists, "public use" really means "public purpose." And the phrase "public purpose" means just about whatever any government wants it to mean. Five of the nine justices voted to diminish private property rights and expand the power of government beyond its constitutional limits.³

As Justice Clarence Thomas wrote in his dissent:

> The Court has elsewhere recognized "the overriding respect for the sanctity of the home that has been embedded in our traditions since the origins of the Republic"... when the issue is... whether the government may search a home. Yet today the Court tells us that we are not to "second-guess the City's considered judgments"... when the issue is, instead, whether the government may take the infinitely more intrusive step of tearing down petitioners' homes. *Something has gone seriously awry with this Court's interpretation of the Constitution. Though citizens are safe from the government in their homes, the homes themselves are not.* [Emphasis added]⁴

While the appointment of more justices who are faithful to the Constitution—lawyers call them "originalists"—to the Court is critical, the problem is that the judiciary has relentlessly expanded its power throughout our history to dictate national policy, especially since the 1930s. The judiciary's seizure of power has become institutionalized. And it's the institution that must be addressed.

Is Criticism Forbidden?

The judicial activists who have exercised this enormous power resent any attempt to restrain their authority. They say it's an assault on "judicial independence" and even on their personal safety. In a speech last year to appellate lawyers, then associate justice Sandra Day O'Connor complained about former House majority leader Tom DeLay (although not by name), because he dared to make the point that "judicial independence does not equal judicial supremacy." She said that death threats against judges have become increasingly common. (She then referred to Senator Jon Cornyn, again without naming him, because he had complained that judicial activism might contribute to public hostility.) And she said that the "experience of developing countries, former Communist countries, and our own political culture teaches that we must be ever vigilant against those who would strong-arm the judiciary into adopting their preferred policies."[5]

The mere discussion of the Supreme Court's unconstitutional excesses evoked panic from O'Connor, who conflated judicial independence with judicial supremacy, which helps explain both her years of activism on the Court and her disdain for the representative branches. O'Connor drew no line where judicial independence ends and judicial supremacy (tyranny) begins.

I want to be clear. Threats against judges are absolutely deplorable, as are threats against any official in government. Those who make them should be prosecuted to the fullest extent of the law. But I reject O'Connor's effort to use these threats to bar debate about the judiciary's role and to intimidate those who think the judiciary is as worthy of discussion as anything else. I have no doubt that the president is threatened frequently. However, criticism of the president, his policies, his power, and everything else about him is robust, if not extreme. And nobody suggests that the debate and criticism have led to the threats on his life.

It's disturbing and absurd that O'Connor would attempt to lump Court critics with the strong-arm tactics of former Communist regimes. If anything evokes the Communist Politburo model, it is not critics of the Court, but nine robed lawyers who can stand in unchallenged judgment on virtually any issue or activity in which they wish to intervene. But O'Connor is not alone in arguing for an unconstrained Supreme Court.

On February 7, 2006, Associate Justice Ruth Bader Ginsburg, a former top lawyer for the American Civil Liberties Union, gave a speech in which she strenuously supported the Court's use of *foreign* law in its proceedings. She denounced efforts to pass congressional resolutions that would prohibit federal courts from engaging in such unconstitutional behavior (unconstitutional because judges are limited to applying U.S. law to most cases and controversies before them). And like O'Connor, Ginsburg attempted to smear opponents of her activism by linking them to death threats. She said, in part, "These [congressional] measures recycle some resolutions and bills proposed before the 2004 elections in the United States, but never put to a vote. Although I doubt the current measures will garner sufficient votes to pass, it is disquieting that they have attracted sizable support. And one not-so-small concern—they fuel the irrational fringe."[6]

I and other originalists argue for a federal government with limited authority, as compelled by the Constitution—and that includes a limited, defined role for the judiciary. And most Americans who read the Constitution for themselves agree. The public is fed up with judges who use their office to exercise power they don't have and who look outside the Constitution to foreign laws and courts for guidance. Under our republican form of government, the people, through their representatives, determine our laws, not judges. Yet Ginsburg, like O'Connor, is blinded by her arrogance and self-righteousness and cannot recognize this plain fact. She prefers to lash out at her critics while providing no evidence to support her allegation that congressional criticisms and proposals have led to threats against her or any other justice.

The framers assumed that all three branches of government would jealously guard their power. While we see this play out every day between the executive and legislative branches, Congress has done little to restrain the judiciary. Most liberal politicians applaud judicial activism, because judges unencumbered by constitutional limitations use their activism to impose a liberal agenda on society, saving liberals the trouble of winning elections. Most libertarian scholars support an activist judiciary as a counterweight to majoritarianism, which they believe is a greater threat to liberty. And most elected Republicans prefer to complain about court decisions rather than actually do something about judicial abuse, lest they be admonished by the media, academics, and Supreme Court justices themselves.

Former Nevada senator and Ronald Reagan confidant Paul Laxalt once told me that each day Congress meets, we lose a little bit of our liberty. I would add that each day the Supreme Court is in session, the Constitution is threatened. Of course, like Congress, the high court is not always wrong or all bad. But when the Court misfires, it does enormous damage that is extremely difficult to reverse. In the past the Supreme Court has endorsed slavery, segregation, and internment. And now it endorses the seizure of your home.

While the people can redress congressional and executive misbehavior at the ballot box, the judiciary is unaccountable and out of reach. As I point out in this book, the concentration of so much power in a mere nine lawyers—well beyond the framers' intent—undermines our system of government and the people's faith in a judiciary that is so obviously out of control. *Men in Black* is a call to reform our judiciary and restore our constitutional government as envisioned by the framers and supported by the people.

INTRODUCTION

BY RUSH LIMBAUGH

Mark "F. Lee" Levin has headed up the "legal division" of Excellence in Broadcasting for years—and for good reason. He is simply the best at what he does. He specializes in an area that is particularly close to my heart: constitutional law. Mark has eaten, breathed, and slept the United States Constitution since he was in junior high school. He loves history, especially American history, and is passionate about this nation's constitutional heritage. He and I share the belief that this is the greatest nation in the history of the world, not because of our geographical blessings, and not even because of our diversity. America's greatness lies in the unique system of government established by the framers to maximize our individual liberties, which has ultimately led to our national strength and prosperity.

Mark tells me he was so fascinated with our constitutional history as a young boy that he used to visit the various historic sites in Philadelphia, where our government was born, and early on began studying our founding documents. Through the years, his love of this carefully crafted system of limited government has not diminished in the slightest, and he remains committed to doing his part to preserve it and the freedom it guarantees.

Mark doesn't just talk the talk. He walks the walk. That's why he serves as president of Landmark Legal Foundation, a superb public interest law firm dedicated to "leading the fight to preserve America's founding principles." Landmark is the leading conservative law firm litigating for school choice—and is the National Education Association's most feared adversary. Landmark Legal serves as the conservative movement's top legal watchdog against government expansion and abuse, including taking on the politically correct Environmental Protection Agency. Landmark has been in the thick of the ongoing battle against voting fraud and has taken on the Internal Revenue Service.

Mark served in the Reagan Justice Department under Attorney General Edwin Meese and has always been involved in the world of politics, mostly as a writer and pundit. Now he has his own very popular radio show on WABC in New York City, where he continues to champion the causes of limited government, the entrepreneurial spirit, and safeguarding America's national security.

Given his strong belief in our constitutional system, which was designed to divide and diffuse governmental power between our federal and state governments and among the three branches of our federal government, Mark has been justifiably concerned over the years as these delicate balances have been eroded. He rightly sees an unaccountable, activist federal judiciary as the primary culprit.

Every honest observer of the political scene knows that since the 1960s, the judicial branch, led by the United States Supreme Court, has accelerated its already well-honed pattern of usurping the authority of the elected branches of government. Constitutionalists like Mark (and me) believe that the judiciary should stay out of politics and policy matters. Federal judges, and especially Supreme Court justices, all of whom are unelected and unaccountable to the people, have rejected their constitutional role. They increasingly legislate from the bench and rewrite the Constitution at will.

Liberal apologists for this kind of judicial tyranny glibly protest that but for the activist Supreme Court we would still be living in the dark ages on issues from slavery to civil rights. But it was the Court that upheld slavery and segregation, setting back race relations in America for more than a century. Every time the Court arrogates power that was properly left to the other branches, it chips away at our constitutional foundation. Every time the federal courts issue rulings over internal matters of the several states, they do lasting damage to our system of federalism—and thus to the rule of law and to our liberties. Besides, judicial activists have a very poor record. They are the ones responsible for upholding such detestable and unconstitutional practices as slavery and segregation. When a small group of men and women donning black robes makes decisions beyond its authority, it is disenfranchising the will of the people, which is properly exercised through the people's duly elected representatives.

This trend must be reversed before it's too late. That's why Mark has written this incredible book: to set out in layman's terms the current state of our runaway judiciary and the threat it poses to our nation. Mark takes us through all of today's hot-button issues and the way they are being shaped by the Supreme Court. In each chapter, he gives us the history of the constitutional development of these issues so that we understand exactly where we are compared with where we started and where we ought to be.

This book couldn't be more timely or important, as liberals continue shamelessly to thwart the people, Congress, the president, and state governments. Increasingly, liberals are also denying the president his judicial appointment power by blocking his well-qualified appointments purely for political reasons. While the informed public—informed primarily thanks to conservative talk radio—understands many of the issues involved in this book, Mark Levin's *Men in Black* provides an indispensable historical and constitutional context. And it offers suggested solutions to remedy the serious problems we face. Let me tell you, folks, this is a subject in need of our urgent attention. And this book provides the ammunition you need to defend your liberty.

I am proud to endorse this book by a constitutional scholar, a brilliant lawyer, a pundit extraordinaire, an exceptional radio talk show host, a patriot, and my very good friend. I hope it sells a million and that twice that many read, absorb, and take to heart its critical message.

MEN, NOT GODS

The biggest myth about judges is that they're somehow imbued with greater insight, wisdom, and vision than the rest of us; that for some reason God Almighty has endowed them with superior judgment about justice and fairness. But the truth is that judges are men and women with human imperfections and frailties. Some have been brilliant, principled, and moral. Others have been mentally impaired, venal, and even racist.

Barely one hundred justices have served on the United States Supreme Court. They're unelected, they're virtually unaccountable, they're largely unknown to most Americans, and they serve for life. They work in a cloistered setting hidden from public view. Yet in many ways the justices are more powerful than members of Congress and the president.

The Supreme Court today is involved in nearly every aspect of modern life, regularly vetoing the decisions of elected federal and state authorities. As few as five justices can and do dictate economic, cultural, criminal, and security policy for the entire nation. So who are these justices? Well, it's

1

impossible to generalize. But here are some of the more stunning personalities who have served on the Supreme Court:

James Wilson

Wilson was appointed by George Washington in 1789. He had been one of the more influential delegates at the Constitutional Convention, but had serious financial troubles after he was appointed to the Court. He put his money into land speculation, fell into serious debt, and was put in debtor's prison. He once had his son pay off a creditor so that he—an associate justice of the Supreme Court—could be sprung from jail in Burlington County, New Jersey. Hounded by creditors, Wilson later left his native Pennsylvania and had to live a life on the run. After "holing up in a series of 'dreary taverns,'" he died broke in North Carolina and was buried in an unmarked grave.[1]

John Rutledge

Rutledge, too, was appointed by Washington in 1795—by recess appointment—and became the nation's second chief justice. A United States senator from Rutledge's native South Carolina wrote that "after the death of his wife, his mind was frequently so much deranged, as to be in a great measure deprived of his senses."[2] There was considerable opposition to Rutledge's appointment, and he was voted down by the Senate. There had been rumors that his "mind was unsettled" and "he was becoming insane."[3] Rutledge's depression was so serious that he made two failed suicide attempts, one shortly before and one soon after the Senate rejected his nomination.[4]

Henry Brockholst Livingston

Appointed by Thomas Jefferson in 1806, Livingston had killed a man in a duel before his appointment to the Court.[5]

Henry Baldwin

Baldwin was appointed by Andrew Jackson in 1830. In 1832, it was reported that he:

"was seized today with a fit of derangement." Less than two weeks later Daniel Webster alerted a friend to "the breaking out of Judge Baldwin's insanity," and another correspondent observed more pithily that "Judge Baldwin is out of his wits." Baldwin was hospitalized for what was called "incurable lunacy" and missed the entire 1833 term of Court. Baldwin's colleague Joseph Story informed Circuit Judge Joseph Hopkinson in May 1833 that "I am sure he cannot be sane. And, indeed, the only charitable view, which I can take of any of his conduct, is, that he is partially deranged at all times." But Justice Baldwin nonetheless returned to active service on the Supreme Court, and remained a voting member of the Court for eleven more years until his death in April 1844 at age sixty-four.[6]

Robert C. Grier

Appointed by James Polk in 1846, Grier suffered paralysis in 1867 and thereafter began a slow mental decline. Grier's case is most troubling because he was the swing vote in one of the more important cases of his era, *Hepburn v. Griswold*, which struck down the law allowing the federal government to print paper money. "Grier's demonstration of mental incapacity during the conference discussion was such that every one of his colleagues acknowledged that action had to be taken."[7]

Nathan Clifford

Clifford was appointed by James Buchanan in 1858. After a period of mental decline, Clifford suffered a stroke in 1880 just before the beginning of the October term of 1880. "Justice Miller described the situation bluntly: 'Judge Clifford reached Washington on the 8th [of] October a babbling idiot. I saw him within three hours after his arrival, and he did not know me or any thing, and though his tongue framed words there was no sense in them.'"[8] Clifford kept his seat until his death in July 1881.

Stephen J. Field

Field, appointed by Lincoln in 1863, was one of the longest-serving justices. As Chief Justice William Rehnquist has written, at the end of Field's service, he "became increasingly lame and often seemed lethargic to his colleagues. During the winter of 1896–97 his condition worsened, and his questions in the courtroom indicated that he had no idea of the issues being presented by counsel."[9]

Joseph McKenna

McKenna was appointed by William McKinley in 1897, and his mental faculties began to decline as he approached his eighties. After Chief Justice William Taft failed to convince McKenna that it was time to retire, Taft called a meeting of the other justices at his home. They decided they could not allow McKenna to cast the deciding vote in the Court's decisions. From then on they agreed that if there was a split vote among them, they would change their votes and not allow the case to go forward. The Court did hold a few cases over until McKenna finally agreed to retire in 1924.[10]

James C. McReynolds

McReynolds, appointed by Woodrow Wilson in 1914, was a notorious anti-Semite. He said he didn't want the Court "plagued with another Jew."[11] There is no official photograph for the Court for 1924 because McReynolds refused to stand next to Justice Lewis Brandeis, the Court's first Jewish justice. He would leave the room whenever Brandeis would speak in conference.[12] He was also openly hostile toward the second Jewish justice, Benjamin Cardozo. "He often held a brief or record in front of his face when Cardozo delivered an opinion from the bench on opinion day."[13]

A McReynolds law clerk, John Knox, also wrote that the justice disapproved of the fact that Knox had been polite to McReynolds's African American servants, Harry and Mary. McReynolds told him:

> I realize that you are a Northerner who has never been educated
> or reared in the South, but I want you to know that you are

becoming much too friendly with Harry. You seem to forget that he is a negro and you are a graduate of the Harvard Law School. And yet for days now, it has been obvious to me that you are, well, treating Harry and Mary like equals. Really, a law clerk to a Justice of the Supreme Court of the United States should have some feeling about his position and not wish to associate with colored servants the way you are doing. . . . I do wish that you would think of my wishes in this matter in your future relations with darkies.[14]

Hugo Black

Black, appointed by FDR in 1937, had been a member of the Ku Klux Klan in Alabama.[15] He stayed on the Court longer than he should have. In 1969, he suffered a stroke, "resulting in a partial loss of memory."[16] His health troubles became worse. "In late March 1971, he started having acute pain in his left ear and a chronic headache over his eye and in the back of his head. Aspirin did not help. He found it more difficult to concentrate. His short-term memory was waning. He would latch onto some event of long ago and reminisce. In conference he began to stumble badly, becoming tired and confused, and unable to remember which case was being discussed."[17]

Black's mental decline seemed to lead to paranoia in the months before his resignation and death. "Black was paranoid about the future, expressing fears of governmental collapse; Nixon was preparing a military coup, he said. 'Anything can happen here. We have small groups fragmenting the government. There may not be a 1972 election—a dictator might take over.'"[18]

Felix Frankfurter

Frankfurter was appointed by Franklin Roosevelt in 1939. He helped launch the career of the notorious spy Alger Hiss. Frankfurter had been a prominent professor at Harvard Law School. Before joining the Court, he had great influence in getting his law students prestigious clerkships for Supreme Court justices. A notable clerk he obtained for Justice Oliver Wendell Holmes was a student named Alger Hiss. At Frankfurter's urging, Hiss began a public service career that included service as a delegate to the Yalta Conference, where FDR, Churchill, and Stalin set the boundaries of postwar Europe. Hiss would later be named by Whittaker Chambers as a spy for the Soviet Union. He was tried for perjury, and Frankfurter, in an unprecedented move for a sitting Supreme Court justice, served as a character witness for Hiss at the trial, as did Associate Justice Stanley Reed, another FDR appointee.[19] Although Frankfurter obviously would not have known of Hiss's eventual ties to the Soviet Union as a Communist spy, he knew of the specific charges when he decided to lend the prestige of his high position to Hiss's defense.

In *Brown v. Board of Education*, Frankfurter behaved in a manner that most legal ethicists would consider extremely troubling. He collaborated with a former clerk, Philip Elman, who was serving in the solicitor general's office in the Executive Branch. (That's the office that represents the administration's position before the Court.) Frankfurter passed confidential information on to Elman about the positions of his fellow justices in *Brown*, and advised him on arguments the government should make to sway the Court.[20]

William O. Douglas

FDR appointed Douglas in 1939. In a particularly bizarre episode, Douglas met a flight attendant on a plane and invited her to visit him at the Court, where he allegedly physically assaulted her.

> Just a short time after she had entered Douglas's chambers, though, members of the staff began hearing strange sounds from inside—shouts, banging furniture, and running feet. A short time later, the office door flew open and out rushed the young woman, her face all flushed and her clothing badly disheveled, shouting at the startled office staff how outraged and disgusted she was. Douglas, she said, had chased her around his desk, grabbing at her clothes and demanding that they go to a motel immediately for a sexual liaison.[21]

Douglas's marriages to young women and his subsequent divorces created financial hardship for him, so he sought income to supplement his Court salary. One significant source of income while he was on the bench came from a questionable source:

> Newspaper reports had established that over the years Douglas had received $101,000 from the foundation of Albert Parvin. Parvin was the former co-owner of the Flamingo Hotel in Las Vegas and a business associate of Meyer Lansky, "Ice Pick Willie" Alderman, and others not usually placed within the category of "nice Jewish boys."[22]

In his last year on the Court, Douglas also suffered, at times, from delusion: "A 1974 stroke incapacitated William O. Douglas at the age of 76 for 2 1/2 months, though he told the press he had been hurt in a fall. Afterwards, he slurred his words, couldn't walk, developed fears that people were trying to kill him, thought he was chief justice and spurned pleas that he quit."[23] Things were so bad that the justices themselves took action: "His refusal to step down despite obvious mental and physical problems led colleagues to decide secretly to stop counting his vote in some cases, until he finally quit at the insistence of his wife and friends,"[24] some ten months after the stroke.

Charles Whittaker

Whittaker, appointed by Eisenhower in 1957, was said to be vacillating and indecisive. The pressures of the Court led him to a nervous breakdown and retirement after five years of service.[25]

Abe Fortas

LBJ appointed Fortas to the Court in 1965. He continued to act as an advisor to Johnson while on the Court. He supplemented his Court salary ($39,500 at the time) by taking money from a foundation set up by a convicted "stock swindler." Fortas "resigned from the Supreme Court after it was revealed that while on the bench he had pocketed a $20,000 retainer from the foundation of jailed financier Louis Wolfson."[26]

> He found a cash cushion in a $20,000-a-year consulting fee from Louis Wolfson, a Florida businessman who was under investigation by the SEC for alleged stock improprieties. In setting the terms for the fee—ostensibly to compensate him for occasional advice to Wolfson's philanthropic foundation and companies—Fortas arranged for [Fortas's wife] Agger to receive the $20,000 each year after his death. In exchange, Fortas had to attend a single annual meeting. (And of course, it was possible that one of Wolfson's cases would end up affected by a decision of the Court.)... [T]wo weeks to the day after the first check was sent, Fortas was writing the White House to boost two of Wolfson's companies—both of which were under federal investigation at the time. It was a quiet deal, and became public only when Johnson tried to make Fortas chief justice in 1968. Fortas, finding himself facing impeachment rather than promotion, resigned.[27]

Thurgood Marshall

Marshall, appointed by LBJ in 1967, stayed on the Court too long. In his final years on the Court, he became indifferent to his judicial duties—he reportedly left much of the writing of opinions to his clerks and sometimes didn't bother to read the briefs submitted by counsel. Instead, he apparently spent many hours watching television in his chambers, especially soap operas.[28] *People* magazine had called him a devotee of *Days of Our Lives* as early as 1982,[29] and he once told fellow justice William Brennan that you could learn a lot about life from soap operas.[30] Despite the fact that he wasn't quite giving it his all, he didn't want to leave, since he would probably be replaced by a conservative. "But despite poor health in recent years—his eyesight is failing, he wears a hearing aid, and he broke his hip in a fall last year—he was determined to keep his seat as long as the likely replacement was another conservative nominee. With cantankerous tongue in cheek, Marshall would tell his clerks, 'If I die, prop me up and keep on voting.' "[31]

In his waning years, Marshall would disparage the framers of the Constitution. At a speech in Hawaii, he said, in part:

> I do not believe that the meaning of the Constitution was forever "fixed" at the Philadelphia Convention.... Nor do I find the wisdom, foresight and sense of justice exhibited by the framers particularly profound. To the contrary, the government they devised was defective from the start, requiring several amendments, a civil war and momentous social transformation to attain the system of constitutional government, and its respect for the individual freedoms and human rights, we hold as fundamental today. They could not have imagined, nor would they have accepted, that the document they were drafting would one day be construed by a Supreme Court to which had been appointed a woman and the descendant of an African slave. "We the people" no longer enslave, but the credit does not belong to the framers. It belongs to those who refused to acquiesce in outdated notions of "liberty," "justice" and "equality," and who strived to better them.[32]

Marshall couldn't have been more wrong, and couldn't have had a weaker grasp of the Constitution. The Constitution established principles of governance. Discrimination, injustice, and inhumanity are not products of the Constitution. To the extent they exist, they result from man's imperfection. Consequently, slavery exists today not in the United States but in places like Sudan. Indeed, the evolution of American society has only been possible because of the covenant the framers adopted, and the values, ideals, and rules set forth in that document.

Many truly great individuals have served on the Supreme Court. Many great rulings have been issued by the Court. But the justices have been frequently and wrongly deified. They have co-opted authority that has not been granted to them; they have usurped the authority that has been granted to Congress, the president, and the states; and they continually behave like an Olympian council.

Men in Black, which refers to the men and women who serve as judges and justices on the federal bench, tells the story of how America has turned from the most representative form of government to a de facto judicial tyranny. From same-sex marriage, illegal immigration, and economic socialism to partial-birth abortion, political speech, and terrorists' "rights," judges have abused their constitutional mandate by imposing their personal prejudices and beliefs on the rest of society. And we, the people, need not stand for it.

CHAPTER ONE

Radicals in Robes

"The American people will never be able to regain democratic self
government—and thus shape public policy—until we curb activist judges."

Edwin Meese III,
attorney general of the United States under President Ronald Reagan[1]

America's founding fathers had a clear and profound vision for what they wanted our federal government to be. They created a republican government strong enough to protect and nurture the young nation but, at the same time, one limited in scope and size so that it could not squelch states' prerogatives or stifle their citizens' liberty. The overarching purpose was to prevent the concentration of power in a relative handful of institutions and individuals.

With respect to the federal judiciary, the framers also had definite intentions. They wanted a central court system free from the political pressures of the legislative and executive branches of the government[2] with a narrow role and limited authority[3]—a judiciary that respected, applied, and preserved the rule of law and the principles of popular sovereignty enshrined in the Constitution.

Were our forefathers to view the American federal government of the twenty-first century, I believe they'd be appalled. Activist judges have taken over school systems, prisons, private-sector hiring and firing practices, and farm quotas; they have ordered local governments to raise property taxes and states to grant benefits to illegal immigrants; they have expelled God, prayer, and the Ten Commandments from the public square; they've endorsed severe limits on political speech; and they've protected virtual child pornography, racial discrimination in law school admissions, flag burning, the seizure of private property without just compensation, and partial-birth abortion. They've announced that morality alone is an insufficient basis for legislation. Courts now second-guess the commander in chief in time of war and confer due process rights on foreign enemy combatants. They intervene in the electoral process.

The Supreme Court in particular now sits in final judgment of essentially all policy issues, disregarding its constitutional limitations, the legitimate roles of Congress and the president, and the broad authority conferred upon the states and the people. The Court has broken through the firewalls constructed by the framers to limit federal and, especially, judicial power.

The plain language of the Constitution should govern judges when rendering constitutional decisions. Judicial decisions should not be based on the personal beliefs and policy preferences of a particular judge. Judges are appointed for life *because* they're not politicians. And because they're not politicians, they're not directly accountable to the people and are not subject to elections. They have a different role, which is to search for answers to the issues presented to them based on what the Constitution and the law compel. They have a duty to approach their responsibilities with restraint. Their decisions carry the weight of law and can have far-reaching consequences. When a judge strays from this obligation, he undermines the very structure of our Constitution, disenfranchises the people, and inserts into law subjective opinions that often lead to inconsistent, illogical, and flawed results. The Constitution defines and establishes the distribution of authority, the structure of government, and the process by which national decisions are to be made.

Generally speaking, judges tend to adhere to one of two philosophies. Too few judges keep their sworn oath to uphold the Constitution. Those who do look to the text of the Constitution and the intent of the framers when deciding a constitutional question, and believe they are bound by them. These judges are known as originalists. Too many judges consider the Constitution a document of broad principles and concepts, one that empowers them to substitute their personal beliefs, values, and policies for those enumerated in the Constitution. They see their role limited only by the boundaries of their imaginations. These judges are activists or non-originalists.

Originalists believe that the powers enumerated specifically in the Constitution are the only powers of the federal government, unless the Constitution is formally amended. Originalists generally interpret provisions of the Constitution (and, when applicable, statutes) narrowly. In other words, these judges attempt to look at the plain meaning of the law. They believe in a clearly delineated separation of powers.

My friend Robert Bork summed it up well when he said that originalism "appeal[s] to a common sense of what judges' roles ought to be in a properly functioning constitutional democracy. Judges are not to overturn the will of legislative majorities absent a violation of a constitutional right, as those rights were understood by the framers."[4] Moreover, "judges may look to the text, structure, and history of the Constitution, but are prohibited from inventing extra-constitutional rights."[5] "Originalism seeks to promote the rule of law by imparting to the Constitution a fixed, continuous, and predictable meaning."[6]

Originalists object to the judiciary grabbing power in the name of advancing a social good or remedying some actual or perceived injustice. To the extent that this framework is compromised, both liberty and the rule of law are jeopardized. The judiciary, operating outside its scope, is the greatest threat to representative government we face today.

A judicial activist, on the other hand, construes the Constitution broadly and rejects some of its provisions outright (or gives them superficial acknowledgment) if they interfere with the desired outcome. In essence, activist judges make, rather than interpret, the law. They substitute their will for the judgment of deliberative bodies. They see their role as "doing justice" or "righting wrongs" when, in fact, they're doing neither. They're no more just or wise than the next guy. Judicial activists simply use their high positions to impose by fiat that which should be determined through the democratic process.

Four landmark decisions by the U.S. Supreme Court stand out as examples of the terrible consequences that can arise when activist Supreme Court justices substitute personal policy preferences for constitutional imperatives. The cases of *Dred Scott v. Sandford, Plessy v. Ferguson, Korematsu v. United States,* and *Roe v. Wade* (which I will discuss in a later chapter) are all examples of judicial activism. In these four cases, the Court either ignored the clear mandates of the Constitution in favor of a desired result or usurped legislative authority. These decisions had tragic and far-reaching consequences.

Dred Scott was decided in 1856. It is one of the most infamous cases in American history.[7] Scott was a slave whose master, an army surgeon, had taken him to posts in Missouri, Illinois, and what is now Minnesota. When Scott's master died, Scott was inherited by his widow. But encouraged by white friends, Scott sued for his freedom on the grounds that he had lived so long in free territory.

The questions before the Court were whether Scott was a citizen of the United States with a right to sue in federal court, whether prolonged residence in a free state had made him free, whether Fort Snelling (part of the Louisiana Purchase, now in Minnesota) was free territory, and whether Congress could enact a law that banned slavery in the land acquired in the Louisiana Purchase.[8]

Chief Justice Roger Taney wrote the majority opinion and ruled that because Scott was not a citizen of the United States he did not have standing to bring suit. Taney argued that when the Constitution was ratified, citizenship "was perfectly understood to be confined to the white race and that they alone constituted the sovereignty in the Government."[9] Thus, blacks were not citizens. The opposite, however, was true, as Abraham Lincoln pointed out in a speech on June 26, 1857. Lincoln cited the dissenting opinion of Supreme Court Justice Benjamin R. Curtis, who showed, "that in five of the then thirteen states, to wit, New Hampshire, Massachusetts, New York, New Jersey and North Carolina, free Negroes were voters, and, in proportion to their numbers, had the same part in making the Constitution that the white people had."[10]

In other words, the "facts" Taney used to support his conclusion were simply wrong.

As for Scott's residence in free territory making him free, Taney rejected that argument, but with little explanation. He devoted only one page of his fifty-five-page opinion to the subject.[11]

On the final point, Taney concluded that the Fifth Amendment prohibited people from being deprived of life, liberty, or property without due process, and because slaves were property, any congressional ban on slavery in the territories of the Louisiana Purchase was unconstitutional because it would be a denial of property without due process.[12]

But Taney's ruling ignored Article IV of the Constitution, which, as Professor Michael McConnell (now a federal judge) has pointed out, "vests in Congress the power to adopt 'all needful Rules and Regulations' for the governance of the territories, and nothing in the language or history suggests that decisions about slavery are an exception. Under traditional canons of constitutional interpretation, the Court should have given effect to the Missouri Compromise and declared Dred Scott a free man."[13] Taney presumed, in McConnell's words, "that a statute can be unconstitutional because it violates unenumerated rights,"[14] in this case an unenumerated right to slavery. With typical activist flair, Taney overruled Congress's power to ban slavery in the territories and imposed his own view on the nation.

McConnell quotes Justice Curtis's dissenting opinion in *Dred Scott*: "When a strict interpretation of the Constitution, according to the fixed rules which govern the interpretation of laws, is abandoned, and the theoretical opinions of individuals are allowed to control its meaning, we have no longer a Constitution; we are under the government of individual men, who for the time being have power to declare what the Constitution is according to their own views of what it ought to mean."[15]

This is precisely the problem we face today.

In 1896, in *Plessy v. Ferguson*, the Supreme Court examined the constitutionality of a Louisiana law requiring railway companies carrying passengers in their coaches to provide equal but separate accommodations for the white and colored races.[16] The law was challenged under the Fourteenth Amendment, which prohibits the states from "making or enforcing any law which shall abridge the privileges and immunities of citizens of the United States, or shall deprive any person of life, liberty or property without due process of law, or deny to any person within their jurisdiction the equal protection of the laws."[17]

The majority, led by Justice Henry B. Brown, upheld the constitutionality of the Louisiana statute. Brown wrote, "We cannot say that a law which authorizes or even requires the separation of the two races in public conveyances is unreasonable, or more obnoxious to the Fourteenth Amendment than the acts of Congress requiring separate schools for colored children in the District of Columbia."[18]

In *Plessy*, an activist Supreme Court upheld a state law that mandated segregation, and forced a private industry (in this case the railroads) to separate individuals on account of race. By failing to invoke the plain language of the Fourteenth Amendment, the Court inserted its own segregationist version of what was just. Like *Dred Scott*, the Court's decision would have terrible consequences. The doctrine of "separate but equal" was the law of the land for the next fifty-eight years, until the Court reversed course in the 1954 decision *Brown v. Board of Education.*[19]

In 1944, in *Korematsu v. United States,* the Supreme Court upheld executive orders (issued by President Franklin Roosevelt) establishing military authority for the forced internment of Americans during World War II.[20]

The Court's opinion, only some twenty pages long, was devoid of any legitimate constitutional basis for upholding Roosevelt's orders. More than 110,000 law-abiding individuals, mostly Japanese Americans and Americans of Japanese ancestry, were removed from their homes on the West Coast, relocated to camps in the interior of the country, and detained without cause.

The Fifth Amendment states that "no person shall be ... deprived of life, liberty, or property without due process of law."[21] If this wasn't a violation of the Fifth Amendment, then what is? Rather than applying the clear language of the Constitution, this activist Court simply upheld FDR's policy. Indeed, the Court dismissively concluded that war demands sacrifices and that certain groups will have to bear certain burdens.[22]

Given the sheer inhumanity of these decisions, it is difficult to understand why so many regard the Supreme Court as the most moral and just of the three branches of government. These cases are crucial to understanding the danger inherent in judicial activism. When the judiciary utilizes outcome-determinative reasoning, rather than adhering to the Constitution, the result can be catastrophic. Activist Supreme Courts have justified slavery, segregation, and racism. They helped precipitate the Civil War and set back race relations for more than a century. But instead of learning the painful lessons of the past—that the Constitution must guide their approach to the law—several current Supreme Court justices are no less committed to judicial activism.

Recently, Justice Anthony Kennedy, in a 2003 speech to the American Bar Association, spoke out against federal mandatory minimum-sentencing laws that the courts—and Kennedy—are obliged to uphold: "I can accept neither the necessity nor the wisdom of federal mandatory minimum sentences. In too many cases, mandatory minimum sentences are unwise and unjust."[23]

Kennedy again decried the Federal Sentencing Guidelines in testimony before the House Appropriations Committee when he said, "I do think federal judges who depart downward are courageous."[24]

This is a remarkable declaration. We have a Supreme Court justice praising judges who violate federal law, and almost no one noticed, and even fewer cared. I doubt Kennedy would be so complimentary about lower court judges—or legislators—defying his Court's rulings.[25]

The late Supreme Court justice Thurgood Marshall, when asked about his judicial philosophy, stated, "You do what you think is right and let the law catch up."[26] Marshall deserves credit for his bluntness. Many judicial activists shroud their approach in bogus legal constructs. Marshall didn't.

When Congress or state legislatures pass laws with which a large segment of the public disagrees, the people have numerous outlets for recourse. They can lobby their representatives, raise funds to run advertisements encouraging their fellow citizens to get involved, organize grassroots movements, participate in voter registration drives, and, above all else, support or oppose candidates for public office based on their viewpoints.

But if the Supreme Court issues a decision holding unconstitutional, say, a federal statute prohibiting partial-birth abortion, as it did in the 2000 case *Stenberg v. Carhart*, there is precious little tens of millions of citizens who oppose this grievously brutal procedure can do to influence that decision.[27] It has been handed down from on high, wrapped in constitutional language by justices who are appointed for life and institutionally immune from accountability.

When judges come between the people and their representatives, they frustrate representative government and poison the body politic. So many of the nation's most far-reaching and contentious issues are now determined by judicial orders, increasing the public's cynicism about government and apathy toward voting. And when justices ignore their sworn obligation to uphold the Constitution, they destroy the very rule of law they claim to enforce and undermine their own credibility and legitimacy. But the judicial activists remain undeterred. Indeed, Supreme Court justices are increasingly relying on international law—not the Constitution—to justify their approaches and actions.

Ruth Bader Ginsburg

Justice Ruth Bader Ginsburg, in a speech discussing the 1948 Universal Declaration of Human Rights, which she described as "the foundation document for contemporary human rights discourse," complained that the U.S. Supreme Court did not have the "same readiness to look beyond one's shores" as other nations. She said:

> The U.S. Supreme Court has mentioned the Universal Declaration of Human Rights a spare five times and only twice in a

majority decision... nor does the U.S. Supreme Court note the laws or decisions of other nations with any frequency.

She continued:

When Justice Breyer referred in 1997 to federal systems in Europe, dissenting from a decision in which I also dissented, the majority responded: "We think such comparative analysis inappropriate to the task of interpreting a constitution." In my view, comparative analysis emphatically is relevant to the task of interpreting constitutions and enforcing human rights. We are losers if we neglect what others can tell us about endeavors to eradicate bias against women, minorities and other disadvantaged groups.[28]

Ginsburg has written that "a too strict jurisprudence of the framers' original intent seems too unworkable." She added that adherence to "our eighteenth-century Constitution" is dependent on "change in society's practices, constitutional amendment and judicial interpretation." She later remarked that "boldly dynamic interpretation departing radically from the original understanding" of the Constitution is sometimes necessary.[29]

Anthony Kennedy

Kennedy referred to international standards when examining Texas sodomy laws in the 2003 case *Lawrence v. Texas*:

The sweeping references by Chief Justice Burger to the history of Western civilization and the Judeo-Christian moral and ethical standards [in a 1986 Supreme Court case, *Bowers v. Hardwick*] did not take account of other authorities pointing in an opposite direction. A committee advising the British Parliament recommended in 1957 repeal of laws punishing homosexual conduct. The Wolfenden Report: Report of the Committee on Homosexual

Offenses and Prostitution (1963). Parliament enacted the substance of those recommendations 10 years later. Sexual Offences Act 1967 § 1. Of even more importance, almost five years before *Bowers* was decided, the European Court of Human Rights considered a case with parallels to *Bowers* and to today's case. An adult male resident in Northern Ireland alleged he was a practicing homosexual who desired to engage in homosexual conduct. The laws of Northern Ireland forbade him that right. He alleged that he had been questioned, his home had been searched, and he feared criminal prosecution. The court held that the laws proscribing the conduct were invalid under the European Convention on Human Rights.[30]

Kennedy continued:

To the extent *Bowers* relied on values we share with a wider civilization, it should be noted that the reasoning and holding in *Bowers* have been rejected elsewhere. The European Court of Human Rights has followed not *Bowers* but its own decision in *Dudgeon v. United Kingdom*. Other nations, too, have taken action consistent with an affirmation of the protected right of homosexual adults to engage in intimate, consensual conduct. The right the petitioners seek in this case has been accepted as an integral part of human freedom in many other countries. There has been no showing that in this country the governmental interest in circumscribing personal choice is somehow more legitimate or urgent.[31]

Sandra Day O'Connor

Here's Justice Sandra Day O'Connor lecturing about the importance of international jurisprudence on the Court, especially in the future: "Although international law and the law of other nations are rarely binding upon our decisions in U.S. courts, conclusions reached by other countries and by the international community should at times constitute persuasive authority in American courts."[32]

She added, "While ultimately we must bear responsibility for interpreting our own laws, there is much to learn from other distinguished jurists who have given thought to the same difficult issues that we face here."[33] Moreover, Justice O'Connor has referred to international law in one of her books, *The Majesty of the Law: Reflections of a Supreme Court Justice.*[34] In the chapter titled "Broadening our Horizons," she wrote, "Nevertheless, I think that American judges and lawyers can benefit from broadening our horizons. I know from my experience at the Supreme Court that we often have much to learn from other jurisdictions."[35] She goes on to say, "As the American model of judicial review of legislation spreads further around the globe, I think that we Supreme Court justices will find ourselves looking more frequently to the decisions of other constitutional courts, especially other common-law courts that have struggled with the same basic constitutional questions that we have: equal protection, due process, the Rule of Law in constitutional democracies."[36] O'Connor recently ratcheted up her rhetoric in a speech at Georgetown Law School: "International law is no longer a specialty.... It is vital if judges are to faithfully discharge their duties."[37]

John Paul Stevens

In 2002, in *Thompson v. Oklahoma*, Stevens referred to international standards for the execution of criminals under sixteen years of age:

> The conclusion that it would offend civilized standards of decency to execute a person who was less than sixteen years old at the time of his or her offense is consistent with the views at have been expressed by respected professional organizations, by other nations that share our Anglo-American heritage, and by the leading members of the Western European community. Thus, the American Bar Association and the American Law Institute have

formally expressed their opposition to the death penalty for juveniles. Although the death penalty has not been entirely abolished in the United Kingdom or New Zealand (it has been abolished in Australia, except in the State of New South Wales, where it is available for treason and piracy), in neither of those countries may a juvenile be executed. The death penalty has been abolished in West Germany, France, Portugal, The Netherlands, and all Scandinavian countries, and is available only for exceptional crimes such as treason in Canada, Italy, Spain and Switzerland. Juvenile executions are also prohibited in the Soviet Union.[38]

It is as if many of these justices will rely on anything but the Constitution to guide their decision-making. And there's a reason for this: The Court has so fundamentally altered its duties, and so completely rejected the limits placed on it by the Constitution's checks and balances and enumeration of powers, that the justices are in an endless search for extra-constitutional justifications and inventions to explain their activism. The power they crave does not exist in the Constitution, which is why they must constantly skirt its provisions.

Reliance on international law is a complete rejection of not only the roles of the other branches, for these are not decisions or laws reflective of their deliberations or actions, but the Constitution itself.

Judicial activists are nothing short of radicals in robes—contemptuous of the rule of law, subverting the Constitution at will, and using their public trust to impose their policy preferences on society. In fact, no radical political movement has been more effective in undermining our system of government than the judiciary. And with each Supreme Court term, we hold our collective breath hoping the justices will do no further damage, knowing full well they will disappoint. Such is the nature of judicial tyranny.

CHAPTER TWO

JUDICIAL REVIEW:
THE COUNTER-REVOLUTION
OF 1803

"This member of the Government was at first considered as the most harmless
and helpless of all its organs. But it has proved that the power of declaring what
the law is ... by sapping and mining slyly and without alarm the foundations of
the Constitution, can do what open force would not dare to attempt."

Letter from Thomas Jefferson to Edward Livingston, 1825[1]

So how did America reach the point where the federal judiciary has
amassed more influence over more areas of modern life than any other
branch of government? From which section of the Constitution were
the courts granted the authority to overrule Congress and the president?

The answer is that the Supreme Court has simply taken such power for
itself. Nowhere in the Constitution is the federal judiciary expressly given the
authority to interject itself into every facet of federal—and state—operation.
Federal courts have accumulated their power under the rubric of judicial
review. Judicial review involves a court overturning an act of Congress or of
the executive branch on the grounds that the act in question contravenes the
federal Constitution. It is founded on the principle that courts will be unbi-
ased guardians of the clear meaning of the Constitution.

At the time of the Constitutional Convention in 1787, there were only a
handful of instances in which state courts overruled legislatures for violating
state constitutions.[2] Moreover, state courts did not assume carte blanche

authority to rule on any subject. The courts followed British common law. They ruled on criminal law, matters of equity between individuals and businesses, and other legal matters.

Courts also, as a rule, regarded the state constitutions as the central legal nervous system of their respective states. Because the constitution of a state had been adopted by the people (generally through a convention and/or direct popular vote), it was considered by judges to be a higher law than an act of a legislature or a state governor.[3]

The Virginia Constitution of 1776 even included a statement of principles that "all power of suspending laws, or the execution of laws, by any authority, without consent of the representatives of the people, is injurious to their rights, and ought not to be exercised."[4]

There was no mechanism in the Articles of Confederation—the forerunner to the Constitution—for the sort of sweeping judicial authority later assumed by federal courts. The Articles, in fact, did not establish a permanent federal judiciary but relied on state courts to resolve disputes.[5]

Most delegates at the Constitutional Convention in 1787 thought a federal court system was necessary, that the federal judiciary should be independent of—and not subordinate to—the other branches of government (that principle was affirmed in nearly every state constitution), and that federal judges should serve "during good behavior" or, essentially, for life. These state constitutions aimed to insulate judges from political pressure, but every state constitution explicitly allowed judges to be impeached, as a check on misbehavior. In other words, judges were expected to be accountable to the constitution and the people who approved it.

The first mention of the judiciary in the Virginia Plan—which served as the initial outline for the Constitutional Convention—was to make it part of a "council of revision" that would examine acts of the national legislature and approve or reject them, though Congress could pass a bill over the council's veto.[6]

Beyond its role in the council of revision, the Virginia Plan had the federal judiciary consisting of a "supreme tribunal" and inferior tribunals as designated by the legislature. The inferior tribunals would be arbiters of fact, while the supreme tribunal would be the final court of appeal. The jurisdiction for the judiciary was also specific: "[A]ll piracies & felonies on the high seas, captures from an enemy; cases in which foreigners or citizens of other States applying to such jurisdictions may be interested; or which respect the collection of the National revenue; impeachments of any National officers, and questions which may involve national peace and harmony."[7]

Within days of the Constitutional Convention beginning its work, on June 4, 1787, the delegates took up the question of the Court's participation in a council of revision, and there was substantial opposition to it. Few delegates spoke in favor of the concept and there were many questions about the judiciary maintaining its objectivity if it were involved in negating legislative acts.[8]

The Convention had its most focused exchange on the topic of judicial authority on August 15, 1787. Again taking up the issue of the judicial veto over acts of Congress, the debate began when James Madison:

> [M]oved that all acts before they become laws should be submitted both to the Executive and Supreme Judiciary Departments, that if either of these should object 2/3 of each House, if both object, 3/4 of each House, should be necessary to overrule the objections and give to the acts the force of law....
>
> [Charles Pinckney, of South Carolina] opposed the interference of the Judges in the Legislative business: it will involve them in parties, and give a previous tincture to their opinions.[9]
>
> John Dickinson of Delaware argued that judges should not be empowered to overturn acts of the national legislature. Roger Sherman of Connecticut disapproved of judges "meddling in politics and parties."[10]

The framers considered and rejected the inclusion of the judiciary in the review process. They did not want judges involved in either the legislative process, with all the political intrigue that would entail, or in reviewing laws they would eventually have to adjudicate. Hugh Williamson, a delegate from

North Carolina, noted that he preferred to give the power to the president alone, rather than "admitting the Judges into the business of legislation."[11] Ultimately, the Convention came up with the presidential veto.[12]

Most important, the framers did not intend to grant general authority to the judiciary to rule on the constitutionality of legislative acts. Madison (who, by August 27, had dropped his initial support for the judiciary being involved in a veto) summed up the Convention's take on judicial review: "[He] doubted whether it was not going too far to extend the jurisdiction of the Court generally to cases arising under the Constitution & whether it ought not to be limited to cases of a Judiciary Nature. The right of expounding the Constitution in cases not of this nature ought not to be given to that Department."[13]

In the final analysis, if the framers had wanted to empower the judiciary with a legislative veto, they could have done so. They did not. Instead, the Convention crafted a federal judiciary, like many other provisions in the final Constitution, as a product of compromise. It was a compromise between the interests of the individual states and the need for a federal government that would be strong enough, and flexible enough, to meet the present and future needs of a nation with diverse interests. It was also the clear intention of the framers that no one branch would be subsumed by any other.[14]

Once the Convention completed its work, the political battle began over the proposed Constitution. The *Federalist Papers*, authored by Alexander Hamilton, James Madison, and John Jay, were among the first and the best post–Revolutionary War examples of American campaign literature. They are a series of eighty-five essays that began appearing in New York newspapers a little more than a month after the Constitutional Convention ended on September 17, 1787, written to persuade members of Congress and the states to adopt the Constitution. Essays 78 to 83, all written by Hamilton, contain the principal discussions of the nature and authority of the new federal judiciary.

Because there was no federal judiciary in existence at that time, and the principal concern was protecting the judiciary from being subsumed by the seemingly more powerful executive and legislative branches, much of the debate centered on creating an independent judiciary, rather than in limiting the scope and authority of federal judges. It is for this reason that much of Hamilton's effort in *Federalist* 78 was dedicated to an explanation of the steps taken by the framers of the new Constitution to ensure that federal judges would be independent and free of control from Congress, the president, the political whims of the day, and the various state governments.

The judiciary did not represent a threat, Hamilton wrote, "so long as the judiciary remains truly distinct from both the legislature and the Executive. For I agree, that there is no liberty, if the power of judging be not separated from the legislative and executive powers." [15]

This is exactly what has happened, but in reverse. Instead of being subsumed by Congress or the president, the judiciary has subsumed substantial authority over the other branches.

While other issues garnered most of the attention in the ratification process, there were commentators on both sides of the debate who addressed the nature and potential problems that could develop in the federal judiciary. Unquestionably, spokesmen such as Hamilton, Madison, and Jay were very persuasive as pro-Constitution voices, but there were also forceful opponents of the Constitution who saw the potential abuses.

Robert Yates, an ardent anti-federalist and delegate to the Constitutional Convention from New York, was an especially articulate opponent of the Constitution. In a series of essays published in the *New York Journal*, which became known as the Anti-federalist Papers, Yates wrote under the name "Brutus." In essay 11, Yates questioned the powers and pitfalls of the proposed federal judicial system. He warned that:

> The real effect of this system of government, will therefore be brought home to the feelings of the people, through the medium of the judicial power. It is, moreover, of great importance, to examine with care the nature and extent of the judicial power, because those who are to be vested with it, are to be placed in a situation altogether unprecedented in a free country. They are to be rendered totally independent, both of the people and the legislature,

both with respect to their offices and salaries. No errors they may commit can be corrected by any power above them, if any such power there be, nor can they be removed from office for making ever so many erroneous adjudications.

The only causes for which they can be displaced, is, conviction of treason, bribery, and high crimes and misdemeanors.

This part of the plan is so modelled, as to authorise the courts, not only to carry into execution the powers expressly given, but where these are wanting or ambiguously expressed, to supply what is wanting by their own decisions. [16]

Yates also warned that the Supreme Court would not be constrained by the strict language of the Constitution, regardless of the assurances being offered at that time by the pro-Constitution writers:

They will give the sense of every article of the constitution, that may from time to time come before them. And in their decisions they will not confine themselves to any fixed or established rules, but will determine, according to what appears to them, the reason and spirit of the constitution. The opinions of the supreme court, whatever they may be, will have the force of law; because there is no power provided in the constitution, that can correct their errors, or con-troul their adjudications. From this court there is no appeal. [17]

And once activist judges found themselves freed from the constraints imposed by the Constitution, Yates predicted, there would be no practicable limit to the Court's reach:

When the courts will have a precedent before them of a court which extended its jurisdiction in opposition to an act of the legislature, is it not to be expected that they will extend theirs, especially when there is nothing in the constitution expressly against it? and they are authorised to construe its meaning, and are not under any controul?

This power in the judicial, will enable them to mould the government, into almost any shape they please.[18]

Yates predicted the process by which the federal judiciary would achieve primacy over the state governments and the other branches of the national government:

Perhaps nothing could have been better conceived to facilitate the abolition of the state governments than the constitution of the judicial. They will be able to extend the limits of the general government gradually, and by insensible degrees, and to accommodate themselves to the temper of the people. Their decisions on the meaning of the constitution will commonly take place in cases which arise between individuals, with which the public will not be generally acquainted; one adjudication will form a precedent to the next, and this to a following one.[19]

While the Constitution created the silhouette of the national judiciary, it was up to the Congress actually to form it with legislation that would constitute a functional system of federal courts. Congress did this with the Judiciary Acts of 1789 and 1801.

The biggest problem with the Judiciary Act of 1801 was timing. The bill was introduced before the presidential election of 1800, but was not passed by the Federalist-controlled Congress until after the election, and while the deadlocked presidential election was being determined by the House of Representatives. President John Adams signed the bill on February 13, 1801, just three weeks before the end of his term of office. He also sent to the Federalist-controlled Senate nominees for the sixteen new judgeships, and they were confirmed shortly before the end of the Adams administration. These judges came to be called Adams's "midnight judges"—some of whom became the subject of the *Marbury v. Madison* case. [20]

On March 8, 1802, just days after Thomas Jefferson's followers—the Republicans—took control of both houses of Congress, Congress repealed the Judiciary Act of 1801. On April 29, 1802, Congress enacted the Judiciary Act of 1802, which, among other things, abolished the sixteen new judgeships created by Adams and the Federalists.[21]

In its 1803 *Marbury v. Madison* decision, the Supreme Court determined that it had the power to decide cases about the constitutionality of congressional (or executive) actions and—when it deemed they violated the Constitution—overturn them. The shorthand label given to this Court-made authority is "judicial review." And this, quite literally, is the foundation for the runaway power exercised by the federal courts to this day. What is far less recognized is that *Marbury* started out as anything but the ominous precedent it has become.

Marbury was a brilliantly conceived political strategy crafted by John Marshall, a master politician. Marshall, the chief justice of the Supreme Court, wrote the decision not to set a revolutionary precedent but to deny the new president, Jefferson, his longtime political rival, an opportunity to rebuff a Supreme Court controlled by Jefferson's Federalist opponents.[22]

Marbury was precipitated by the election of 1800, in which Thomas Jefferson, the incumbent vice president and leader of the Republicans,[23] ran for president against the incumbent president, John Adams, leader of the Federalists. The Federalists controlled both houses of Congress, but were torn between the followers of Adams and Alexander Hamilton. Hamilton's faction withheld its support for Adams's reelection bid in 1800, and the race ended in an electoral college tie between Jefferson and his vice presidential running mate, Aaron Burr. Adams came in third. The election was then thrown into the House of Representatives.[24]

Realizing he would not win reelection, Adams moved to solidify his party's influence in the federal government. The passage of the Judiciary Act of 1801, creating sixteen new federal circuit judgeships, was part of his strategy. Just prior to leaving office, Adams selected, and the Federalist-controlled, lame duck Senate confirmed, nominees to fill the posts. Adams's term ran out, however, before John Marshall, who was then secretary of state, could actually deliver the commissions of office to some of the designees.[25] Marshall's successor as secretary of state, James Madison, refused to deliver the commissions (at President Jefferson's direction) and William Marbury, among others, filed suit in federal court seeking an order (writ of mandamus) directing Madison to deliver his commission as justice of the peace. [26]

Marshall, long a rival of Jefferson's in Virginia politics, was one of the most articulate leaders in the Federalist Party. Marshall had served in the Virginia state house, the U.S. House of Representatives, as one of President Adams's representatives to France in 1797, and then as secretary of state.[27] He was nominated to be chief justice by President Adams and assumed the post on February 4, 1801, exactly one month before Adams's term ended.[28]

With a Republican majority elected to both houses of Congress in 1800, Marshall realized that Jefferson and his Republicans could denude the Supreme Court of authority and that he, as chief justice, could be impeached and removed from office. Marshall understood that, in the Marbury case, if he ordered Secretary of State Madison to deliver Marbury's commission to office, Jefferson would order Madison to ignore the Supreme Court's writ, and the Court's authority would be seriously weakened.[29] Marshall was also concerned that he not be seen as protecting the interests of Federalist jurists like Marbury, who had assumed his position as a justice of the peace and had been hearing cases and issuing judgments for a year.[30]

Bearing all this in mind, Marshall's decision in *Marbury*—while upsetting the Constitution's balance of power and the relationship between the federal government and the states—was a master political stroke. Marshall stated that Marbury, consistent with legal doctrine at the time, had something akin to a property right to the office to which he had been nominated and confirmed. Marshall also said that the federal judiciary should be able to issue an order directing the appointment of Marbury, but because the Constitution did not enumerate such an original right for the Supreme Court, the Court was powerless to do so.[31]

Marshall went well beyond the specific issues in the case. He said that the Court had a responsibility to set aside acts of Congress that violate principles enumerated in the Constitution:

> Between these alternatives there is no middle ground, the constitution is either a superior, paramount law, unchangeable by ordinary means, or it is on a level with ordinary legislative acts, and like other acts, is alterable when the legislature shall please to alter it.
>
> If the former part of the alternative be true, then a legislative act contrary to the constitution is not law: if the latter part be true, then written constitutions are absurd attempts, on the part of the people, to limit a power in its own nature illimitable.
>
> Certainly all those who have framed written constitutions contemplate them as forming the fundamental and paramount law of the nation, and consequently the theory of every such government must be, that an act of the legislature repugnant to the constitution is void.[32]
>
> The judicial power of the United States is extended to all cases arising under the constitution. Could it be the intention of those who gave this power, to say that, in using it, the constitution should not be looked into? That a case arising under the constitution should be decided without examining the instrument under which it arises? This is too extravagant to be maintained.[33]

Marshall's Federalist Party had lost the presidency and Congress, but Marshall was determined to fight back. And so the doctrine of judicial review was born. Yes, the Constitution is indeed the supreme law of the land. But now the Court, by its own fiat, would decide what is or is not constitutional. The Constitution's structure, including the balance of power between the three branches, was now broken.

Although Jefferson is claimed by modern Democrats as the father of their political party, he was a leading opponent of judicial activism. After *Marbury*, Jefferson became an even more vocal critic of what he viewed as the over-reaching of the judiciary under Marshall's leadership.

To Abigail Adams, John Adams's wife, Jefferson wrote a year after *Marbury*: "The Constitution . . . meant that its coordinate branches should be checks on each other. But the opinion which gives to the judges the right to decide what laws are constitutional and what not, not only for themselves in their own sphere of action but for the Legislature and Executive also in their spheres, would make the Judiciary a despotic branch."[34]

Jefferson's concern about judicial power grew stronger as he passed into old age. From Monticello, in 1820, the author of the Declaration of Independence wrote to William C. Jarvis:

> To consider the judges as the ultimate arbiters of all constitutional questions [is] a very dangerous doctrine indeed, and one which would place us under the despotism of an oligarchy. Our judges are as honest as other men and not more so. They have with others the same passions for party, for power, and the privilege of their corps . . . and their power the more dangerous as they are in office for life and not responsible, as the other functionaries are, to the elective control. The Constitution has erected no such single tribunal, knowing that to whatever hands confided, with the corruptions of time and party, its members would become despots. It has more wisely made all the departments co-equal and co-sovereign within themselves.[35]

Neither the history of our founding nor the establishment of our government supports the current arrangement in which the judiciary rules supreme. Indeed, Marshall's ruling in *Marbury* was nothing short of a counter-revolution. For 200 years, the elected branches have largely acquiesced to the judiciary's tyranny.

CHAPTER THREE

IN THE COURT WE TRUST?

"The Constitution was never meant to prevent people from praying;
its declared purpose was to protect their freedom to pray."

Ronald Reagan[1]

The First Amendment provides that "Congress shall make no law respecting an establishment of religion, or prohibiting the free exercise thereof."[2] The framers thought that religious faith was important to our system of government. They believed in the protection of religious minorities and sought to avoid the intolerance and threat to religious liberty that might arise from a nationally established church.

But we've come a long way since the First Amendment was ratified. As Chief Justice William Rehnquist has written, the Court "bristles with hostility to all things religious in public life."[3] For the last several decades, the Court, based on a misreading of Thomas Jefferson's now famous letter to the Danbury Baptists[4] (which we will discuss in due course), has seized on the mistaken idea that the Constitution requires a severe "wall of separation" between church and state.

As a result, the Supreme Court's cases involving the religion clauses are hopelessly complicated and riddled with inconsistent conclusions. But there is one conclusion we can draw: The Supreme Court has simply abolished your right to the free exercise of your religion in public. And unless the courts are called to account on this, religious freedom in this country is seriously endangered.

Many of the men who founded America came here to escape religious persecution, and when the Constitution's Bill of Rights was drafted, their goal was to make sure every American maintained his right to practice his faith free from government interference and with no federal favoritism to a particular creed. So the federal government was prohibited from establishing a religion and equally prohibited from interfering with the people's free expression of their religion.

What does it mean to "establish" a religion? Liberals today believe the government establishes religion if a nativity scene is placed on a town square at Christmas. But the framers had a much different understanding. They had in mind the Church of England: a formal union of political and ecclesiastical authority in the hands of the state.

The First Amendment's establishment clause—"Congress shall make no law respecting an establishment of religion"—was written to prevent the federal government from establishing a *national* church. States, however, retained the right to have established churches—and in fact, several of them did. The Puritans (later the Congregationalists), for instance, were the officially established church in Massachusetts.[5]

Not only did many colonies collect taxes for maintaining established churches, religious orthodoxy was upheld as well. When the doctrines of a church were enforced by the state, the results could be quite severe. The punishment and execution of religious heretics continued in the New World in Massachusetts, with the expulsion of Roger Williams and Anne Hutchinson in the 1630s and the execution of Mary Dyer and other Quakers in the 1660s.[6]

The Quakers found similar treatment at the hands of the Anglicans, the established church in Virginia, where a series of anti-Quaker laws passed in the late 1600s criminalized the refusal of Quakers to baptize their children, prohibited their assembly, and provided for their execution if they returned after expulsion.[7]

The nonconformists in the colonies continued to suffer under the established churches during the Revolutionary era and beyond. In Virginia, non-Anglican preachers were required to obtain a license from the state. Baptists refused as a matter of principle, and more than forty-five Baptist ministers were jailed for this offense in Virginia between 1765 and 1778.[8] Among the Virginians who took notice of the Baptists' suffering was James Madison. As a result, he became one of the strongest advocates of disestablishment.

In Connecticut, the union of religious and political interests between the Congregationalists and the Federalists was known as "The Standing Order."[9] Professor Daniel L. Dreisbach of American University has written, "[A]ll citizens, Congregationalists and dissenters alike, had to pay taxes for the support of the established church, civil authorities imposed penalties for failure to attend church on Sunday or to observe public fasts and thanksgivings, and positions of influence in public life were reserved for Congregationalists. Dissenters were often denied access to meetinghouses, their clergy were not authorized to perform marriages, and dissenting itinerant preachers faced numerous restrictions and harassment by public officials."[10]

These religious dissenters, such as the Danbury Baptists, weren't exempted from supporting Connecticut's established church until the Toleration Act of 1784.[11]

Against this backdrop, the framers contemplated the role of religion in the new republic. Although the original Constitution did not include a Bill of Rights, in 1789 Congress proposed twelve amendments to the states, ten of which were ratified in 1791, including the First Amendment with its establishment and free exercise clauses. James Madison, the primary author of the Bill of Rights, believed the intent of the religion clauses to be quite clear. He "apprehended the meaning of the words to be, that Congress should not establish a religion, and enforce the legal observation of it by law, nor compel men to worship God in any manner contrary to their conscience."[12]

But neither Madison nor Jefferson, the framers most secular in outlook, were hostile to religion. It was widely believed at the nation's founding that faith was a necessary predicate to liberty. As Jefferson wrote in the Declaration of Independence, human beings have certain unalienable rights endowed by God. Rights are not conferred on us by a monarch or the state. Without faith, he later wrote, liberty was vulnerable: "And can the liberties of a nation be thought secure when we have removed their only firm basis, a conviction in the minds of the people that these liberties are the gift of God? That they are not violated but with his wrath?"[13]

Furthermore, Madison wrote near the end of his life that belief in God was "essential to the moral order of the world."[14] Opposition to an established church is not opposition to religion in general—though this concept has been completely lost on today's secularists.

Madison interpreted the "free exercise" of religion, according to American Enterprise Institute scholar Vincent Phillip Muñoz, "to mean no privileges and no penalties on account of religion."[15] The establishment clause, Muñoz writes, was "intended to end things like special religious taxes, religious qual-ifications for public office, and the enforcement of religious orthodoxy through Sabbath-breaking laws."[16] The establishment clause was never intended to ban the invocation of God in public forums or the voluntary par-ticipation in "ceremonies or rites that recognized God."[17] In other words, it was never intended to create a strict wall of separation between church and state (a phrase, of course, that appears nowhere in the Constitution).

In fact, Madison noted how avoiding the establishment of one religion had actually *helped* religion in general. He wrote, "Religion flourishes in greater purity, without than with the aid of government."[18]

At the time of the ratification of the Constitution, America was an extremely religious nation. The framers never envisioned a time where the mention of God in the public square would be controversial, let alone illegal in certain circumstances. The historical record is filled with examples of offi-cials of the federal government invoking God during the same period that the Bill of Rights was ratified.

Chief Justice William Rehnquist has written of one exceptionally persua-sive example: "On the day after the House of Representatives voted to adopt the form of the First Amendment Religion Clauses which was ultimately proposed and ratified, Representative Elias Boudinot proposed a resolution asking President George Washington to issue a Thanksgiving Day proclamation. Boudinot said he 'could not think of letting the session pass over without offering an opportunity to all citizens of the United States of joining with one voice, in returning to Almighty God their sincere thanks for the many blessings he had poured down upon them.'"[19]

Within two weeks, President Washington issued the following proclamation:

> Now therefore, I do recommend and assign Thursday, the 26th day of November next, to be devoted by the people of these States to the service of that great and glorious Being who is the beneficent author of all the good that was, that is, or that will be; that we may then unite in rendering unto Him our sincere and humble thanks for His kind care and protection of the people of this country previous to their becoming a nation; for the signal and manifold mercies and the favorable interpositions of His providence in the course and conclusion of the late war; for the great degree of tranquility, union, and plenty which we have since enjoyed; for the peaceable and rational manner in which we have been enabled to establish constitutions of government for our safety and happiness, and particularly the national one now lately instituted; for the civil and religious liberty with which we are blessed, and the means we have of acquiring and diffusing useful knowledge; and, in general for all the great and various favors which He has been pleased to confer upon us.
>
> And also that we may then unite in most humbly offering our prayers and supplications to the great Lord and Ruler of Nations, and beseech Him to pardon our national and other transgressions; to enable us all, whether in public or private stations, to perform our several and relative duties properly and punctually; to render our National Government a blessing to all

the people by constantly being a Government of wise, just, and constitutional laws, discreetly and faithfully executed and obeyed; to protect and guide all sovereigns and nations (especially such as have shown kindness to us), and to bless them with good governments, peace, and concord; to promote the knowledge and practice of true religion and virtue, and the increase of science among them and us; and, generally, to grant unto all mankind such a degree of temporal prosperity as He alone knows to be best.[20]

So, our first president called for a national prayer to God within days of the vote on the Bill of Rights.

Government interference with religion was relatively modest until the twentieth century. There were few, if any, significant court decisions regarding the religion clauses of the First Amendment for the first 150 years of the republic. During this period, the federal government actually provided direct funding to religious organizations. As Rehnquist has noted: "As the United States moved from the eighteenth into the nineteenth century, Congress appropriated time and again public moneys in support of sectarian [religious] Indian education carried on by religious organizations. Typical of these was Jefferson's treaty with the Kaskaskia Indians, which provided annual cash support for the tribe's Roman Catholic priest and church. It was not until 1897, when aid for sectarian education for Indians had reached $500,000 annually, that Congress decided thereafter to cease appropriating money for education in sectarian schools."[21]

In 1947, however, the Supreme Court upended the long-standing balance between the government and religion in a case called *Everson v. Board of Education.*[22] Justice Hugo Black, a longtime admirer of Jefferson, revived a previously obscure metaphor from Jefferson's writings.[23] While president, Jefferson had written to a Baptist community in Danbury, Connecticut, which had congratulated him on his election. Jefferson used his letter to explain why he didn't call for national days of fasting and thanksgiving, as

George Washington and John Adams, his predecessors in office, had done. Jefferson wrote:

> Believing with you that religion is a matter which lies solely between Man & his God, that he owes account to none other for his faith or his worship, that the legitimate powers of government reach actions only & not opinions, I contemplate with sovereign reverence that act of the whole American people which declared that *their* legislature should "make no law respecting an establishment of religion, or prohibiting free exercise thereof," *thus building a wall of separation between Church & State.*[24] [Emphasis added.]

Interestingly, two days after writing to the Danbury Baptists, Jefferson attended church services held in the House of Representatives and continued as a regular attendant throughout his presidency.[25] Although the point of the Danbury letter was to explain why he didn't issue proclamations for thanksgiving and fasting as president, he used "virtually indistinguishable" language invoking God in other official statements, such as in his annual messages to Congress.[26]

But in writing for the court in *Everson*, Black seized on this idea that a "wall of separation" existed between church and state. Black also declared that the religion clauses of the First Amendment, which were intended to be a check on the federal government, were now applicable to state and local governments. The term "wall of separation" was to attach thereafter to every case or controversy arising under the establishment clause or the free exercise clause.

Everson involved a New Jersey statute that permitted local school districts to create their own rules for transporting children to and from school. The board of education for Ewing Township, New Jersey, which relied on public buses, reimbursed parents for their children's fares.[27] A portion of this money was distributed to parents who enrolled their children in Catholic parochial schools. As one would expect, these schools instructed their students in Catholic religious teachings.

A taxpayer who lived in Ewing Township brought suit, alleging that the New Jersey statute violated the establishment clause. The Court, however, disagreed. Justice Hugo Black, delivering the majority opinion wrote:

> [New Jersey] cannot exclude individual Catholics, Lutherans, Mohammedans, Baptists, Jews, Methodists, Non-believers, Presbyterians, or the members of any other faith, because of their faith, or lack of it, from receiving the benefits of public welfare legislation. While we do not mean to intimate that a state could not provide transportation only to children attending public schools, we must be careful, in protecting the citizens of New Jersey against state-established churches, to be sure that we do not inadvertently prohibit New Jersey from extending its general state law benefits to all its citizens without regard to their religious belief.[28]

While this affirmed fair treatment of religion in the public sphere, other portions of Black's opinion established the anti-religious precedent that has done so much damage to religious freedom. He wrote, "No tax in any amount, large or small, can be levied to support any religious activities or institutions, whatever they may be called, or whatever form they may adopt to teach or practice religion."[29] He added, "The First Amendment has erected a wall between church and state. That wall must be kept high and impregnable. We could not approve the slightest breach."[30]

According to his biographer, Roger K. Newman, although Black wrote the majority opinion upholding the use of public funds to transport children to Catholic schools, he did so for the purpose of undercutting the true meaning of the religion clauses:

> [Justice Black's opinion in *Everson v. Board of Education*] drew criticism from all quarters. Black's rhetoric and dicta contrasted

too sharply with his conclusion and holding to satisfy anyone. If he had not written it as he did, he later said, "[Supreme Court Justice Robert] Jackson would have. I made it as tight and gave them as little room to maneuver as I could." [Justice Black] regarded it as going to the verge. His goal, he remarked at the time, was to make it a Pyrrhic victory and he quoted King Pyrrhus, "One more victory and I am undone."[31]

Black, therefore, joined the majority in order to thwart them from the inside—and he succeeded. Today, *Everson* is remembered more for the easily understood "wall" metaphor than for the fact that state funds were used to reimburse the parents of parochial students.

Black might have had darker motives behind his opinion. He had been a member of the Ku Klux Klan in the 1920s, when the Klan was deeply resentful of the growing influence of Catholicism in the United States. According to Hugo Black, Jr., his father shared the Klan's dislike of the Catholic Church: "The Ku Klux Klan and Daddy, so far as I could tell, had one thing in common. He suspected the Catholic Church. He used to read all of Paul Blanshard's books exposing the power abuse in the Catholic Church. He thought the Pope and the bishops had too much power and property. He resented the fact that rental property owned by the Church was not taxed; he felt they got most of their revenue from the poor and did not return enough of it."[32]

Whatever the motivation, *Everson* is an inherently flawed opinion. The implications of Black's absolutist language lead to absurd outcomes. Bruce Fein, a former associate deputy attorney general of the United States, provided this withering critique:

> On the one hand, Black insisted that the establishment clause prohibited government from offering any type of financial or other support to religion either directly or indirectly: Neither a state nor the federal government can set up a church, whatever form they adopt to teach or practice religion.

Black, however, seemed to sense the absurdity of his categorical prohibition, which would have required public ambulances to deny service to a cleric who suffered a heart attack while preaching from the pulpit. Accordingly, he immediately retreated from his unbending stance—but without saying so.[33]

The fallacy of the "wall" metaphor is plain, but it is still a constant of constitutional law. Such is the power of Supreme Court precedent. In his dissent in the 1985 case *Wallace v. Jaffree*, Rehnquist pointed this out again:

It is impossible to build sound constitutional doctrine upon a mistaken understanding of constitutional history, expressly freighted with Jefferson's misleading metaphor for nearly forty years. Thomas Jefferson was of course in France at the time the constitutional Amendments known as the Bill of Rights were pressed by Congress and ratified by the States. His letter to the Danbury Baptist Association was a short note of courtesy, written fourteen years after the Amendments were passed by Congress. He would seem to any detached observer as a less than ideal source of contemporary history to the meaning of the Religion Clauses of the First Amendment.[34]

Yet liberals constantly rely on Jefferson's words to justify their opposition to virtually any government intersection with religion.

For example, Robert Chanin, general counsel for the National Education Association (NEA), explained that the NEA opposed school voucher programs that include religious institutions because "if a state can take millions of dollars, hand it over to sectarian schools, which is then used to provide a religious education, it seems to me you've punched a gaping hole in the wall of separation between church and state."[35] Barry Lynn, the executive director of Americans United for Separation of Church and State, criticized the Supreme Court's decision to uphold a school voucher program, saying, "The

Supreme Court has taken a wrecking ball to the wall of separation between church and state."[36] Ralph Neas, president of a group calling itself People for the American Way, complained about politicians "campaigning from the pulpit," which "clearly violates the spirit of the founders' wall of separation between church and state."[37] These left-wing groups and their leadership are clearly out of the mainstream of American thought and tradition, but their views often resonate in judicial chambers.

As Rehnquist has written:

> The Establishment Clause did not require government neutrality between religion and irreligion nor did it prohibit the Federal Government from providing nondiscriminatory aid to religion. There is simply no historical foundation for the proposition that the Framers intended to build the "wall of separation" that was constitutionalized in *Everson*. . . .
>
> . . . The "wall of separation between church and State" is a metaphor based on bad history, a metaphor which has proved useless as a guide to judging. It should be frankly and explicitly abandoned.[38]

Despite this, the "wall" is part of the lexicon of many Supreme Court cases that involve religion and it has led to an inconsistent and illogical series of decisions.

Once again, Justice Rehnquist explained, in his 1985 opinion in *Wallace v. Jeffree*:

> [I]n the thirty-eight years since *Everson* our Establishment Clause cases have been neither principled nor unified. Our recent opinions, many of them hopelessly divided pluralities, have with embarrassing candor conceded that the "wall of separation" is merely a "blurred, indistinct, and variable barrier," which "is not wholly accurate" and can only be "dimly perceived."[39]

...[A] State may lend to parochial school children geography textbooks that contain maps of the United States, but the State may not lend maps of the United States for use in geography class. A State may lend textbooks on American colonial history, but it may not lend a film on George Washington, or a film projector to show it in history class. A State may lend classroom workbooks, but may not lend workbooks in which the parochial school children write, thus rendering them nonreusable. A State may pay for bus transportation to religious schools but may not pay for bus transportation from the parochial school to the public zoo or natural history museum for a field trip. A State may pay for diagnostic services conducted in the parochial school but therapeutic services must be given in a different building; speech and hearing "services" conducted by the State inside the sectarian school are forbidden, but the State may conduct speech and hearing diagnostic testing inside the sectarian school. Exceptional parochial school students may receive counseling, but it must take place outside of the parochial school such as in a trailer parked down the street. A State may give cash to a parochial school to pay for the administration of state-written tests and state-ordered reporting services, but it may not provide funds for teacher-prepared tests on secular subjects. Religious instruction may not be given in public school, but the public school may release students during the day for religion classes elsewhere, and may enforce attendance at those classes with its truancy laws.[40]

It is almost impossible to discern a consistent thread of logic in these cases. This is because the Supreme Court has once again intervened in matters not on sound constitutional grounds, but because it wishes to dictate policy. And in this area of law, lacking a consistent rationale for its decisions, the Court is flailing. Having rejected the plain meaning of the religion clauses, it is forced to concoct ever more nuanced arguments to support its rulings. Two recent cases highlight the problem.

In 2002, in *Zelman v. Simmons-Harris*, the Supreme Court ruled that the state of Ohio could provide education vouchers to low-income parents so they could send their children to private secular or religious schools.[41]

Writing for a 5–4 majority, Rehnquist noted that the Ohio program did not favor one religion over another: The choice was completely up to the parents. "In keeping with an unbroken line of decisions rejecting challenges to similar programs, we hold that the program does not offend the Establishment Clause."[42]

Still, four of the justices would have overturned the program. Predictably, Justice John Paul Stevens, the most senior (and arguably most liberal) member of the Court, argued, "Whenever we remove a brick from the wall that was designed to separate religion and government, we increase the risk of religious strife and weaken the foundation of our democracy."[43]

Only two years later, in the 2004 case *Locke v. Davey*, the Supreme Court ruled that a Washington State scholarship program could specifically bar state scholarship funds to students pursuing a degree in theology.[44] Joshua Davey—who had won such a scholarship—sued the state and argued that its prohibitions on religious study violated the free exercise, establishment, and free speech clauses of the First Amendment. The Supreme Court's majority opinion against Davey was written by Rehnquist. On the surface, this seems remarkable, given Rehnquist's grasp of constitutional history and his past opinions. However, it's possible that Rehnquist, seeing that a majority of his fellow justices had lined up against Davey, decided that he would write the decision with the intention of limiting its scope and, therefore, its damage to the religion clauses.

In any event, Rehnquist wrote:

> The Religion Clauses of the First Amendment provide: "Congress shall make no law respecting an establishment of religion,

or prohibiting the free exercise thereof." These two Clauses . . . are frequently in tension. Yet we have long said that "there is room for play in the joints" between them. In other words, there are some state actions permitted by the Establishment Clause but not required by the Free Exercise Clause. . . .

Under our Establishment Clause precedent, the link between government funds and religious training is broken by the independent and private choice of recipients. As such, there is no doubt that the State could, consistent with the Federal Constitution, permit Promise Scholars to pursue a degree in devotional theology.[45]

Rehnquist reasoned that while the state could provide scholarship funds for a student to major in theology, refusing to do so—while funding other majors—is neither discriminatory nor violates the First Amendment.

The schools, of course, have been a particular battleground in the assault on the free exercise of religion and even mere references to God. The battles started in earnest with the 1962 Supreme Court ruling of *Engel v. Vitale*, which outlawed state-sponsored prayer in a controversial and dubious decision that was at odds with American history.[46]

Over the years, state restrictions on prayer in school have grown more oppressive and ridiculous, as two recent cases help highlight. In 1992, in *Lee v. Weisman*,[47] Justice Anthony Kennedy wrote the Supreme Court's majority decision that struck down the long-standing practice by Providence, Rhode Island, schools of inviting clergy to give invocations and benedictions at high school graduation ceremonies. Kennedy said that such prayers violated the establishment clause and was specifically concerned with the "coercive" nature of such prayer. Kennedy wrote, "The undeniable fact is that the school district's supervision and control of a high school graduation ceremony places public pressure, as well as peer pressure, on attending students to stand as a group or, at least, maintain respectful silence during the invocation and benediction. This pressure, though subtle and indirect, can be as real as any overt compulsion."[48]

This absurdity was picked apart by Professor Vincent Phillip Muñoz in testimony before the Senate Judiciary Committee:

> In *Lee v. Weisman*, the Court eliminated non-denominational invocations and benedictions at public school graduations. According to Kennedy, to ask public school children to stand respectfully while others pray "psychologically coerces" religious practice. In 2000, the Court prohibited the Texas tradition of non-denominational prayer before high school football games, because, it said, some fans might feel like "outsiders." Thus interpreted, the "coercion test" secures "the right not to feel uncomfortable" because of others publicly expressing their religious beliefs.[49]

So the nonexistent constitutional right not to feel uncomfortable trumped, in the Court's logic, the First Amendment's guarantee of the free exercise of religion, which Providence, Rhode Island, had exercised for a very long time.

A related controversy made national headlines in 2004 when the Supreme Court heard the case of the *Elk Grove Unified School District v. Newdow*. The question before the Court was whether voluntary recitation of the Pledge of Allegiance—with the phrase "under God"—in a public school classroom unlawfully violates the establishment clause.[50]

Michael Newdow, who brought the case, was "ordained" in the Universal Life Church, a ministry that "espouses the religious philosophy that the true and eternal bonds of righteousness and virtue stem from reason rather than mythology."[51] He now calls himself the head of the "First Amendmist [sic] Church of True Science."[52]

Newdow also has a law degree and is determined to have his beliefs imposed on society through the courts. He told *Newsweek* magazine that he had the idea to begin his crusade in a checkout line in 1996. After buying some soap, he looked at the change in his hand and saw "In God We Trust" on it. He thought to himself, "This is offensive. I don't trust in God."[53] He did some legal research and decided that it would be easier to challenge the Pledge than the motto on currency. In 1998, he brought a legal challenge to the Pledge's recitation in Florida public schools but failed because his daughter wasn't school-age,[54] and she was living with her mother, Sandra Banning, in California.[55]

After Newdow moved to California, his daughter was enrolled in kindergarten in the Elk Grove School District. As in most public schools across America, the school led the children in the Pledge every morning. On behalf of his daughter—who, ironically, had no objection at all to reciting the Pledge—Newdow filed suit in March 2000 in federal district court against everyone he could think of: the president, Congress, the state of California, and the Elk Grove Unified School District and its superintendent. He claimed his daughter was harmed because she was forced to "watch and listen as her state-employed teacher in her state-run school leads her classmates in a ritual proclaiming that there is a God, and that our's [sic] is 'one nation under God.'"[56] The district court threw out his case, declaring that the Pledge was constitutional. Newdow appealed to the Ninth Circuit Court of Appeals. In an opinion that caused shock waves across the country, the Ninth Circuit held that the Pledge ran afoul of the establishment clause because it was an endorsement of monotheism.[57] The court found that the Pledge failed all the varying judicial tests created to determine establishment clause violations, including the state endorsement of religion and the state coercion of religious activity. Furthermore, the court found that Newdow had standing "to challenge a practice that interferes with his right to direct the religious education of his daughter."[58]

Sandra Banning, the child's mother, whom Newdow had never married, became aware of the case for the first time in the newspapers. Although she and Newdow shared physical custody, she obtained sole legal custody in February 2002.[59] A parent granted legal custody by a family court has the right to make decisions about the child's upbringing. Once Banning had sole legal custody, Newdow had no standing to bring a lawsuit in the child's name. Moreover, Banning said that she and the child were Christians with no objections to saying the Pledge. In fact, Banning's daughter led her class in the Pledge the day after the first Ninth Circuit ruling.[60] Newdow's claim that his child had been harmed by watching and listening to the Pledge was patently untrue.

The Ninth Circuit reconsidered Newdow's standing and ruled that while Newdow no longer represented the child, he still had standing as a noncustodial parent "to object to unconstitutional government action affecting his child."[61]

When the case reached the Supreme Court, Newdow asked Justice Antonin Scalia to remove himself from the case, because Scalia had commented on the subject in public. Scalia did so. Newdow, who doesn't practice law, demanded the right to argue the case, even though attorneys normally need three years of legal experience before they can appear before the Supreme Court. The Court bent its own rules and gave Newdow permission to argue the case himself.[62] What happened next was an illustration of the Court's confusion.

The Supreme Court ruled unanimously against Newdow, but the justices couldn't unite behind an opinion. Stevens wrote that Newdow simply did not have standing to file suit. So there was no reason for the Court to decide whether the Pledge violates the establishment clause. Rehnquist dismissed that argument, pointing out that the Supreme Court defers to lower courts on questions of standing.[63]

Rehnquist went further and argued that the Pledge *was* constitutional. Justices Sandra Day O'Connor and Clarence Thomas agreed, although for different reasons. Rehnquist wrote that, "reciting the Pledge, or listening to others recite it, is a patriotic exercise, not a religious one; participants promise fidelity to our flag and our Nation, not to any particular God, faith or church."[64]

O'Connor urged the Court to create yet another test for deciding religion clause cases. The Pledge's reference to God was "ceremonial deism" in her view, and she invented a new test for ceremonial deism based on history and ubiquity, absence of worship or prayer, absence of reference to a particular religion, and minimal religious content.[65] Absent in her decision was why these tests were necessary when the language and intent of the First Amendment should have been the only test that mattered.

Kennedy joined the most liberal justices in *Elk Grove*, ruling against Newdow on standing grounds.[66] He could not do otherwise because the Ninth Circuit relied, in part, on the logic behind *his* coercion test in *Lee v. Weisman*. He either had to affirm the ridiculous—that the Pledge represented an establishment of religion (based on a precedent established by his own decision)—or dodge the issue by dismissing Newdow's standing to bring the case. So Kennedy dodged.

Thomas took the most intellectually honest approach. He candidly admitted that if you followed Kennedy's coercion test and the related cases to their logical ends, then the Pledge would have to be struck down. He argued it would be better to discard the many layers of ill-considered opinions and "begin the process of rethinking the Establishment Clause."[67]

Unfortunately, Thomas's advice isn't likely to fall on receptive ears any time soon. And the Pledge—with its phrase "under God"—remains in a state of judicial limbo.[68] Like the public is now, the framers would be appalled. This is the point to which judicial activism has brought us. In the meantime, the assault on religion in American life accelerates.

Most infamously, judges are now the tool by which the American Civil Liberties Union (ACLU) pursues its obsession against displays of the Ten Commandments on public property. The ACLU, in fact, has filed so many suits against public display of the Ten Commandments that a separate page on its website is devoted to them.[69] Its legal victories or pending cases against the Ten Commandments stretch the length and breadth of the land, from Montana to Georgia, from California to Kentucky.

And the ACLU is not alone. Americans United for the Separation of Church and State has filed similar actions. Their most notable case was the challenge to the courthouse display of the Ten Commandments by the chief justice of the Alabama Supreme Court, Roy Moore. The case resulted in the removal of both the Ten Commandments and Moore from the bench.

By the standard activist judges use today, I wouldn't be surprised if at some point displaying the Declaration of Independence on public property is challenged. After all, the Declaration speaks of "Laws of Nature and of Nature's God" and that "all men . . . are endowed by their Creator with certain unalienable Rights." It declares that the founders are "appealing to the Supreme Judge of the world" and relying "on the protection of divine Providence." Rabbis, ministers, and priests at public high school graduation ceremonies can be legally barred from saying as much.

We should remember that the Declaration of Independence is not merely a historical document. It is an explicit recognition that our rights derive not from the King of England, not from the judiciary, not from government at all, but from God. The keystone of our system of popular sovereignty is the recognition, as the Declaration acknowledges, that "all men are created equal" and "endowed by their Creator with certain unalienable Rights." Religion and God are not alien to our system of government, they're integral to it.

The intensive and concerted effort to exclude references to religion or God from public places is an attack on our founding principles. It's an attempt to bolster a growing reliance on the government—especially the judiciary—as the source of our rights. But if our rights are not unalienable, if they don't come from a source higher than ourselves, then they're malleable at the will of the state. This is a prescription for tyranny.

CHAPTER FOUR

DEATH BY PRIVACY

"Our nationwide policy of abortion-on-demand through all nine months
of pregnancy was neither voted for by our people nor enacted by our
legislators—not a single state had such unrestricted abortion before
the Supreme Court decreed it to be national policy in 1973."

Ronald Reagan, 1983[1]

oday, legalized abortion is the law of the land because the Supreme
Court decided in 1973 that its recently created constitutional right to
privacy also included a new constitutional right to abortion. If you
look in the Constitution, however, you will find no general "right to privacy"
any more than you will find a right to abortion—and for good reason: It's
not there. The framers assumed no general right to privacy because, to state
the obvious, criminal and evil acts can be committed in privacy. Criminal
codes are full of such examples—from murder to incest to rape and other
crimes.

How Judges Make Law

The modern argument for a right to privacy began in 1961 in Justice John
Marshall Harlan's dissent in *Poe v. Ullman*.[2] The case was brought by
Planned Parenthood on behalf of a carefully selected group of people: a
married couple, a single woman, and a Planned Parenthood obstetrician,

C. Lee Buxton. Planned Parenthood's suit was directed against a Connecticut law that prohibited the sale and use of contraceptives.[3] The Supreme
Court dismissed the case because the law had not been enforced against the
people in Planned Parenthood's case. It is a basic judicial principle that
there has to be an actual legal dispute to be adjudicated. But Justice Harlan
issued a dissent, writing, "I believe that a statute making it a criminal
offense for married couples to use contraceptives is an intolerable and
unjustifiable invasion of privacy in the conduct of the most intimate concerns of an individual's personal life."[4]

Harlan provided an extensive rationale for his position, which became the
theoretical cornerstone for the right to privacy. Where did Harlan derive his
notions about privacy rights? Melvin L. Wulf, a lawyer for the American Civil
Liberties Union, claims credit for first raising the idea with Harlan in the
ACLU's friend-of-the court brief in *Poe v. Ullman*. Wulf later explained his
strategy for getting the Court to adopt the privacy rights approach:

> Judges dislike breaking entirely new ground. If they are consider-
> ing adopting a novel principle, they prefer to rest their decision
> on earlier law if they can, and to show that the present case
> involves merely an incremental change, not a wholesale break
> with the past. Constitutional litigators are forever trying to per-
> suade courts that the result they are seeking would be just a short
> step from some other case whose decision rests soundly on
> ancient precedent.
>
> Since the issue of sexual privacy had not been raised in any
> earlier case, we employed the familiar technique of argument by
> analogy: If there is no exact counterpart to the particular case
> before the Court, there are others that resemble it in a general sort
> of way, and the principles applied in the similar cases should also
> be applied—*perhaps even extended a little bit*—to the new case.[5]
> [Emphasis added.]

In other words, Wulf understood that the Court would be open to rewriting the Constitution by pretending to uphold it. Although Harlan's was a minority opinion, and had no immediate legal effect, its impact would soon become clear. After *Poe* was decided, Planned Parenthood officials found a way to get arrested so they could mount another challenge to Connecticut law.[6] In 1965, Justice William O. Douglas adopted Harlan's reasoning in the majority opinion in the case of *Griswold v. Connecticut*, and the right to privacy became constitutional law.[7] Douglas, who was appointed by President Franklin Roosevelt in 1939, is most famous for being the longest-serving justice and, to conservatives, for writing one of the most parodied phrases in Supreme Court history. In order to strike down the Connecticut law prohibiting the sale of contraceptives, Douglas wrote that "specific guarantees in the Bill of Rights have penumbras, formed by emanations from those guarantees that help give them life and substance."[8]

Don't be embarrassed if you don't know what emanations from penumbras are. Young lawyers across America had to pull out their dictionaries when reading *Griswold* for the first time. A penumbra is an astronomical term describing the partial shadow in an eclipse or the edge of a sunspot—and it is another way to describe something unclear or uncertain. "Emanation" is a scientific term for gas made from radioactive decay—it also means "an emission."[9]

Douglas's decision not only found a right to privacy in a penumbra of an emanation, it manipulated the facts of the case: Estelle Griswold, the executive director of the Planned Parenthood League of Connecticut, and Dr. C. Lee Buxton, the group's medical director, gave information and prescribed birth control to a married couple. Griswold and Buxton, not the married couple, were later convicted and fined $100 each. The relationship at issue, then, was doctor-patient, not husband-wife. Yet Douglas framed his opinion around a presumed right to *marital* privacy. He expounded at length about the sanctity of marriage but used vague phrasing to describe the rights at issue, never explicitly stating that married couples have a right to use contraceptives. He even raised the ugly specter of sex police, though no police had intruded into anyone's bedroom. "Would we allow the police to search the sacred precincts of marital bedrooms for telltale signs of the use of contraceptives?"[10] This little phrase has been used as holy writ by judicial activists ever since to further expand the right to privacy in a variety of areas, including abortion and sodomy, as we'll see.

Justice Hugo Black, in his dissent, was not impressed. He attacked the way Douglas had turned constitutional law into semantics by replacing the language of actual rights with the phrase "right to privacy." He wrote, "The Court talks about a constitutional 'right of privacy' as though there is some constitutional provision or provisions forbidding any law ever to be passed which might abridge the 'privacy' of individuals. But there is not. There are, of course, guarantees in certain specific constitutional provisions which are designed in part to protect privacy at certain times and places with respect to certain activities."[11]

Black, normally an ally of Douglas, feared that using such a phrase as "right to privacy" could be a double-edged sword. "One of the most effective ways of diluting or expanding a constitutionally guaranteed right is to substitute for the crucial word or words of a constitutional guarantee another word or words, more or less flexible and more or less restricted in meaning. . . . 'Privacy' is a broad, abstract and ambiguous concept which can easily be shrunken in meaning but which can also, on the other hand, easily be interpreted as a constitutional ban against many things other than searches and seizures."[12] Black concluded by saying, "I like my privacy as well as the next one, but I am nevertheless compelled to admit that government has a right to invade it unless prohibited by some specific constitutional provision."[13]

Seven years after the issue of married couples and contraceptives was decided in *Griswold*, the Court considered contraceptives and unmarried couples in 1972 in *Eisenstadt v. Baird*.[14] Although he quoted *Griswold* frequently in the majority opinion, Justice William Brennan nonetheless found that Massachusetts law could be overturned on Fourteenth Amendment equal protection grounds without having to rely on the marital privacy rights created by *Griswold*. While Connecticut's law in *Griswold* prohibited the use of contraceptives, Massachusetts had laws restricting their distribution. Married people could obtain contraceptives only from doctors or pharmacists by prescription, while single people could obtain them only to prevent the spread of disease. Massachusetts law was challenged when William Baird gave a speech at Boston University about birth control and overpopulation. He exhibited contraceptives and gave "Emko vaginal foam" to a young woman in the audience, both of which actions were illegal, and Baird was convicted. His conviction for showing contraceptives was overturned by the Massachusetts Supreme Judicial Court on First Amendment grounds, so distribution was the sole issue before the U.S. Supreme Court.

Brennan found that the statute was a prohibition on contraception per se and ruled that "whatever the rights of the individual to access contraceptives may be, the rights must be the same for the unmarried and the married alike."[15] Yet again, a major Supreme Court decision rested on a naked assertion of opinion instead of legal reasoning. Nowhere does the Constitution require that married couples and single people be treated the same where contraception is involved.

Brennan then argued for expanding the right to privacy: "If under *Griswold* the distribution of contraceptives to married persons cannot be prohibited, a ban on distribution to unmarried persons would be equally impermissible. It is true that in *Griswold* the right of privacy in question inhered in the marital relationship. Yet the marital couple is not an independent entity with a mind and heart of its own, but an association of two individuals each with a separate intellectual and emotional makeup."[16]

In other words, Douglas's rhetoric about the sanctity of marriage was essentially irrelevant. The right to privacy belonged to individuals, not the couple.

Brennan continued, "If the right of privacy means anything, it is the right of the individual, married or single, to be free from unwarranted governmental intrusion into matters so fundamentally affecting a person as the decision whether to bear or beget a child."[17]

So the right to privacy means everything and nothing. It has no constitutional basis and no tangible form. But what is clear is that the Supreme Court, by usurping the legislature's authority to set social policy, has seized from the people the power to make such determinations. A mere five justices are now able to substitute their personal judgments for those of Congress and every state government in the name of privacy rights. This quiet revolution against representative government has gone largely unnoticed. The exception is the occasional Court decision on "hot button" issues in which the attention is mostly on the Court's ruling, not on its abuse of power.

Also notice how Brennan inserted the phrase to "bear or beget a child" in the opinion. The case was about contraceptives, which affect only the begetting of children. Yet Brennan explicitly added the concept of bearing a child as well. He was subtly laying the foundation to extend the right of privacy to encompass the right to abortion. This occurred at a time when *Roe v. Wade*— a case involving abortion—had twice been argued before the Court but had not yet been decided. Notice how the judicial activists work—inserting a word in a majority opinion here and there, inserting a phrase in a dissenting opinion, all the while biding their time until five justices can be convinced to join the cause.

The facts of *Roe* are straightforward. "Roe" (the pseudonym for Norma McCorvey, a pregnant woman from Texas) could not legally obtain an abortion in Texas, where it was a crime to procure an abortion or to attempt to perform an abortion, except "by medical advice for the purpose of saving the life of the mother."[18] The central issue was whether Roe had a right to abort her baby although her life was not at risk.

Roe provides an opportunity to explore how external influences, as well as a justice's personal foibles and prejudices, contribute to judicial activism. Justice Harry Blackmun, who wrote the majority opinion, was nominated by President Richard Nixon in 1970 as a judicial conservative. Indeed, one of Nixon's campaign issues in 1968 was the liberalism of the Supreme Court under Chief Justice Earl Warren. What particularly annoyed Nixon and other Republicans was that some of the Court's staunchest liberals, Justices Earl Warren and William Brennan among them, had been nominated by President Dwight Eisenhower, a Republican. Nixon thought the Court was a "disaster," filled with "senile old bastards" and "fools." He was disgusted at how Justice Potter Stewart, another Eisenhower appointee, had been "overwhelmed by the Washington Georgetown social set" and had turned out to be "weak" and "dumb."[19] Nixon wanted to make sure he appointed justices to the Supreme Court who believed in following the original intent of the Constitution. He replaced the retiring Earl Warren with Warren Burger of Minnesota.

Filling Justice Abe Fortas's seat was more difficult. The Senate rejected Nixon's first two nominees, Clement Haynsworth of South Carolina and Harrold Carswell of Florida. Nixon abandoned his attempts to name a southerner to the Court and considered Blackmun, another Minnesotan, who was a judge on the Eighth Circuit Court of Appeals and former counsel to the prestigious Mayo Clinic. As Nixon's third choice, Blackmun later called himself "Old Number 3."[20] Assistant Attorney General William Rehnquist vetted Blackmun and found him competent but not exceptional. Blackmun was called to Washington and met with Nixon by the Rose Garden window. "So I went over and we looked out and he asked a couple of questions, among which—I'll never forget this—he said, 'What kind of a woman is Mrs. Blackmun?' And I said, 'What do you mean?' He said, 'She will be wooed by the Georgetown crowd. Can she withstand that kind of wooing?' I said I thought she could."[21]

Blackmun and others sneered at Nixon for asking questions about his wife. Yet Nixon was quite insightful about how conservatives are continually seduced by the liberal establishment once they move inside the Beltway. They "grow" or "evolve" in office, meaning they become receptive to the liberal elitism of the establishment. (Nixon was soon able to put two more justices on the Court after Blackmun: William Rehnquist and Democrat Lewis Powell.)

During his first full term on the Court, Blackmun voted with Burger 89 percent of the time.[22] Blackmun and Burger, who had been close friends in childhood, were called the Minnesota Twins. Blackmun resented the nickname, believing it unfairly implied he was dominated by Burger. Soon after he was on the Court, Burger assigned Blackmun to write the opinion in *Roe*. It was a major opportunity for Blackmun to prove his intellectual heft and display his constitutional prowess.

According to Bob Woodward's book *The Brethren*, Blackmun suffered from a profound sense of insecurity:

> From his first day at the Court, Blackmun had felt unworthy, unqualified, unable to perform up to standard. He felt he could equal the Chief and [Thurgood] Marshall, but not the others. He became increasingly withdrawn and professorial. He did not enjoy charting new paths for the law. He was still learning. The issues were too grave, the information too sparse. Each new answer was barely answered, even tentatively, when two more questions appeared on the horizon. Blackmun knew that his colleagues were concerned about what they perceived as his indecisiveness.[23]

Blackmun also brought enormous respect for doctors to the Court from his many years as counsel for the Mayo Clinic. He saw abortion laws as state meddling with a doctor's professional judgment.[24]

In *Roe*, Blackmun plunged himself into the history of abortion and even returned to the libraries of the Mayo Clinic to research the medical opinion. Blackmun had other influences working on him—most notably his wife. Nixon had been quite prescient about the effect of Blackmun's wife on his judicial role. While Blackmun was dithering over the opinion, Dorothy Blackmun told one of his pro–abortion rights clerks "that she was doing everything she could to encourage her husband in that direction. 'You and I are working on the same thing,' she said. 'Me at home and you at work.'"[25] Blackmun later claimed that she (and his three daughters) never tried to influence his decision.[26]

Other justices were also predisposed to dismantle the nation's abortion laws, including another Nixon appointee, Lewis Powell. As Bob Woodward noted: "Powell came quickly to the conclusion that the Constitution did not provide meaningful guidance. The right to privacy was tenuous; at best it was implied. If there was no way to find an answer in the Constitution, Powell felt he would just have to vote his 'gut.'... When he returned to Washington, he took one of his law clerks to lunch.... The abortion laws, Powell confided, were 'atrocious.' His would be a strong and unshakable vote to strike them. He needed only a rationale for his vote."[27]

Powell's vote, in other words, was not dictated by a serious effort to interpret the Constitution. Instead, he made a policy decision and then set out to justify it.

Justice Potter Stewart was also in favor of striking down abortion laws. Although he had some misgivings, Stewart thought abortion reform was necessary for various policy reasons.

> As Stewart saw it, abortion was becoming one reasonable solution to population control. Poor people, in particular, were consistently victims of archaic and artificially complicated laws....
>
> Still, these were issues of the very sort that made Stewart uncomfortable. Precisely because of their political nature, the Court should avoid them. But the state legislatures were always so far behind. Few seemed likely to amend their abortion laws. Much as Stewart disliked the Court's being involved in this kind of controversy, this was perhaps an instance where it had to be involved.[28]

Blackmun acknowledged some of the policy issues at stake in the abortion debate, like overpopulation, in the introduction of his opinion:

> We forthwith acknowledge our awareness of the sensitive and emotional nature of the abortion controversy, of the vigorous

opposing views, even among physicians, and of the deep and seemingly absolute convictions that the subject inspires. One's philosophy, one's experiences, one's exposure to the raw edges of human existence, one's religious training, one's attitudes toward life and family and their values, and the moral standards one establishes and seeks to observe, are all likely to influence and to color one's thinking and conclusions on abortion.

In addition, population growth, pollution, poverty, and racial overtones tend to complicate and not to simplify the problem.[29]

Nice speech, but it had nothing to do with a constitutional analysis of Roe. From this inauspicious beginning, Blackmun began a comprehensive, multi-page review of the history of abortion from the beginning of time to the present day. He led with the attitudes of the Persian Empire, the ancient Greeks, and the ancient Romans and tried to divine the real meaning behind the Hippocratic Oath. He moved on to the old common law of England, and examined Christian theology and the works of Catholic theologian Thomas Aquinas. From Europe, he proceeded to the history of abortion law in the individual states. Not stopping there, he outlined the positions of the American Medical Association since the 1800s, as well as the position of the American Public Health Association and the American Bar Association as expressed in the ABA House of Delegates. Once the history lesson was completed, Blackmun sought to refute the various policy reasons given for America's abortion laws.

Finally, Blackmun focused on his legal rationale in Roe. He began with a review of the right to privacy, writing, in part:

The Constitution does not explicitly mention any right of privacy. In a line of decisions, however...the Court has recognized that a right of personal privacy, or a guarantee of certain areas or zones of privacy, does exist under the Constitution. In varying contexts, the Court or individual Justices have, indeed, found at least the

> roots of that right in the First Amendment . . . in the Fourth and
> Fifth Amendments . . . in the penumbras of the Bill of Rights . . .
> in the Ninth Amendment . . . or in the concept of liberty guaran-
> teed by the first section of the Fourteenth Amendment. . . . These
> decisions make it clear that only personal rights that can be
> deemed "fundamental" or "implicit in the concept of ordered lib-
> erty" . . . are included in this guarantee of personal privacy. They
> also make it clear that the right has some extension to activities
> relating to marriage . . . procreation . . . contraception . . . family
> relationships . . . and child rearing and education. . . . [30]

Blackmun *felt* that the right of privacy, wherever it comes from, includes the right to abortion. Do not look any further for legal argument amidst the voluminous opinion, because it does not exist. Perhaps the extensive historical analysis was included to compensate for the lack of legal analysis.

But Blackmun went further, and the Court followed. Not satisfied to strike down the Texas law, Blackmun began to write what seemed to be a new federal statute. According to Blackmun's opinion, a woman's right to abortion could only be abridged by a compelling state interest. In effect, Blackmun argued that there was an inverse relationship between a woman's interest and the state's interest that ranged across a spectrum from conception to birth. Therefore, the state's interest at conception was minimal but increased as the pregnancy progressed, reaching its peak at the end of the pregnancy. A woman's interest, paramount at conception, began to give some ground to the state's interest in protecting the fetus as it matured toward being able to live outside of the mother. But Blackmun specifically declared that the unborn child was not a "person" under the Fourteenth Amendment, and thus had no equal protection rights.

Blackmun wrote that what really mattered was the unborn baby's viability outside the womb. A fetus capable of life outside the womb, Blackmun believed, was more deserving of protection than one in its earliest stages of development. He also shot down Texas's attempt to define life as beginning at conception, which "by adopting one theory of life,"[31] would have then allowed Texas to extend its interest to the earliest stage of pregnancy. Blackmun wrote, "We need not resolve the difficult question of when life begins. When those trained in the respective disciplines of medicine, philosophy, and theology are unable to arrive at any consensus, the judiciary, at this point in the development of man's knowledge, is not in a position to speculate as to the answer."[32]

Blackmun gave deference to medicine, philosophy, and theology (from his own perspective), but not to the Constitution, the people, the states, or the other branches of the federal government. In truth, Blackmun did establish, at least for constitutional purposes, when life begins by recognizing abortion as a constitutionally protected right to privacy. He did precisely what he lectured should not be done.

Blackmun constructed a hyper-technical trimester analysis to break down the rights of the mother and the state. In the first trimester, the decision to abort must be left to the woman's physician. In the second trimester, the state may regulate abortion procedures to promote its interest in the mother's health. In the third trimester, in the interest of protecting the unborn child, the state can regulate and even ban abortion, except where, by medical judgment, it is necessary to preserve the mother's life or health.

The trade-offs inherent in the trimester system smack of the bargaining and dealing that legislators engage in to pass a highway construction bill. It is no wonder that activists justify *Roe* on policy and not legal grounds. But since this policy decision was disguised as a constitutional pronouncement by the Court, American law has been prevented from keeping up with rapid improvements in medical technology. Repeatedly, the Court has shown no willingness to recognize an earlier concept of viability to limit the reach of the abortion right.

Of course, from an analytical and logical point of view, a ban on abortion could have been upheld regardless of whether a fetus is protected by the Fourteenth Amendment as a "person." Americans are fined or imprisoned for destroying endangered wildlife or even wetlands, and these laws have been ruled constitutional.

In any event, Blackmun's stated deference to medicine, in which a doctor can authorize or perform an abortion for the health of the mother, belies his third-trimester framework. This point was driven home in 2000, in *Stenberg v. Carhart*, when the Supreme Court struck down a Nebraska law prohibiting partial-birth abortion.[33] Justice Stephen Breyer, in writing the majority opinion, stated, "We conclude [that the law banning partial-birth abortions violates the Constitution] for two independent reasons. First, the law lacks any exception 'for the preservation of the . . . health of the mother.' Second, it 'imposes undue burden on a woman's ability' to choose."[34] Consequently, the Supreme Court upheld a particularly vicious method of performing an abortion.

A Court historian believes Blackmun's leftward drift from moderate to liberal jurist was a result of *Roe*. "It was not just the criticism and the hate mail he received, but also thank-you letters he received from women. Over time, he came to think he had done a great thing for women, and it made him much more attuned to the cause of protecting individual rights."[35] Another way to describe Blackmun's shift is less charitable: He was moved and thereby seduced by public opinion in much the same way a politician is. There is evidence that Blackmun was particularly vulnerable to this type of lobbying. Chai Feldblum clerked for Blackmun during the term after he had issued his dissent in *Bowers v. Hardwick* (1986), in which he argued that the right to privacy protected homosexual sodomy. His office was once again flooded with letters from across the country.

"I believe he was radicalized by the response to the case," says Feldblum, now a professor of disability law at the Georgetown University Law Center in Washington, D.C. "The hate mail told him that prejudice existed and sodomy laws were part of the problem. The fan mail came from gay people who said things like,

'I am gay, and your dissent meant so much to me.' I'll never forget how much that meant to him."[36]

There is something truly absurd and, frankly, repugnant, about a judge being swayed by fan mail.

After *Roe*, Blackmun saw his role as championing a cause, not interpreting the Constitution. At the end of his career, he dramatically announced, without a trace of irony, that he was morally opposed to the death penalty. "From this day forward, I no longer shall tinker with the machinery of death,"[37] said the author of *Roe*, as if his ruling in *Roe* did not constitute a tinkering with the machinery of death.[38] Blackmun continued to issue self-congratulatory, pompous, and maudlin statements about *Roe*'s importance and vulnerability. "If it goes down the drain, I'd still like to regard *Roe v. Wade* as a landmark in the progress of the emancipation of women,"[39] he said. In 1992, with a presidential election looming, Blackmun made a dramatic call—*within a Supreme Court opinion*—to the supporters of abortion. He piously intoned, "And I fear for the darkness as four Justices anxiously await the single vote necessary to extinguish the light!"[40]

Yet *Roe* has survived, despite attempts to overturn it. Blackmun's personal papers reveal that Justice Anthony Kennedy made a last-moment switch and abandoned one such attempt in *Planned Parenthood v. Casey*,[41] decided in 1992, thereby providing the crucial fifth vote to uphold *Roe*.[42]

There are some interesting parallels between Kennedy and Blackmun. Both were their presidents' third choice for the Supreme Court and were considered competent but not exceptional when vetted by the White House. And, like Blackmun, Kennedy is going through a leftward evolution on the Court.

Kennedy, Justice Sandra Day O'Connor, and Justice David Souter issued jointly the majority opinion of the Court in *Casey*—a very unusual move. The Court allowed certain restrictions on abortion, but left the essential holding in *Roe* intact.[43]

The three justices began by stating the Court's obligations: "Some of us as individuals find abortion offensive to our most basic principles of morality, but that cannot control our decision. *Our obligation is to define the liberty of all, not to mandate our own moral code.* The underlying constitutional issue is whether the State can resolve these philosophic questions in such a definitive way that a woman lacks all choice in the matter, except perhaps in those rare circumstances in which the pregnancy is itself a danger to her own life or health, or is the result of rape or incest."[44] (Emphasis added.)

Of course, defining and establishing parameters for liberty (and life) do involve moral questions. Justice Kennedy, like Justices Douglas, Brennan, and Blackmun before him, delivered his own speech on the right to privacy: "These matters, involving the most intimate and personal choices a person may make in a lifetime, choices central to personal dignity and autonomy, are central to the liberty protected by the Fourteenth Amendment. At the heart of liberty is the right to define one's own concept of existence, of meaning, of the universe, and of the mystery of human life. Beliefs about these matters could not define the attributes of personhood were they formed under compulsion of the State."[45]

These words have been ridiculed by many, including Justice Antonin Scalia, as the "sweet-mystery-of-life" passage.[46] Scalia later wrote, in a different case, "I have never heard of a law that attempted to restrict one's 'right to define' certain concepts; and if the passage calls into question the government's power to regulate actions based on one's self-defined 'concept of existence, etc.,' it is the passage that ate the rule of law."[47]

The "right to define one's concept of the universe" is the modern incarnation of the emanations from penumbras that allegedly provided a right to privacy. It is just another meaningless, pseudo-sophisticated phrase by which justices evade our constitutional framework and impose their personal views on the rest of us. Almost ten years later, Kennedy, in concluding that homosexual sodomy is a constitutional right in *Lawrence v. Texas*, declared, "Liberty presumes an autonomy of self that includes freedom of thought, belief, expression, and certain intimate conduct."[48] Liberty also presumes, indeed requires, something our courts lack: fidelity to the rule of law and respect for the legislative branch of government, where controversial issues can be resolved through the elected representatives of the people, rather than a handful of unelected justices.

There are no more emotional and controversial moral and societal issues than those related to privacy, personal behavior, and liberty. And it's for this reason that public influence on government policy, exercised through the respective branches of government, is so crucial to ensuring the legitimate and proper functioning of a constitutional republic. To be true to its constitutional role, the Supreme Court should refuse to be drawn into making public policy, and it should strike down legislation only when a clear constitutional violation exists. When judicial activists resort to various inventions and theories to impose their personal views on privacy and liberty, they jeopardize the legitimacy of the judiciary as an institution and undermine the role of the other branches of government.

CHAPTER FIVE

Justices in the Bedroom

"The Court has taken sides in the culture war,
departing from its role of assuring, as neutral observer,
that the democratic rules of engagement are observed."

Justice Antonin Scalia, 2003[1]

How did "gay marriage" become a major public policy issue? After all, there has never been any popular movement to change the country's marriage laws. Even in New York, a liberal city with a large homosexual population, a 2004 *New York Daily News* poll showed a majority of voters opposed gay marriage.[2] The push for gay marriage is coming not from the people and their legislatures but from a small minority attempting to impose its view on society through the least democratic branch of government: the judiciary.

Gay advocacy groups don't hide the fact that they seek to advance their agenda by judicial fiat. A brochure distributed by the Lambda Legal Defense and Education Fund makes no pretense of trying to enact its wishes through the democratic process. It focuses only on the courts, stating, "The power of fighting for the freedom to marry is undeniable—and we've just begun! Considering it took until 1967 for the Supreme Court to finally overturn state bans on interracial marriage, it has been just a historical eye-blink since 1996 when a Hawaii court found there is no reason to ban gay people from civil marriage."[3]

Much of the rhetoric surrounding gay marriage has been wrapped in the language of civil rights (homosexuals should have the same right to marry as heterosexuals), economic equity arguments (homosexual couples should have the same access to financial benefits as married heterosexual couples), and child welfare claims (it's better that a parentless child be adopted by a loving homosexual couple than be left to languish in foster care). But these are not questions for the nine unelected justices of the U.S. Supreme Court to decide. They are questions for the people to resolve through their elected representatives.

Although the debate over gay marriage began in the states, the Supreme Court has ruled on related matters that will have serious ramifications on how the issue is ultimately decided. Over the last twenty years, it has decided two cases addressing the constitutionality of state sodomy laws: *Bowers v. Hardwick* (1986)[4] and *Lawrence v. Texas* (2003).[5] And it has ruled on a state constitutional amendment that denied special rights to homosexuals: *Romer v. Evans* (1996).[6]

The issue in these cases is whether we, as Americans, can enact into law basic moral beliefs, shared by an overwhelming majority of our fellow citizens, without the Supreme Court's interference.

Of course, some activities, even if they occur in the privacy of one's bedroom, should be (and are) outlawed because they violate the widely shared moral principles of Americans. As William F. Buckley wrote recently:

> What if a civil-rights hate act was being conducted in the bedroom? For that matter, what if Daddy was forcing his way with a 10-year-old girl? Or Mom was starving her 10-month-old boy?
>
> The phrase is an idiotic invocation of a taboo whose single purpose, in current usage, is to illegitimate concern about sexual activity....

That government should stay out of the bedrooms of America has come to mean an ever-increasing area of official non-concern. There is to be no concern over sodomy in the bedroom. But are there limits? What about incest? We know that infanticide is just plain illegal, even if undertaken in the bedroom—provided the infant is at least one day old.[7]

To argue, as some do, that the government should stay out of the bedroom, or that we have an absolute right to privacy in our own homes, is to demand more than constitutional protection for homosexual behavior or homosexual marriage. The fact is that the government is in our bedrooms when it criminalizes certain conduct. The debate is over which branch of government gets to decide how, when, and why it can be there.

In recent cases, the Court has laid the groundwork for ruling that any laws governing morality are constitutionally suspect, which would appear to put traditional marriage at risk.

In *Bowers v. Hardwick*, the facts belie the hysteria about puritanical sex police bursting into people's bedrooms with flashlights and nightsticks. (Even the *New York Times* noted that, "Sodomy laws are rarely enforced even where they remain on the books, in part because of the difficulty of proving violations."[8]) In 1982, an Atlanta police officer went to Michael Hardwick's home with an arrest warrant because Hardwick had not paid a fine for public drunkenness. Another man who lived with Hardwick answered the door and gave the policeman permission to enter and "look around" for him. The unwitting police officer found Hardwick in a room having sex with a man. He arrested Hardwick for violation of Georgia's sodomy statute, which applied to both heterosexual and homosexual sodomy. Hardwick spent twelve hours in jail and was released. The prosecution dropped the charges against him without ever going to trial. A year later, Hardwick brought a civil suit in federal district court for a ruling that the sodomy law was unconstitutional.[9]

After the Court of Appeals for the Eleventh Circuit agreed with Hardwick that homosexual conduct was a fundamental right free from state regulation, the Supreme Court decided to hear the case. Justice Byron White, appointed by President John Kennedy, wrote the majority opinion for the Court, split 5–4, rejecting the claim that homosexual sodomy is a fundamental right. White noted that the rights announced in prior cases involving family, marriage, and procreation had no relationship with a right to engage in homosexual sodomy. Furthermore, he wrote, "any claim that these cases nevertheless stand for the proposition that any kind of private sexual conduct between consenting adults is constitutionally insulated from state proscription is unsupportable."[10]

Hardwick wanted the Supreme Court to find a fundamental constitutional right to engage in homosexual sodomy. It refused. White noted dryly that despite the fact that the due process clauses of the Fifth and Fourteenth Amendments appear to focus only on the processes by which life, liberty, or property can be taken by the government, there have been many cases in which those clauses have been found to have substantive content—that is, they have become vehicles by which judges create new rights "that have little or no textual support in the constitutional language."[11] When a judge decides that the state has done something he disagrees with but which is not explicitly prevented by the Constitution, he can invent a new fundamental right that requires the court to step in and reverse a legislature's decision.

The Court has tried, White continued, to assure itself and the public that these new pronouncements of rights never before recognized in the Constitution involve more than the naked imposition of the individual justices' values on the states and the federal government. It has done so through various attempts to identify the nature of these new fundamental rights that require heightened judicial protection. These are said to be fundamental liberties that are "implicit in the concept of ordered liberty" or those that are "deeply rooted in this Nation's history and tradition."[12] This is mere window dressing, of course, because these phrases can be twisted and contorted to meet any individual's subjective beliefs. Thomas Jefferson's vision of "ordered liberty" might be quite different from Alexander Hamilton's, or from Justice Sandra Day O'Connor's, for that matter. The only vision of ordered liberty that should matter to a judge is the one enshrined in the Constitution.

As White argued, sodomy was a criminal offense under the common law and was prohibited by the original thirteen states when they ratified the Bill of Rights. When the Fourteenth Amendment was ratified, thirty-two of the thirty-seven states in the Union had criminal sodomy laws. Furthermore, until 1961, all fifty states criminalized sodomy. "Against this backdrop, to claim that a right to engage in such conduct is 'deeply rooted in this Nation's history and tradition,' or 'implicit in the concept of ordered liberty' is, at best, facetious."[13]

White refused to expand the Court's authority to find new fundamental rights in the due process clause. "The Court is most vulnerable and comes nearest to illegitimacy when it deals with judge-made constitutional law having little or no recognizable roots in the language or design of the Constitution."[14]

Hardwick had argued that his conduct, having occurred in the privacy of his own home, warranted special consideration. White summarily rejected the idea that the Constitution created an inviolable zone of privacy around the home, pointing out that "victimless crimes, such as the possession and use of illegal drugs, do not escape the law when they are committed at home."[15] Furthermore, White noted that if Hardwick's argument was limited to consensual sexual conduct, "it would be difficult, except by fiat, to limit the claimed right to homosexual conduct while leaving exposed to prosecution adultery, incest, and other sexual crimes even though they are committed in the home. We are unwilling to start down that road."[16]

Justice John Paul Stevens, in his dissent, wrote, "The fact that the governing majority in a State has traditionally viewed a particular practice as immoral is not a sufficient reason for upholding a law prohibiting the practice."[17] White countered, "The law, however, is constantly based on notions of morality, and if all laws representing essentially moral choices are to be invalidated under the Due Process Clause, the courts will be very busy indeed."[18] Unfortunately, the courts have been very busy since White's prediction.

In 1992, the citizens of White's home state of Colorado passed an amendment to their constitution by a statewide referendum. It prohibited the inclusion of "sexual orientation" in civil rights laws that ban racial and religious discrimination. The amendment was prompted by the enactment of municipal ordinances in Denver, Boulder, and Aspen banning discrimination against sexual orientation much the same way racial and religious discrimination is outlawed. It passed 53 percent to 47 percent. Although a majority of the voters of Colorado had voted for the proposal, *Newsweek* magazine declared, "in Colorado the voices of hate have taken on a new edge."[19] The *New York Times* later advocated a boycott of Colorado's tourism industry to "send a potent warning to other states" that might pass similar measures.[20] The night the amendment (Amendment 2) passed, Colorado governor Roy Romer, who later served as head of the Democratic National Committee during the Clinton administration, spoke to a gathering of homosexuals at the state capitol. With a bullhorn in hand, Romer said that if any state employees tried to enforce the measure he would fire them.[21] But Romer didn't need to carry out his threat. Amendment 2 never went into effect. It was challenged almost immediately and its enactment was stopped by a Colorado state court.

The case eventually reached the U.S. Supreme Court as *Romer v. Evans.*[22] Justice Anthony Kennedy wrote the opinion for the majority of the Court, which upheld the permanent injunction issued by the Colorado court against the amendment.[23] Kennedy based his argument on the equal protection clause of the Fourteenth Amendment, which was originally intended to protect the newly freed slaves after the Civil War. Equal protection of the law, it should be emphasized, does not mean that every law must treat each group of people the same. As Kennedy himself admitted, "most legislation classifies for one purpose or another, with resulting disadvantage to various groups or persons."[24] For this reason, laws challenged under the equal protection clause are generally analyzed by the Court under the rational basis test: The law must be reasonably related to a legitimate state purpose. If, however, the law affects a fundamental right, like voting, or a suspect class, like a racial minority, then the law is subject to the strict scrutiny test: It must be narrowly tailored to meet a compelling state interest.

Kennedy dismissed the primary rationale for the amendment: freedom of association for landlords or employers who have objections to homosexual behavior. The reasons offered for the amendment, he wrote, were "inexplicable by anything but animus toward the class it affects"[25] and the amendment served no legitimate state interest.

Justice Antonin Scalia, in his dissent, argued that Amendment 2 was merely an attempt by the people of Colorado to maintain traditional morality. This attempt was not only constitutional, it was specifically approved by Congress within federal statutes and the Supreme Court in the *Bowers v. Hardwick* decision. He noted how Kennedy and the other justices had ignored *Bowers* and instead imposed their own political sensibilities on Colorado:

> In holding that homosexuality cannot be singled out for disfavorable treatment, the Court contradicts a decision, unchallenged here, pronounced only 10 years ago [in *Bowers v. Hardwick*], and places the prestige of this institution behind the proposition that opposition to homosexuality is as reprehensible as racial or religious bias. Whether it is or not is precisely the cultural debate that gave rise to the Colorado constitutional amendment (and to the preferential laws against which the amendment was directed). Since the Constitution of the United States says nothing about this subject, it is left to be resolved by normal democratic means, including the democratic adoption of provisions in state constitutions. This Court has no business imposing upon all Americans the resolution favored by the elite class from which the Members of this institution are selected, pronouncing that "animosity" toward homosexuality . . . is evil.[26]

Scalia punctured the central thesis of the majority with the following observation:

> If it is constitutionally permissible for a State to make homosex-
> ual conduct criminal, surely it is constitutionally permissible for
> a State to enact other laws merely disfavoring homosexual con-
> duct.... And a fortiori it is constitutionally permissible for a State
> to adopt a provision not even disfavoring homosexual conduct,
> but merely prohibiting all levels of state government from
> bestowing special protections upon homosexual conduct.[27]

He concluded, "Today's opinion has no foundation in American constitutional law, and barely pretends [that].... Striking [Amendment 2] down is
an act, not of judicial judgment, but of political will."[28]

Of course, Scalia was right. How could Amendment 2 possibly be unconstitutional in light of the Court's holding in *Bowers*? Kennedy understood
this, and he, on behalf of a majority of the justices, would soon strike back
by overruling *Bowers*, the case they couldn't square with their desired result
in *Romer*. They seized on a case called *Lawrence v. Texas*.[29]

In 1998, a Texas sheriff's deputy responded to a report of a man going
crazy "with a gun."[30] The deputy entered the suspect's apartment through the
unlocked front door. Although he found no one with a gun, he saw John
Lawrence and Tyron Garner engaging in anal sex. He arrested them for violation of Texas's sodomy statute, a Class C misdemeanor, and they spent the
night in jail. Notably, the sodomy statute in Texas, unlike the Georgia statute,
prohibited conduct between same-sex couples but not different-sex couples.
Lawrence and Garner were charged and convicted before a justice of the
peace. Roger Nance, who had called in the complaint, was also arrested for
filing a false police report, for which he spent fifteen days in jail. After a new
trial in criminal court, the convictions of Lawrence and Garner were upheld
by the Texas Court of Appeals. The two men sought protection under the
equal protection and due process clauses of the Fourteenth Amendment, as
well as the repeal of *Bowers*.[31]

The U.S. Supreme Court took up the case, hearing oral argument in March
2003. The questions posed by the justices during oral argument revealed

much about their thinking. The transcript shows Justice Stephen Breyer quoting a childish poem to mock the idea that a state could ban certain conduct simply because it didn't like it.[32] He also badgered the lawyer representing Texas for trying to justify the sodomy statute: "You've not given a rational basis except to repeat the word morality," Breyer said, as if morality is an insufficient basis for law. Breyer summed up the main argument for overruling *Bowers*: It was not about sodomy per se, but that "people in their own bedrooms . . . have their right to do basically what they want, [if] it's not hurting other people."[33] This is wrong as a matter of law and fact.

Before *Lawrence* was decided, Senator Rick Santorum of Pennsylvania provoked a firestorm of criticism in the media with his opinion about the case. "If the Supreme Court says that you have the right to consensual [gay] sex within your home, then you have the right to bigamy, you have the right to polygamy, you have the right to incest, you have the right to adultery. You have the right to anything," he said. "All of those things are antithetical to a healthy, stable, traditional family."[34]

Although Santorum was making an accurate prediction about the legal ramifications of overturning *Bowers*, he was denounced as "a bigot who spreads lies."[35] The *New Republic* stated, "It's hard to characterize Santorum's remarks as anything other than those of a homophobic bigot; but, rest assured, Santorum's staff has tried."[36]

In June 2003, the U.S. Supreme Court's majority opinion in *Lawrence* overruled *Bowers*. Kennedy wrote the opinion for the majority, which was long on philosophy and short on precedent. Kennedy's opinion in *Lawrence* is a result in search of a rationale. He began with "Liberty protects the person from unwarranted government intrusions into a dwelling or other private places."[37] This statement means absolutely nothing from a constitutional perspective. Every criminal or immoral act can be justified on the grounds of exercising liberty. But Kennedy has a purpose in such an approach. By using the catchall word "liberty" rather than applying the Constitution to the issue, he seeks to expand the plain meaning of the due process clause of the Fourteenth Amendment (which prohibits the states from depriving any "person of life, liberty, or property, without due process of law") to grant rights not mentioned elsewhere in the Constitution.

Kennedy and the majority explicitly overruled *Bowers* and wrote that Stevens's original reasoning, *in dissent*, that morality alone is not a legitimate basis to support a law was right. Scalia countered, "This effectively decrees the end of all morals legislation. If, as the Court asserts, the promotion of majoritarian sexual morality is not even a legitimate state interest, [no law against fornication, bigamy, adultery, adult incest, bestiality, and obscenity] can survive rational-basis review."[38]

Kennedy, traveling further and further away from his judicial responsibility to interpret the Constitution, wrote of an "emerging awareness that liberty gives substantial protection"[39] to sexual decisions and reviewed how sodomy laws had been repealed in most states and even in Europe, where the European Court of Human Rights found sodomy laws invalid under the European Convention on Human Rights.[40] Kennedy concluded with a lecture about liberty: "The petitioners are entitled to respect for their private lives. The State cannot demean their existence or control their destiny by making their private sexual conduct a crime. Their *right to liberty under the Due Process Clause* gives them the full right to engage in their conduct without intervention of the government.... The Texas statute furthers no legitimate state interest which can justify its intrusion into the personal and private life of the individual."[41] (Emphasis added.)

Justice O'Connor was faced with a problem. How could she vote with the majority in *Lawrence* when seventeen years earlier she had voted with the majority in *Bowers*? She attempted to solve this dilemma with a laughable approach. She concurred in *Lawrence*'s result but provided a different rationale for her vote, arguing that the Texas sodomy statute, which prohibited *same*-sex sodomy but not heterosexual sodomy, violated the equal protection clause.[42]

As Scalia wrote, the Texas statute could not possibly be a denial of equal protection "since it is precisely the same distinction regarding partner that is drawn in state laws prohibiting marriage with someone of the same sex while permitting marriage with someone of the opposite sex."[43]

Scalia's conclusion describes how the Supreme Court has effectively set the terms for the gay marriage debate. He wrote:

> Today's opinion dismantles the structure of constitutional law that has permitted a distinction to be made between heterosexual and homosexual unions, insofar as formal recognition in marriage is concerned. If moral disapprobation of homosexual conduct is "no legitimate state interest" for purposes of proscribing that conduct ... and if, as the Court coos (casting aside all pretense of neutrality), "when sexuality finds overt expression in intimate conduct with another person, the conduct can be but one element in a personal bond that is more enduring,"... what justification could there possibly be for denying the benefits of marriage to homosexual couples exercising "[t]he liberty protected by the Constitution"...? Surely not the encouragement of procreation, since the sterile and the elderly are allowed to marry. This case "does not involve" the issue of homosexual marriage only if one entertains the belief that principle and logic have nothing to do with the decisions of this Court. Many will hope that, as the Court comfortingly assures us, this is so.[44]

These three cases—*Bowers*, *Romer*, and *Lawrence*—demonstrate some undeniable and unpleasant facts that need to be considered if traditional marriage is to be preserved. The Supreme Court is clearly in the business of vetoing state (and federal) legislation by inventing new and increasingly more absurd justifications. It does not feel bound by the Constitution or even precedent. It is abandoning the constitutional framework that supports the moral foundation of our laws. In the future, statutes and even state constitutional provisions that uphold the public's moral consensus and traditions will be open to challenge.

None of this was lost on the Lambda Legal Defense and Education Fund, which saw *Lawrence* as the truly radical decision that it was:

> Lambda Legal will announce its aggressive plan for turning this landmark ruling into a reality in LGBT [lesbian, gay, bisexual, and transgender] people's everyday lives. From couples and families to kids in school, we're sharing our vision for how this decision will touch every LGBT person in America—and we're sharing the Lambda Legal plan for making that happen. Celebrate our victory this week...together, we're going to use it to win even greater equality for LGBT people for generations to come.[45]

Susan Sommer, a supervising attorney for the group, hailed the decision as an opportunity: "But even beyond what we can do with it [the Supreme Court's decision] technically as a legal precedent, which is quite a bit, it also simply changes the landscape, changes the culture, and reflects an enormous shift in this nation. The court has sent a very powerful message to courts around the land, to legislatures around the land and to every community that gay men and women should be afforded the same dignities and liberties as everyone else. It is now a new day."[46]

Scalia and Sommer are right. The Supreme Court has set the stage for imposing gay marriage on every state under a distorted reading of the Fourteenth Amendment. And the Supreme Judicial Court of Massachusetts might have created the circumstances under which the U.S. Supreme Court could eventually act.

In 2001, seven gay couples sued the Massachusetts Department of Public Health when they were denied marriage licenses. The couples claimed that they had a fundamental right under the Massachusetts Constitution to pick the spouse of their choice. Therefore, they argued, the Massachusetts marriage statutes could not be interpreted to exclude same-sex couples.[47]

In November 2003, by a narrowly split vote of 4 to 3, the Supreme Judicial Court of Massachusetts found that the denial of marriage to gay couples violated the Massachusetts Constitution. The court wrote, "Barred access to the protections, benefits, and obligations of civil marriage, a person who enters into an intimate, exclusive union with another of the same sex is arbitrarily deprived of membership in one of our community's most rewarding and cherished institutions. That exclusion is incompatible with the constitutional principles of respect for individual autonomy and equality under law."[48]

To rectify this supposed injustice, the Supreme Judicial Court changed the common-law definition of civil marriage to mean "the voluntary union of two persons as spouses to the exclusion of all others."[49] While explaining their action, the court claimed that it would not be "appropriate" to strike down the existing marriage laws. Their concern rings hollow, considering that instead of striking them down, the court drastically changed a fundamental aspect of the state marriage laws. Moreover, the court explicitly adopted the approach taken by the Court of Appeal for Ontario, Canada, in a gay marriage case, by changing the common-law definition.[50] Not only did the court usurp the state legislature, but it looked beyond its own constitution to a foreign legal system for guidance.

After it altered the definition of marriage that had existed in Massachusetts for centuries, the Supreme Judicial Court went a step further. The Court gave the state legislature 180 days to "take such action as it may deem appropriate in light of this opinion."[51] The legislature was, in effect, given a deadline to fix the legal mess the Court had created.

The Massachusetts legislature scrambled to come up with a possible solution. An attempt by the legislature to protect traditional marriage through a constitutional amendment required longer than 180 days. The legislature decided to propose the enactment of civil union laws, which would provide many, if not all, of the benefits of marriage, except one—the name.

By a quirk of the Massachusetts Constitution, "each branch of the legislature, as well as the governor or the council, shall have authority to require the opinions of the justices of the supreme judicial court, upon important questions of law, and upon solemn occasions."[52] The Massachusetts Senate asked the court to consider if the civil union proposal was constitutional, to which the court responded in February 2004 with a forceful "no." Central to its reasoning was the terminology of the bill:

> The bill's absolute prohibition of the use of the word "marriage" by "spouses" who are the same sex is more than semantic. The dissimilitude between the terms "civil marriage" and "civil union" is not innocuous; it is a considered choice of language that reflects a demonstrable assigning of same-sex, largely homosexual, couples to second-class status. . . . The bill would have the effect of maintaining and fostering a stigma of exclusion that the Constitution prohibits. It would deny to same-sex "spouses" only a status that is specially recognized in society and has significant social and other advantages. The Massachusetts Constitution, as was explained in the *Goodridge* opinion, does not permit such invidious discrimination, no matter how well intentioned.[53]

Despite the opinion, the Massachusetts legislature was not deterred. It went ahead with a constitutional convention. It passed the civil union law and an amendment to the state constitution banning same-sex marriage, but the earliest it will appear on the ballot for ratification is 2006.

Nevertheless, shortly after midnight on May 17, 2004—the end of the court's deadline to institute gay marriage—municipal clerks began handing out marriage licenses to same-sex couples in Massachusetts. As the Associated Press reported, "As of Monday, Massachusetts joins the Netherlands, Belgium, and Canada's three most populous provinces as the only places worldwide where gays can marry."[54]

Four of seven justices of the Supreme Judicial Court of Massachusetts—with the stroke of a pen—abolished hundreds of years of tradition and law over the strong objections of the legislature. And as these activist justices undoubtedly intended, their ruling will have consequences well beyond their jurisdiction and Massachusetts's borders.

Unfortunately, without federal intervention, the prospect of one state imposing gay marriage on other states is quite real. The Constitution requires each state to honor a sister state's public acts and judgments under the full faith and credit clause.[55] If a gay couple marries in Massachusetts, what prevents them from moving to Alabama and demanding that their marriage be recognized there? The existing legal impediments to gay marriage nationally can be easily circumvented.

For example, in 1996 Congress overwhelmingly passed the federal Defense of Marriage Act (DOMA), which was signed into law by President Bill Clinton. Congress acted because of rumblings that Hawaii's state courts were going to recognize a constitutional right to gay marriage. The DOMA states, "No State, territory, or possession of the United States, or Indian tribe, shall be required to give effect to any public act, record, or judicial proceeding of any other State, territory, possession, or tribe respecting a relationship between persons of the same sex that is treated as a marriage under the laws of such other State, territory, possession, or tribe, or a right or claim arising from such relationship."[56] In essence, a state does not have to honor a same-sex marriage performed in a sister state.

Thirty-nine states have also passed equivalent versions of the DOMA, thereby refusing to recognize gay marriages performed elsewhere.[57] In August 2004, Missouri became the fifth state to pass an amendment to its state constitution banning gay marriage.[58] There are more constitutional amendment efforts under way in numerous other states.

The possibility also exists that a state could argue, if challenged in court, that the recognition of gay marriage is not compelled by the full faith and credit clause because it goes against the "public policy" of the objecting state. Even heterosexual marriages have not been uniformly enforced in the United States. For example, the age of consent differs among the states, so some states declare a marriage from a sister state invalid if a spouse is too young.[59]

Yet all these legal obstacles to gay marriage will crumble before an activist U.S. Supreme Court. The U.S. Constitution is the highest law in the land, and the Court routinely strikes down state and federal law, and even state constitutional provisions, by invoking the federal Constitution. Given the Supreme Court's rulings in *Lawrence* and *Romer*, a homosexual couple could plausibly argue that denying recognition of their marriage would be a violation of the Fourteenth Amendment's equal protection clause. In fact, "equality under the law" was the cornerstone of the Massachusetts court's ruling.

There are essentially two options available to the elected branches of government to prevent the judiciary from seizing the ultimate authority to define marriage—to amend the federal Constitution, or for Congress to pass a law denying the federal courts jurisdiction to rule on this subject.[60]

A federal marriage amendment was put forth by Senator Wayne Allard and Representative Marilyn Musgrave, both Colorado Republicans. It stated: "Marriage in the United States shall consist only of the union of a man and a woman. Neither this Constitution, nor the constitution of any State, shall be construed to require that marriage or the legal incidents thereof be conferred upon any union other than the union of a man and a woman."[61]

In February 2004, President Bush called for a constitutional amendment to protect traditional marriage. He noted that "some activist judges and local officials have made an aggressive attempt to redefine marriage."[62] Although he did not specifically mention it, he announced his support for an amendment that followed the Musgrave/Allard approach.[63]

A primary criticism of this approach, however, is that it violates the principles of federalism by defining marriage for the states. Senator John McCain, among others, said it was "antithetical in every way to the core philosophy of Republicans."[64] The procedure for amending the Constitution, however, apart from holding a constitutional convention, which no one endorses, requires the vote of two-thirds of both houses of Congress and then ratification by three-fourths of the states. The amendment process itself—involving all state legislatures and requiring a super-majority for passage—*is* federalism.[65]

On July 14, 2004, the Senate voted 50–48 against a procedural motion to bring the federal marriage amendment to the floor for a vote.[66] A week later, House Republicans tried the alternative approach: limiting the Court's jurisdiction to rule on marriage. Representative John Hostettler of Indiana sponsored the Marriage Protection Act, which would strip jurisdiction from all federal courts over the Defense of Marriage Act. The bill passed 233–194.[67]

House Minority Leader Nancy Pelosi of California derided the measure, citing *Marbury v. Madison* for the proposition that the judiciary has final say over the constitutionality of congressional acts. She said, "Subsequent decisions and the court's role as an equal branch strongly suggest that Congress cannot prohibit the court from determining the validity of a law in the first place."[68] Hostettler countered, "Anyone [who] actually reads the Constitution and has a basic understanding of grammar and the English language in general can find the fact that the Constitution grants the Congress the authority."[69]

For now, the issue is stalled. Not a single state legislature has recognized homosexual marriage, and most states have taken steps to defend themselves against activist courts that would impose it. This issue, like few others, will determine whether Congress has the will finally to defend its constitutional role as the public's federal representative body.

CHAPTER SIX

ENDORSING RACISM

"You guys have been practicing discrimination for years. Now it is our turn."

Justice Thurgood Marshall[1]

"**A**ffirmative action" has been around since the 1960s. In Executive Order 10925, President John Kennedy instructed federal contractors to take "affirmative action to ensure that applicants are treated equally without regard to race, color, religion, sex, or national origin." Several years later, President Lyndon Johnson issued Executive Order 11246, which required government contractors to take affirmative steps to "expand job opportunities for minorities." President Richard Nixon went even further. He ordered federal agencies to set up a national Minority Business Enterprise contracting program.[2] In his autobiography, Nixon wrote, "A good job is as basic and important a civil right as a good education. . . . I felt that the plan [Labor Secretary] George Shultz devised, which would require such [affirmative] action by law, was both necessary and right. We would not impose quotas, but would require federal contractors to show affirmative action to meet the goals of increasing minority employment."[3]

The problem with affirmative action is that it invariably involves reverse discrimination. Discriminating against people because of their race is repugnant and unconstitutional. But remedying the wrong of past discrimination by inflicting new discrimination undermines the very principle of racial non-prejudice that is the professed goal of American law and public policy.

The *Bakke* Case

Starting in the late 1960s, educational institutions began to establish affirmative action programs designed to increase minority enrollment. The first Supreme Court decision to directly address affirmative action in education was the landmark 1978 case *Regents of the University of California v. Bakke.*[4] *Bakke* involved the admissions program of the University of California at Davis's medical school. Students applying to the school had to have a minimum 2.5 grade point average, and only one in six who met that minimum standard were invited for an interview. Applicants were given a total admission score that included their overall grade point average, grade point average in science courses, graded interview score, Medical College Admission Test (MCAT) scores, and other criteria, including letters of recommendation and extracurricular activities. In 1973, a perfect score was 500 points. In 1974, it was increased to 600 points.[5]

There was, however, a special admissions program run by a separate admissions committee for minority group applicants, in which the 2.5 grade point average cutoff did not apply. When the medical class size was fifty, eight slots were reserved for minority candidates Both numbers were doubled in 1973.[6]

Allan Bakke was a white male who applied to the medical school in 1973. His combined score was 468 out of 500. His application for admission was denied because it was late in the year and the admissions program had ruled that any candidates who scored below a 470 would not be accepted.[7]

Bakke applied again the following year; this time, his application was early and his combined score was 549 out of 600. He was placed on the waiting list but ultimately rejected. In both years, candidates who had lower grade point averages, lower MCAT scores, and lower total combined scores than Bakke were admitted under the special admissions process.[8]

The issue presented to the Supreme Court in *Bakke* was whether the special admissions program violated the equal protection clause of the Fourteenth Amendment. The Fourteenth Amendment prohibits all state discrimination based on race, without exception. The Court has ruled that the Fourteenth Amendment protects Celtic Irishmen,[9] Chinese,[10] Austrian resident aliens,[11] Japanese,[12] and Mexican-Americans.[13] It has said that "Congress was intent upon establishing in the federal law a broader principle than would have been necessary simply to meet the particular and immediate plight of the newly freed Negro slaves."[14] But what about Bakke, a white male who was denied admission to a state medical school because of a racially discriminatory policy? Wouldn't the Fourteenth Amendment protect him?

Not necessarily, because over the years the Supreme Court has taken the clear language of the Fourteenth Amendment and twisted it into a pretzel. It has held that when a government entity makes a law that provides for a classification based on race, the law is subject to a type of judicial examination known as strict scrutiny. This is the highest level of scrutiny that a court can invoke when deciding whether a particular law is constitutional. In order to pass muster under a strict scrutiny analysis, such a law must be "narrowly tailored" to meet a "compelling government interest."[15]

Laws that are subject to the strict scrutiny standard are, in most cases, overturned because the burden falls on the government to show how and why the law serves a compelling state interest. California argued that its compelling state interest in the special admissions program was to (1) increase minority representation in medicine, (2) counter racial discrimination in society, (3) increase the number of doctors in minority areas, and (4) reap the educational benefits of a more ethnically diverse student body.

Justice Lewis Powell, who wrote the opinion for the majority of the Court, dismissed the first justification, because it was "discrimination for its own sake which is prohibited by the Constitution."[16] As to the second point,

Powell conceded that the state has a recognized interest in remedying past discrimination, but the "purpose of helping certain groups whom the faculty of the Davis Medical School perceived as victims of 'societal discrimination' does not justify a classification that imposes disadvantages upon persons like respondent [Mr. Bakke], who bear no responsibility for whatever harm the beneficiaries of the special admissions program are thought to have suffered."[17]

As for the argument that minority physicians would practice in communities that are underserved, Powell concluded that the state had not demonstrated "that it must prefer members of particular ethnic groups over all other individuals in order to promote better health care delivery to deprived citizens."[18]

Powell, however, found California's final argument persuasive, at least up to a point. He wrote that because promoting a diverse student body encourages "speculation, experiment and creation" it is a constitutionally permissible goal. But he wrote that diversity "encompasses a far broader array of qualifications and characteristics of which racial or ethnic origin is but a single though important element."[19]

Powell decided that since the special admissions program focused solely on ethnic diversity, it actually hindered diversity and was, therefore, unconstitutional. He wrote:

> In summary, it is evident that the Davis special admissions program involves the use of an explicit racial classification never before countenanced by this Court. It tells applicants who are not Negro, Asian or Chicano that they are totally excluded from a specific percentage of the seats in an entering class. No matter how strong their qualifications, quantitative and extracurricular, including their own potential for contribution to educational diversity, they are never afforded the chance to compete with applicants from the preferred groups for the special admissions

seats. At the same time, the preferred applicants have the opportunity to compete for every seat in the class.[20]

Consequently, the Court outlawed racial quotas, or the setting aside of a certain number of classroom seats exclusively for minorities. But proponents of affirmative action won a partial victory nevertheless, because admissions programs could in the future use racial classifications if they are narrowly tailored and are one of several factors in the attainment of a diverse student body. Although California lost, affirmative action survived.

Bakke would have significant and lasting consequences. Powell's decision "served as the touchstone for constitutional analysis of race-conscious admission policies. Public and private universities across the Nation modeled their own admissions programs on Powell's views."[21]

In 2003, the Supreme Court again took up the issue of affirmative action in education when it decided the cases of *Grutter v. Bollinger* and *Gratz v. Bollinger.*[22] The cases involved admissions programs at the University of Michigan Law School and undergraduate school.

In *Grutter*, Barbara Grutter applied for admission to the law school. She had a 3.8 grade point average and a score of 161 out of 180 on the Law School Admission Test (LSAT). Grutter was initially placed on a waiting list for admission but her application was subsequently rejected. She challenged the law school's admission policy, alleging that she was discriminated against because she was white.

The law school's admissions procedures bore the stamp of the *Bakke* decision, referring "to the educational benefits that diversity is designed to produce."[23] The former dean of admissions "testified that he did not direct his staff to admit a particular percentage or number of minority students, but rather to consider an applicant's race along with all other factors."[24] He also "testified that at the height of the admissions season, he would frequently consult the so-called 'daily reports' that kept track of the racial and ethnic composition of the class."[25] He said he sought "to ensure that a critical mass of underrepresented minority students would be reached so as to realize the educational benefits of a diverse student body."[26] Another former dean of law school admissions testified that there was "no number, percentage, or range of numbers or percentages" sought by the school to reach what it deemed a "critical mass" of minority students.[27]

Against this backdrop, Justice Sandra Day O'Connor, writing for a majority of the Supreme Court, concluded that "we endorse Justice Powell's view [in *Bakke*] that student body diversity is a compelling state interest that can justify the use of race in university admissions."[28] O'Connor stated that the law school program was sufficiently tailored to survive a strict scrutiny analysis and wrote, "attaining a diverse student body is at the heart of the Law School's proper institutional mission."[29] Diversity, according to O'Connor, "'promotes cross-racial understanding,' helps to break down racial stereotypes and 'enables [students] to better understand persons of different races.'"[30]

O'Connor next examined whether the school's policy was narrowly tailored to achieve the compelling interest. Unlike the "special admissions" program in *Bakke*, O'Connor concluded that the school's admission policy was sufficiently tailored and did not operate as a quota system. The policy "is flexible enough to ensure that each applicant is evaluated as an individual and not in any way that makes an applicant's race or ethnicity the defining feature of his or her application."[31] But she also placed a time constraint on "race conscious admission policies":

> We are mindful, however, that "[a] core purpose of the Fourteenth Amendment was to do away with all governmentally imposed discrimination based on race." Accordingly, race-conscious admissions policies must be limited in time. This requirement reflects that racial classifications, however compelling their goals, are potentially so dangerous that they may be employed no more broadly than the interest demands. Enshrin-

ing a permanent justification for racial preferences would offend this fundamental equal protection principle. We see no reason to exempt race-conscious admissions programs from the requirement that all governmental use of race must have a logical end point. The Law School, too concludes that all "race conscious programs must have reasonable durational limits."[32]

O'Connor and the Supreme Court majority recommended "periodic reviews" in order to determine whether the race-conscious admission policy was still necessary in order to attain the goal of diversity.[33]

Of course, there's nothing in the Fourteenth Amendment about different scrutiny tests, diversity, and all the other judicial creations designed to get around the clear prohibition against racial discrimination.

Diversity had never been a constitutional basis for government-sanctioned racial discrimination. As Justice Antonin Scalia stated in his dissent:

> The educational "benefit" that the University of Michigan seeks to achieve by racial discrimination consists, according to the Court, of "cross-racial understanding," and "better prepar[ation of] students for an increasingly diverse workforce and society,"... all of which is necessary not only for work, but also for good "citizenship." This is not of course an "education benefit" on which students will be graded on their Law School transcript (Works and Plays Well with Others, B+) or tested by the bar examiners (Q: Describe in 500 words or less your cross-racial understanding). For it is a lesson of life rather than law—essentially, the same lesson taught to (or rather learned by, for it cannot be "taught" in the usual sense) people three feet shorter and twenty years younger than the full-grown adults at the University of Michigan Law School, in institutions ranging from Boy Scout troops to public-school kindergartens.[34]

There is another point to make here, and Brian Fitzpatrick, a former Supreme Court law clerk, has made it. It is that many universities practicing affirmative action in their admissions programs (and justifying such programs under the rubric of "diversity") actually work to segregate races within the institution, thereby defeating the very purpose they claim to pursue. For example, in 1999, Princeton University held a separate graduation ceremony for minorities. Certain universities have separate "multicultural" dormitories. These dorms allow members of minority groups to segregate themselves from the general student population. Even the University of Michigan, a party in *Grutter*, holds a separate graduation ceremony for black seniors.[35]

And as Samuel Issacharoff, a law professor at Columbia Law School, has stated, "The commitment to diversity is not real. None of these universities has an affirmative-action program for Christian fundamentalists, Muslims, Orthodox Jews, or any other group that has a distinct viewpoint."[36] "Diversity" is just the clever label the Court gives to reverse discrimination.

Besides, Americans don't need government-orchestrated diversity. We are a racially and ethnically diverse populace, and are becoming more so every year. In 2004, the U.S. Census Bureau projected that America's Hispanic and Asian populations would triple over the next fifty years. By the year 2050, whites would represent half of the total population.[37] One in six adopted children is racially different from his or her parents. In 2000, one in fifteen marriages in the U.S. was interracial. This is up from one in twenty-three in 1990.[38]

More to the point, as a matter of law, O'Connor's decision fails her own stated requirement that the Law School program be "narrowly tailored" to achieve the purported "compelling government interest" of diversity. As Chief Justice William Rehnquist argued in his dissent, any program that seeks a "critical mass" of "underrepresented minority" students is essentially a quota system. Rehnquist wrote:

> From 1995 through 2000 the percentage of admitted applicants
> who were [underrepresented minorities—African Americans,

Native Americans and Hispanics] closely tracked the percentage of individuals in the school's applicant poll who were from the same groups.... For example, in 1995, when 9.7% of the applicant pool was African American, 9.4% of the admitted class was African American. By 2000 only 7.5% of the applicant pool was African American and 7.3% of the admitted class was African American. This correlation is striking.[39]

Justice Clarence Thomas, in his dissent, pointed out the essential unfairness of the quota system: "No one would argue that a university could set up a lower general admission standard and then impose heightened requirements only on black applicants. Similarly, a university may not maintain a high admission standard and grant exemptions to favored races." If the school wanted to encourage "diversity" all it had to do, Thomas noted, was lower its admission standards.[40] Thomas also repudiated Justice O'Connor's twenty-five-year time limit on her decision, writing that "the Law School's current use of race violates the Equal Protection Clause and that the Constitution means the same thing today as it will in 300 months."[41]

Apart from violating the Fourteenth Amendment, as a practical matter O'Connor's decision uses nebulous terms and applies subjective analysis that will predictably result in further litigation and inconsistent decisions.

A companion case to *Grutter v. Bollinger* was *Gratz v. Bollinger*.[42] In *Gratz*, the Supreme Court decided that the University of Michigan's undergraduate admissions program—which had a "selection index" (its preferred mislabeling of racial discrimination)—failed the strict scrutiny analysis. The majority in *Gratz* found that the "selection index" was not narrowly tailored to meet the state's compelling interest to promote diversity, so it violated the equal protection clause of the Fourteenth Amendment.[43] The majority's reasoning is summarized best by Rehnquist:

The current policy automatically distributes 20 points to every single applicant from an "underrepresented minority" group, as defined by the University. The only consideration that accompanies this distribution of points is a factual review of an application to determine whether an individual is a member of one of these minority groups. Moreover, unlike Justice Powell's example, where the race of a "particular black applicant" could be considered without being decisive ... the automatic distribution of 20 points has the effect of making "the factor of race ... decisive" for virtually every minimally qualified underrepresented minority applicant.[44]

While the Court reached the right conclusion in *Gratz*, it did so by an overly convoluted reading of the Fourteenth Amendment. The Fourteenth Amendment is not about charts and indexes and statistics; the distinction the Court finds between the *Grutter* and *Gratz* admissions programs are hypertechnical. The Court seems to believe that government-sponsored racial discrimination is okay as long as it is done on an individual rather than a group basis. But where is that distinction in the Constitution?

The fact that universities consider many factors in enrolling students is no excuse for including race among those factors. The Fourteenth Amendment explicitly provides for equal protection of all races. Government-sponsored racial discrimination violates the Constitution.

Reacting to recent Court decisions, Ward Connerly, one of America's leading advocates for merit-based admissions policies, wrote:

Let it be said that when given a chance to complete the liberation of black Americans, on June 23, 2003, five justices consigned them to another generation—or, perhaps, a term of indefinite duration—of virtual enslavement to the past. Instead of being free to just be Americans, the Court has entrapped American-born blacks in a seemingly inescapable web of being set apart from the rest of America, as well as prolonging the suspicion and stigmatization that is visited on the accomplishments of high-achievers who are perceived to benefit from "diversity" and "affir-mative action" just because of their skin color.[45]

At various times in our history, the Court has promoted slavery, segrega-tion, and internment based on race and ethnicity. Today it promotes reverse discrimination. Mark up yet another victory for judicial activism and a set-back for the rule of law and individual liberty.

CHAPTER SEVEN

CITIZENSHIP UP FOR GRABS

"The Constitution does not constitute us as 'Platonic Guardians' nor does it vest in this Court the authority to strike down laws because they do not meet our standards of desirable social policy, 'wisdom,' or 'common sense.'...We trespass on the assigned function of the political branches under our structure of limited and separated powers when we assume a policymaking role."

Chief Justice Warren Burger, 1982[1]

I f there is one area of law that should be universally understood as being largely outside the purview of the Supreme Court's social engineering reach, it is immigration. Article I, Section 8 of the Constitution states that Congress shall have the power "to establish an uniform Rule of Naturalization."[2]

That, however, is not how events have transpired. For the last several decades, the Supreme Court has effectively trampled on Congress's constitutionally mandated, separate, and exclusive power and taken upon itself the task of rewriting America's immigration laws. The Court has abused its limited authority and has become, effectively, the architect of the rules governing not only how immigrants enter and remain in America, but whether those immigrants can avail themselves of social benefits that states and even Congress have sought to limit to U.S. citizens.

Thanks to succeeding Supreme Courts, illegal immigrants—not legal immigrants but aliens who have broken U.S. law to enter this country—are entitled to a public school education at the U.S. taxpayers' expense. The Court has also ruled that despite laws to the contrary, noncitizens who are legally in the U.S. can qualify for welfare, can seek tuition assistance to attend colleges and universities, and can take competitive civil service jobs and practice law.

According to the Federation for American Immigration Reform (FAIR), Arizona spends $1.3 billion each year on illegal immigration.[3] The same FAIR study reported that every Arizonan essentially pays a $700 annual tax to support the direct costs of illegal immigration. The *New York Times* reported in 2002 that "a wave of immigrants in the last 10 years, particularly in rural areas far from traditional immigration hubs, has left school districts across the country desperately short of people qualified to teach English."[4] In fact, the number of students who have limited English skills has doubled to approximately five million in the last ten years.[5] Educating illegal immigrants in the public schools costs the states at least $7.4 billion annually, according to FAIR.[6] California alone spends an estimated $2.2 billion annually to educate illegal immigrant children.[7] And the *Washington Times* reported that hospitals near the U.S.-Mexican border spent, in 2000, almost $190 million to treat illegal aliens and another $113 million in ambulance and follow-up fees.[8]

Before American independence, each of the thirteen colonies developed its own immigration policies. Most of these policies were geared toward encouraging immigration from Europe to help alleviate severe labor shortages throughout the vast expanse of the colonial territories.[9] Land grants and exemptions from taxes were popular enticements to immigrants to settle in the New World. However, most of the colonies also had laws in place to discourage certain types of immigrants—specifically Roman Catholics.[10] Many of the colonies levied head taxes on ship captains for any Catholic they brought ashore. Certain colonies offered land grants and tax benefits only to Protestants.[11] As a result, the majority of the early immigrants came from Protestant England and Germany.

After 1776, the new Congress did not preempt the states' existing immigration and naturalization policies.[12] The only modification to the status quo came in Article IV of the Articles of Confederation (the forerunner to the

Constitution), which provided that the citizens of each state were given the same privileges and immunities as citizens of every other state. But each state retained its own naturalization and immigration laws and standards. This arrangement created a de facto briar patch of policies and practices that inhibited commerce and limited America's potential role on the world stage. The problem was rectified at the Constitutional Convention in 1787. Article I, Section 8 of the new Constitution gave Congress the power "To establish an uniform Rule of Naturalization."[13]

The noted nineteenth-century associate justice of the Supreme Court and constitutional scholar Joseph Story spoke eloquently of the need for congressional oversight and exclusive jurisdiction over immigration:

> The power of naturalization is, with great propriety, confided to Congress, since, if left to the States, they might naturalize foreigners upon very different, and even upon opposite systems; and, as the citizens of all the States have common privileges in all, it would thus be in the power of any one State to defeat the wholesome policy of all the others in regard to this most important subject. Congress alone can have power to pass uniform laws, obligatory on all the States; and thus to adopt a system, which shall secure all of them against any dangerous results from the indiscriminate admission of foreigners to the right of citizenship upon their first landing on our shores. And, accordingly, this power is exclusive in Congress.[14]

The first effort to control immigration and naturalization came with the Naturalization Act of 1790, when Congress set the residency requirement for U.S. citizenship at two years. In 1795, the requirement was increased to five years. The Alien and Sedition Acts of 1798 were dramatic attempts by Congress, then controlled by the Federalist Party of John Adams and Alexander Hamilton, to address both a national security threat and a political challenge to the Federalists' power.[15] The first was the imminent threat of war with

France and the second was the trend of new immigrants to ally with the Republican Party headed by Thomas Jefferson. Among the many things these acts did was criminalize criticism of the federal government and increase the time an immigrant had to live in the United States before becoming a citizen from five to fourteen years. They also provided for the deportation of aliens from "enemy" states and allowed the president to imprison enemy aliens during wartime.[16]

When Jefferson won the presidency and his party took control of both houses of Congress in 1800, the Alien and Sedition Acts were repealed. Congress also returned the residency requirement for U.S. citizenship to five years. Beyond these actions, no real effort was made by Congress to limit immigration in this country until 1875, when Congress passed the first immigration act that restricted entry of aliens to the United States.[17] The act prohibited immigration by slaves, prostitutes, and Chinese "coolies."[18] Later laws imposed temporary or permanent restrictions on entry by Chinese emigrants and other groups.

Congressional legislation has repeatedly, over the last two centuries, added, modified, or removed the residency, gender, race, and age requirements to become a U.S. citizen. The Naturalization Act of 1855, for example, opened U.S. citizenship to immigrant women who married a citizen or whose husbands became naturalized.[19]

More recently, in 1996, Congress enacted the Illegal Immigration Reform and Immigrant Responsibility Act (IIRIRA), which gave immigration officers the authority to summarily deport an alien if the officer determines that the alien has engaged in fraud or misrepresentation, or that the alien does not possess valid documents.[20] It also delegated to the attorney general—not to the Supreme Court—*sole* authority to naturalize individuals. Congress specifically stated in the IIRIRA that courts could no longer review an attorney general's decision to remove an alien "on the basis of most criminal convictions."[21]

Congress's rationale for keeping naturalization an executive branch function is that deportation hearings do not determine whether an alien is guilty of any crime. By simply kicking someone out of our country, the federal government is not, in a legal sense, punishing that person.

Unfortunately, while recognizing in some cases Congress's basic authority to write immigration law, a majority of justices on the Supreme Court have on several occasions used two constitutional provisions to insert the Court's institutional nose under the immigration tent. The Court discovered that the equal protection and due process clauses in the Fifth[22] and Fourteenth[23] Amendments granted the judiciary all of the authority it will ever need to rewrite America's immigration laws.

However, the Supreme Court has chosen in successive decisions to extend the premise of equal protection and due process to include equal access to social benefits as well. In fact, in *Graham v. Richardson*,[24] a 1971 case, the Court said, "this Court now has rejected the concept that constitutional rights turn upon whether a governmental benefit is characterized as a 'right' or as a 'privilege.'"[25]

This wasn't always the case. The Court, particularly in the years leading up to World War I, recognized the importance of distinguishing between citizens and noncitizens in making and managing public policy. In 1915, in *Heim v. McCall*, the Supreme Court decided in favor of New York's authority to show preference in hiring citizens for transit authority projects. Justice Joseph McKenna wrote:

> The basic principle of the decision of the Court of Appeals was that the State is a recognized unit and those who are not citizens of it are not members of it. Thus recognized it is a body corporate and, like any other body corporate, it may enter into contracts and hold and dispose of property. In doing this, it acts through agencies of government. These agencies, when contracting for the State, or expending the State's moneys, are trustees for the people of the State. . . . And it has hence decided that in the control of such agencies and the expenditure of such moneys it

could prefer its own citizens to aliens without incurring the con-
demnation of the National or the state constitution.[26]

In *Heim*, in fact, the Court specifically rejected the argument that the
Fourteenth Amendment precluded states from discriminating against noncitizens in the distribution of public benefits. "[I]t belongs to the State, as the
guardian of its people, and having control of its affairs, to prescribe the conditions upon which it will permit public work to be done on its behalf, or on
behalf of its municipalities."[27]

In other words, the Supreme Court of 1915 deferred to the judgment of
the state governments to determine how public funds should be distributed—exactly as the framers of the Constitution intended.

In 1927, in *Ohio ex rel. v. Clarke Deckebach Auditor*, the Court reinforced
the *Heim* decision, specifically rejecting the equal protection argument
advanced under the Fourteenth Amendment, and rejected the premise that
the Court should exercise unfounded authority and write new law through
its opinions.[28] An 1815 treaty between the United States and Britain guaranteed that "the merchants and traders of each nation . . . shall enjoy the most
complete protection and security for their commerce."[29] A merchant in
Cincinnati, who was a resident alien and a subject of the British Empire, was
denied a license to operate a pool hall because city ordinances required that
such licenses be issued only to U.S. citizens. Justice Harlan Stone, in a unanimous decision, stated:

> Some latitude must be allowed for the legislative appraisement of
> local conditions . . . and for the legislative choice of methods for
> controlling an apprehended evil. It was competent for the city to
> make such a choice, not shown to be irrational, by excluding from
> the conduct of business an entire class rather than its objection-
> able members selected by more empirical methods.[30]

But the Court, in a number of cases over the last four decades, has determined not only that aliens—even illegal aliens—are "persons" as defined in

the Fifth and Fourteenth Amendments, but also that their status is increasingly indistinguishable from that of citizens. So while the Constitution gives to Congress the sole authority to determine how many immigrants may enter the country, how immigrants can become citizens of the United States, and whether those immigrants should be able to avail themselves of the benefits of U.S. citizenship, the Court has chosen on several occasions to ignore the express direction of the founders and usurp that authority for itself.

The first of these cases was *Graham v. Richardson*, which involved the rules established by two states for aliens to receive welfare benefits.[31] In the 1960s, Pennsylvania and Arizona required that permanent, resident aliens in those states meet minimum residency requirements in order to receive certain welfare benefits. Arizona, for example, required that to qualify for welfare a resident alien must have lived in the state for fifteen years.[32] State officials were concerned that, without minimum residency requirements, aliens would move from state to state depending on the benefits they could receive.[33]

In 1969, Carmen Richardson, a sixty-four-year-old Mexican native who had legally emigrated to Arizona thirteen years before, became disabled. She filed for welfare benefits but was turned down because she did not meet the state's fifteen-year residency requirement.[34] Richardson subsequently filed suit in federal court in Arizona, claiming that the residency requirement violated the equal protection clause of the Fourteenth Amendment and her constitutionally protected right to travel. Richardson's case was joined with other cases in Arizona and Pennsylvania and heard by the U.S. Supreme Court after lower courts accepted her arguments and ruled in her favor.[35]

In rejecting the established principle that states have a right and a responsibility to husband their limited resources for their citizens and long-standing legal residents, Justice Harry Blackmun wrote:

> We agree with the three-judge court in the Pennsylvania case that
> the justification of limiting expenses is particularly inappropriate
> and unreasonable when the discriminated class consists of aliens.
> Aliens like citizens pay taxes and may be called into the armed
> forces . . . aliens may live within a state for many years, work in the

> state and contribute to the economic growth of the state.... There
> can be no "special public interest" in tax revenues to which aliens
> have contributed on an equal basis with the residents of the
> state.... Accordingly, we hold that a state statute that denies wel-
> fare benefits to resident aliens and one that denies them to aliens
> who have not resided in the United States for a specified number
> of years violate the Equal Protection Clause.[36]

Blackmun also invoked a test for courts to use to decide whether a citizenship requirement for benefits from a state or federal agency is permissible. "The Court's decisions have established that classifications based on alienage, like those based on nationality or race, are inherently suspect and subject to close judicial scrutiny."[37] In other words, lawmakers could only use noncitizenship if they could demonstrate a compelling government interest in doing so—a hurdle that would be nearly impossible to overcome.

The real question the Court should have addressed—and the one that would have profound constitutional implications—is: Who gets to determine whether aliens are eligible for certain benefits? Who sets policy? Clearly, if there is a desire to create a national standard for the eligibility of federal programs, Congress should make that decision. If the program is exclusive to a particular state, the relevant state government should make that decision. The Court simply abrogated the explicit and inherent authority of those elected legislative bodies and imposed its own preference.

The Court also found that the Civil Rights Act of 1866, which guaranteed equal rights to every citizen in every state, included a protected right to travel among the states.[38] The Court ruled that creating residency requirements for aliens would inhibit their right to travel. Again, the Court simply created a new constitutional right—the right to travel—and then extended that "right" to aliens.

In 1976, the Supreme Court ruled in the case *Hampton v. Mow Sun Wong* that citizenship was an unconstitutional requisite to holding a government job.[39] In 1970, five resident alien civil service employees were dismissed from their jobs in the Post Office,[40] the Health, Education, and Welfare Department,[41] and other federal agencies because it was discovered that they were not U.S. citizens as required by Civil Service Commission regulations. The five sued the commission in federal court.

The Supreme Court ruled unanimously that the citizenship requirement violated the due process and equal protection clauses and legal aliens' right to liberty. Justice John Paul Stevens wrote:

> The rule enforced by the Commission has its impact on an iden-
> tifiable class of persons who, entirely apart from the rule itself,
> are already subject to disadvantages not shared by the remainder
> of the community. Aliens are not entitled to vote and, as alleged
> in the complaint, are often handicapped by a lack of familiarity
> with our language and customs. The added disadvantage result-
> ing from the enforcement of the rule—ineligibility for employ-
> ment in a major sector of the economy—is of sufficient
> significance to be characterized as a deprivation of an interest in
> liberty.... By reason of the Fifth Amendment, such a deprivation
> must be accompanied by due process...It follows that some
> judicial scrutiny of the deprivation is mandated by the Consti-
> tution.[42]

The unanimous vote of the Court notwithstanding, the reasoning behind the *Hampton* decision is another example of the Court reaching into an area the Constitution reserves for Congress—and that Congress in successive immigration and naturalization acts delegated to the executive branch. The legislative history cited—yet ignored—by Stevens in the *Hampton* decision even demonstrated that it was the intention of Congress that civil service jobs be reserved for U.S. citizens or, at least, to aliens who had pledged permanent allegiance to the country.[43]

The Court had to manufacture the premise that denying resident aliens a civil service job somehow infringed on their liberty to obtain a job at all, and that there was no valid reason for ensuring that government jobs go primar-ily to U.S. citizens.

In 1973, in *Sugarman v. Dougall,* New York's civil service law included the requirement that all state civil servants be U.S. citizens.[44] Four low-level state employees, who were resident aliens, were dismissed from their positions once their citizenship status became known.[45] They then sued the state, claiming that the statute violated their Fourteenth Amendment due process rights.[46]

In an 8–1 decision (only Justice William Rehnquist dissented) the Supreme Court built on the *Graham* decision and continued to reverse the position it took in the 1915 cases that states have the right to distinguish between citi-zens and noncitizens in their public expenditures. In *Sugarman,* the Court found that while states could indeed differentiate between citizens and nonci-tizens in certain types of jobs, those jobs had to be very narrowly defined and limited specifically to the functions of the government—such as law enforce-ment and senior policymaking positions. Citizenship was not a material requirement for other civil service positions, so requiring it for those posi-tions violated an immigrant's Fourteenth Amendment rights.[47]

Rehnquist, however, offered a brilliant response in his solitary dissent:

> The Court, by holding ... that a citizen-alien classification is "sus-pect" in the eyes of our Constitution, fails to mention, let alone rationalize, the fact that the Constitution itself recognizes a basic difference between citizens and aliens. That distinction is consti-tutionally important in no less than 11 instances in a political document noted for its brevity.... Not only do the numerous classifications on the basis of citizenship that are set forth in the Constitution cut against both the analysis used and the results reached by the Court in these cases; the very Amendment which the Court reads to prohibit classifications based on citizenship establishes the very distinction which the Court now condemns as "suspect."[48]

The 1982 *Plyler v. Doe* decision is perhaps the most egregious of the Court's immigration rulings.[49] In the 1960s and 1970s, a rising tide of illegal immigrants crossed the border from Mexico into Texas to take advantage of the better economic climate and quality of life in the United States. By 1975, the financial strain of the influx had started to choke the already crowded school systems in Texas border towns. In response, Texas enacted a new law concerning children not legally admitted to the United States that allowed local school districts to deny their enrollment and withheld from local school districts state funds to educate these children.[50]

Numerous lawsuits were brought on behalf of several children challenging the new law, which were consolidated in the case *Plyler v. Doe*. In a 5–4 decision, Justice William Brennan, writing for the majority, went so far as to extend the term "person" in the Fourteenth Amendment to include illegal aliens, by virtue of their physical presence in the United States.[51]

Moreover, Brennan found that the children of illegal immigrants weren't responsible for their illegal entry into the country, therefore, "legislation directing the onus of a parent's misconduct against his children does not comport with fundamental conceptions of justice."[52]

While the Court recognized that there is no constitutionally enumerated "right" to a free public education, Brennan stated:

> [N]either is [a public education] merely some governmental "benefit" indistinguishable from other forms of social welfare legislation. Both the importance of education in maintaining our basic institutions, and the lasting impact of its deprivation on the life of the child, mark the distinction. The American people have always regarded education and [the] acquisition of knowledge as matters of supreme importance.... We have recognized the public schools as a most vital civic institution for the preservation of a democratic system of government.... And these historic perceptions of the public schools as inculcating fundamental values

necessary to the maintenance of a democratic political system have been confirmed by the observations of social scientists.[53]

But Brennan wasn't done. When he moved to the question of whether the equal protection clause applied to extending social benefits to illegal aliens, he determined that because Texas had essentially delineated illegal aliens as a distinct "class" of people, they must be treated equally with every other person in the state. Not to do so in this instance—the provision of a free public education—would violate the equal protection clause.[54] In *Plyler*, the Court decided that any conglomeration of people, regardless of the reason for their classification under law, had to be treated identically with every other class of people.

Brennan also said that irrespective of the financial burden imposed on the community or the state by illegal aliens, the cost was not sufficient to justify preventing illegal immigrants from availing themselves of a free public education.[55]

Chief Justice Warren Burger, writing the dissenting opinion for himself and Justices Byron White and Rehnquist, summed up the true nature of the Court's action:

> The Court makes no attempt to disguise that it is acting to make up for Congress' lack of "effective leadership" in dealing with the serious national problems caused by the influx of uncountable millions of illegal aliens across our borders. The failure of enforcement of the immigration laws over more than a decade and the inherent difficulty and expense of sealing our vast borders have combined to create a grave socioeconomic dilemma. It is a dilemma that has not yet even been fully assessed, let alone addressed. However, it is not the function of the Judiciary to provide "effective leadership" simply because the political branches of government fail to do so.[56]

The Supreme Court has reached into other areas to find rights for immigrants that the Constitution, Congress, and the executive branch never intended. In 1973, in *In Re Griffiths*, the Court ruled that a state could not deny noncitizens the right to take the bar exam and become licensed, practicing attorneys—again thanks to the hidden meaning the Court found in the equal protection clause.[57]

In 1977, in *Nyquist v. Mauclet*, the Court decided by a 5–4 vote that it was unconstitutional for New York to require resident aliens to at least apply for U.S. citizenship before becoming eligible for financial aid for education.[58]

The Court, as a practical matter, is in no position to substitute its policy objectives for that of a legislature or Congress. It sits as an adjudicative body, insulated from the kind of give-and-take that occurs between the citizenry and their representatives. It has no responsibility for the kind of balancing act elected officials must undertake in weighing public priorities.

September 11, 2001, underscored that we need greater government scrutiny over our borders and immigration. Congress's role in drafting and the executive's authority in enforcing immigration law have never been more important, and the judiciary's interference with these constitutional roles has never been more dangerous.

CHAPTER EIGHT

AL QAEDA GETS A LAWYER

"Terrorism is the preferred weapon of weak and evil men."

Ronald Reagan, 1986[1]

After September 11, 2001, President George W. Bush took several steps to enhance U.S. security both here and abroad. One step was to detain "enemy combatants" who were captured by the U.S. military while fighting for the Taliban and al Qaeda in Afghanistan. The president designated them "illegal combatants" because they are not conventional soldiers: They don't wear uniforms, they don't carry weapons in the open, and they often hide among the civilian population.[2] They're being held at the U.S. naval base in Guantanamo Bay, Cuba.

Alberto R. Gonzales, former counsel to the president, whom President Bush nominated in November 2004 to succeed John Ashcroft as attorney general, explained the Bush administration's detention policy this way:

> Under [the laws of war] captured enemy combatants, whether soldiers or saboteurs, may be detained for the duration of hostilities. They need not be "guilty" of anything; they are detained

simply by virtue of their status as enemy combatants in war. This detention is not an act of punishment but one of security and military necessity. It serves the important purpose of preventing enemy combatants from continuing their attacks. Thus, the terminology that many in the press use to describe the situation of these combatants is routinely filled with misplaced concepts. To state repeatedly that detainees are being "held without charge" mistakenly assumes that charges are somehow necessary or appropriate. But nothing in the law of war has ever required a country to charge enemy combatants with crimes, provide them access to counsel, or allow them to challenge their detention in court—and states in prior wars have generally not done so. It is understandable, perhaps, that some people, especially lawyers, should want to afford the many due process protections that we have grown accustomed to in our criminal justice system to the individuals captured in our conflict with al Qaeda. It has been many years, fortunately, since the United States has been in a conflict that spans the globe, where enemy combatants have been captured attempting to attack our homeland. But the fact that we have not had occasion to apply the well-established laws of war does not mean that they should be discarded. The United States must use every tool and weapon—including the advantages presented by the laws of war—to win the war against al Qaeda.[3]

Moreover, as William J. Haynes, general counsel of the Department of Defense, has written:

The president has unquestioned authority to detain enemy combatants, including those who are U.S. citizens, during wartime. *Ex Parte Quirin* (1942); *Colepaugh v. Looney* (1956); *In re Territo* (1946)...*Hamdi v. Rumsfeld* (2002). The authority to detain enemy combatants flows primarily from Article II of the Constitution [in which the president is designated the commander in chief]. In the current conflict, the president's authority is bolstered by Congress's joint resolution of September 15, 2001, which authorized "the President...to use all necessary and appropriate force" against al Qaeda and against those nations, organizations, or persons he determines "committed or aided in the September 11 attacks." This congressional action clearly triggers (if any trigger were necessary) the president's traditional authority to detain enemy combatants as commander in chief.

Presidents (and their delegates) have detained enemy combatants in every major conflict in the Nation's history, including recent conflicts such as the Gulf, Vietnam, and Korean wars. During World War II, the United States detained hundreds of thousands of POWs in the United States (some of whom were U.S. citizens) without trial or counsel. Then as now, the purposes of detaining enemy combatants during wartime are, among other things, to gather intelligence and to ensure that detainees do not return to assist the enemy.[4]

Before these individuals were detained in Guantanamo Bay, they were subjected to a thorough vetting process. As the government explained to the U.S. Supreme Court, "When an individual is captured, commanders in the field, using all available information, make a determination as to whether the individual is an enemy combatant, i.e., whether the individual 'is part of or supporting forces hostile to the United States or coalition partners, and engaged in an armed conflict against the United States.' Individuals who are not enemy combatants are released by the military."[5]

After being identified as enemy combatants, "[They] are sent to a centralized holding in the area of operations where a military screening team reviews all available information with respect to the detainees, including information derived from interviews of the detainee. That screening team looks at the circumstances of capture, the threat the individual poses, his intelligence value, and with assistance from other U.S. government officials on the ground, determines whether continued detention is warranted."[6]

After this review, the screening team's recommendations were examined by a general officer. If he recommended detention at Guantanamo Bay, this decision was again examined by a Defense Department review panel. The overwhelming number of individuals who were initially detained were released. Even fewer wound up in Guantanamo Bay. The government reported that "approximately 10,000 individuals have been screened in Afghanistan and released from U.S. custody."[7]

Once enemy combatants arrived at Guantanamo Bay, they were "subject to an additional assessment by the military commanders regarding the need for their detention."[8] It included a review "by a team of interrogators, analysts, behavioral scientists, and regional experts, and a further round of review by the commander of the Southern Command."[9] The commander of Southern Command then sent his recommendations to "an interagency group composed of representatives from the Department of Defense, Department of Justice, and Department of State. This recommendation was then reviewed by the Secretary of Defense or his designee."[10]

Clearly, the process for identifying and detaining an enemy combatant has been thorough and extensive. Moreover, the government has stated that some of these individuals are "direct associates of Osama Bin Laden; al Qaeda operatives with specialized training; bodyguards, recruiters, and intelligence operatives for al Qaeda; and Taliban leaders."[11]

Several enemy combatants filed petitions—called writs of habeas corpus— with federal courts challenging the executive branch's authority to detain them. These challenges made their way to the Supreme Court. In 2004, two such cases were decided: *Rasul v. Bush*[12] and *Hamdi v. Rumsfeld*.[13] They represent egregious examples of judicial activism. In *Hamdi*, the Supreme Court briefly described Yaser Esam Hamdi's background:

> Born as an American citizen in Louisiana in 1980, Hamdi moved
> with his family to Saudi Arabia as a child. By 2001, the parties

agree, he resided in Afghanistan. At some point that year, he was seized by members of the Northern Alliance, a coalition of military groups opposed to the Taliban government, and eventually was turned over to the United States military. The Government asserts that it initially detained and interrogated Hamdi in Afghanistan before transferring him to the United States Naval Base in Guantanamo Bay in January 2002. In April 2002, upon learning that Hamdi is an American citizen, authorities transferred him to a naval brig in Norfolk, Virginia, where he remained until a transfer to a brig in Charleston, South Carolina.[14]

According to the government, Hamdi was "affiliated with a Taliban military unit and received weapons training." He "remained with his Taliban unit following the attacks of September 11." While the Taliban was in conflict with the U.S. military, Hamdi's unit surrendered. Hamdi was subsequently labeled an enemy combatant:

> [The government contends] that Hamdi was labeled an enemy combatant "based upon his interviews and in light of his association with the Taliban." According to the declaration, a series of "U.S. military screening teams" determined that Hamdi met "the criteria for enemy combatants," and "a subsequent interview of Hamdi has confirmed that he surrendered and gave his firearm to Northern Alliance forces, which supports his classification as an enemy combatant."[15]

Hamdi's father, who challenged the detention in federal court, asserted that his son went to Afghanistan to do "relief work," and because he was in Afghanistan for only two months prior to the September 11 attacks could not have received military training.[16]

The Court concluded that Congress had approved the use of military force and had authorized the president to "use all necessary and appropriate force [against] nations, organizations, or persons [that the president determines] planned, authorized, committed, or aided [in the September 11, 2001, al Qaeda terrorist attacks]."[17] In essence, Congress had declared war.[18]

The Court also found that members of the Taliban fit the definition of enemy combatants.[19] Therefore, the government was authorized to detain as enemy combatants individuals who were fighting American (and Northern Alliance) forces in Afghanistan.

In addition, the Court ruled that the detention of enemy combatants was not punitive, but was done to prevent their return to the battlefield and for interrogation purposes: "The capture and detention of lawful combatants and the capture, and trial of unlawful combatants by 'universal agreement and practice,' are 'important incidences of war.' It is now recognized that Captivity is neither a punishment nor an act of vengeance, but merely a temporary detention which is devoid of all penal character. . . . A prisoner of war is no convict; his imprisonment is a simple war measure."[20] And how long can the government incarcerate detainees? The Court held it "may detain, for the duration of these hostilities, individuals legitimately determined to be Taliban combatants who 'engaged in armed conflict against the United States.'"[21]

Nevertheless, the Supreme Court concluded that Hamdi was entitled not only to challenge the circumstances of his detention before a court, but also to present arguments against his detention. As the Court put it, "We therefore hold that a citizen-detainee seeking to challenge his classification as an enemy combatant must receive notice of the factual basis for his classification, and a fair opportunity to rebut the Government's factual assertions before a neutral decision-maker."[22]

In his dissent, Justice Clarence Thomas contended that the constitutional authority of the president to wage war and protect the security interests of the American people should take precedence over the perceived authority of the courts. National security and the president's constitutional authority and duty to wage war for the protection of the United States, Thomas pointed out, are matters over which the courts should have no jurisdiction:

The President, both as Commander-in-Chief and as the Nation's organ for foreign affairs, has available intelligence services whose reports are not and ought not to be published to the world. It would be intolerable that courts, without the relevant information, should review and perhaps nullify actions of the Executive taken on information properly held secret. Nor can courts sit in camera in order to be taken into executive confidences. But even if courts could require full disclosure, the very nature of executive decisions as to foreign policy is political, not judicial. Such decisions are wholly confided by our Constitution to the political departments of the government, Executive and Legislative. They are delicate, complex, and involve large elements of prophecy. They are and should be undertaken only by those directly responsible to the people whose welfare they advance or imperil. They are decisions of a kind for which the Judiciary has neither aptitude, facilities nor responsibility and which has long been held to belong in the domain of political power not subject to judicial intrusion or inquiry.[23]

Thomas raised two other practical issues resulting from the Court's decision—the diversion of wartime personnel and the exposure of classified information:

It also does seem quite likely that, under the process envisioned by the [Court], various military officials will have to take time to litigate this matter. And though the [Court] does not say so, a meaningful ability to challenge the Government's factual allegations will probably require the Government to divulge highly classified information to the purported enemy combatant, who might then upon release return to the fight armed with our most closely held secrets.[24]

Nothing in the Constitution gives parity, much less primacy, to the courts over war-related matters. Indeed, as Thomas argues, the Constitution assigns such authority to the president. The Supreme Court somehow believes that courts are more qualified or trustworthy to rule on detentions. But why is that? Why is it assumed that judges are more competent in weighing the rights of individuals against national-security needs? The ingrained bias against the elected branches and their ability to make well-reasoned and just judgments is destructive to the entire notion of representative government. If elected officials cannot be trusted to make wise decisions about national security, then they cannot be trusted to make decisions at all. There is no evidence that the president has abused his constitutional authority in detaining Hamdi or anyone else. There has been no widespread detention of U.S. citizens—only two, to the best of my knowledge—and only after an extensive vetting process. This hardly justifies the Court's intervention and usurpation of executive authority.

The issues in *Hamdi* do not present garden-variety criminal matters, yet the Supreme Court couldn't resist treating Hamdi's detention this way by cobbling together an unclear due-process requirement, which will be left to the lower courts to figure out.

These days, a single U.S. citizen working in collaboration with al Qaeda or other terrorist groups is potentially more dangerous to more people in this nation than any foreign standing army. And information he might have about future attacks—combined with the government's need for secrecy to thwart them—justifies a decision by the president to detain "illegal combatants" without judicial second-guessing.[25]

As bad as the *Hamdi* decision was, the Supreme Court went even further in *Rasul v. Bush*. In *Rasul*, the Court determined that federal courts could hear cases in which *foreign* enemy combatants challenge their detention.[26] *Rasul* involved two Australian citizens and twelve Kuwaiti citizens "who were captured abroad during hostilities between the United States and the Taliban."[27]

These enemy combatants have also been detained at Guantanamo Bay. Justice John Paul Stevens, writing for the majority, ruled that they had the right to petition the federal courts to review their status as detainees.[28] Stevens devoted considerable verbiage attempting to distinguish the facts in *Rasul* from the 1950 Supreme Court opinion in *Johnson v. Eisentrager*.[29] *Eisentrager* established the principle that aliens detained outside the sovereign territory of the United States could not ask federal courts to review their status. The reasoning of the Court was explained by Robert D. Alt, a fellow in legal and international affairs at the John Ashbrook Center for Public Affairs:

> [Proceedings by alien detainees] would hamper the war effort and bring aid and comfort to the enemy. They would diminish the prestige of our commanders, not only with enemies but with wavering neutrals. It would be difficult to devise more effective fettering of a field commander than to allow the very enemies he is ordered to reduce to submission to call him to account in his own civil courts and divert his efforts and attention from the military offensive abroad to the legal defensive at home. Nor is it unlikely that the result of such enemy litigiousness would be [a] conflict between judicial and military opinion highly comforting to enemies of the United States.[30]

In *Eisentrager*, twenty-one German nationals were taken into custody in China at the conclusion of World War II. They were tried and convicted of war crimes by a U.S. military tribunal in China. They were then remitted to a military prison in Germany. These individuals sought to bring their case to America by filing a writ of habeas corpus in the U.S. District Court for the District of Columbia.[31] The issue was whether alien combatants should have access to civilian courts.[32]

Justice Robert Jackson, writing for the Supreme Court's majority, was adamant in denying aliens this access: "We are cited to no instance where a court in this or any other country where the writ [of habeas corpus] is known, has issued it on behalf of an alien enemy who, at no relevant time and in no stage of his captivity, has been within its territorial jurisdiction."[33]

Jackson realized the danger enemy combatants posed. "But these prisoners were actual enemies, active in the hostile service of an enemy power. There is no fiction about their enmity."[34] The German soldiers were denied the ability to petition civilian courts for review of their status.

War limits the right of certain aliens to access U.S. courts, or at least it used to. As Jackson wrote:

> It is war that exposes the relative vulnerability of the alien's status. The security and protection enjoyed while the nation of his allegiance remain in amity with the United States are greatly impaired when his nation takes up arms against us. While his lot is far more humane and endurable than the experience of our citizens in some enemy lands, it is still not a happy one. But disabilities this country lays upon the alien who becomes also an enemy are imposed temporarily as an incident of war and not as an incident of alienage.[35]

Obviously, we are not at war with the home countries of the individuals who initiated the *Rasul* case (they are citizens of Australia and Kuwait). However, the principle is the same. When these men joined the Taliban and fought for al Qaeda, they became part of an organization that is at war with the United States. Denying foreign enemy combatants access to U.S. courts is an "incident of war."

Eisentrager was clear. The enemy combatants in *Rasul* should never have been granted the right to challenge their detentions in federal courts. Stevens dismantled the precedent established in *Eisentrager,* claiming that the facts in *Rasul* were sufficiently different to compel a contrary result:

> Petitioners [in *Rasul*] differ from the *Eisentrager* detainees in important respects: They are not nationals of countries at war with the United States, and they deny that they have engaged in or plotted acts of aggression against the United States; they have

never been afforded access to any tribunal, much less charged with and convicted of wrongdoing; and for more than two years they have been imprisoned in territory over which the United States exercised exclusive jurisdiction and control.[36]

The fact is that *Eisentrager* and *Rasul* are identical in two significant respects—both involved foreign enemy combatants who never set foot in America, and both involved the detention of foreign enemy combatants outside the United States. There was no reason for the Court to take up this case, and no reason to reverse *Eisentrager*. Stevens and the majority were bent on substituting their preferred view for the president's.

Stevens also attempted to distinguish *Eisentrager* by relying on a statute, which states, in part: "Writs of habeas corpus may be granted by the Supreme Court, any justice thereof, the district courts and any circuit judge *within their respective jurisdiction.*[37] (Emphasis added.)

This, too, is disingenuous. Stevens decided that "within their respective jurisdiction" means any territory over which the United States exercises complete control, but not "ultimate sovereignty," such as on a military base located in a foreign country.[38] Clearly, however, "within their respective jurisdiction" means the territorial locations that demarcate each federal court's reach.[39] Guantanamo Bay is outside such locations; consequently, the law has no application. No matter. Here is how Stevens rewrote the statute: "[B]ecause the writ of habeas corpus does not act upon the prisoner who seeks relief, but upon the person who holds him in what is alleged to be unlawful custody, a district court acts within [its] respective jurisdiction within the meaning [of the law] as long as the custodian can be reached by service of process."[40]

Any enemy combatant can now challenge his detention in a federal court provided the combatant (or the combatant's relatives or friends) is able to deliver a lawsuit to the Department of Defense or the Department of Justice.

The practical implications of this decision are immense. As Justice Antonin Scalia explained:

The consequence of this holding, as applied to aliens outside the country, is breathtaking. It permits an alien captured in a foreign theater of active combat to [bring a suit] against the Secretary of Defense. Over the course of the last century, the United States has held millions of alien prisoners abroad. A great many of these prisoners would no doubt have complained about the circumstances of their capture and the terms of their confinement. The military is currently detaining over 600 prisoners at Guantanamo Bay alone; each detainee undoubtedly has complaints—real or contrived—about those terms and circumstances. The Court's unheralded expansion of federal-court jurisdiction is not even mitigated by a comforting assurance that the legion of ensuing claims will be easily resolved on the merits.... From this point forward, federal courts will entertain petitions from these prisoners, and others like them around the world, challenging actions and events far away, and forcing the courts to oversee one aspect of the Executive's conduct of a foreign war.[41]

Former federal prosecutor Andrew C. McCarthy made an excellent point when he wrote:

[W]hen our military fighting overseas, at the height of active hostilities, grants quarter by apprehending rather than destroying the forces arrayed against it, those forces, those alien enemies trying to kill Americans—alien enemies who secrete themselves among civilians; who use humanitarian infrastructure like ambulances, hospitals and schools to carry out their grisly business; who make a mockery of the laws and conventions of civilized warfare; who torture and kill their captives with a bestiality that defies description; whose only contact with America is to regard her with this savagery—have resort to the courts of the United States to protest their detention and to compel the executive branch, while it is conducting battle, to explain itself. Just to describe this breath-taking claim of entitlement should be to refute it. Yet the United States Supreme Court has ruled in favor of the enemy.[42]

So now, for the first time in American history, captured alien enemy combatants will have access to our courts. They will be afforded some kind of due process hearing and one day I expect they'll have a right to competent counsel, paid for by the American taxpayer, and the right to compel testimony from the soldiers who apprehended them. Even for the Supreme Court, this is a grotesque perversion of the Constitution.

In truth, despite allegations of vast civil liberties violations, President Bush has conducted this war with great restraint, when compared with the actions of past presidents. For example, Article I of the Constitution describes the legislative powers of Congress. Among those powers, Section 9, Clause 2 provides that, "The Privilege of the Writ of Habeas Corpus shall not be suspended, unless when in Cases of Rebellion or Invasion the public Safety may require it."[43] Yet, on several occasions during the Civil War, President Abraham Lincoln suspended the writ to silence or punish those who were sympathetic to slavery or states' rights.[44] As author Craig Smith describes:

> During the Civil War, President Lincoln suspended the writ of habeas corpus first in Maryland and then in southern Ohio because of its sympathy for slavery and states' rights and its geographic location. Reluctantly, Lincoln took the action against Maryland so that he could prevent its legislature from meeting and voting for secession. In September of 1861, nine members of the Maryland legislature were arrested. It was the first time a president of the United States had prevented a state legislature from meeting and was a clear violation of their constitutional rights. However, the threat of Civil War was so severe that Lincoln felt justified in his unprecedented action.

The same would be true in Ohio. During his campaign for governor of Ohio, Congressman Clement L. Vallandigham gave a fiery speech in southern Ohio in support of the rebel effort. When General Burnside read reports of the speech in the newspaper, he had Vallandigham arrested and sent to Boston for trial. Lincoln eventually exiled the Congressman to the South because he had some doubts about incarcerating a sitting congressman for delivering a political campaign speech.[45]

Lincoln's suspension of the writ of habeas corpus was eventually challenged by John Merryman, a secessionist and citizen of Maryland. The case reached the Supreme Court, where the chief justice was Roger B. Taney (author of the 1856 *Dred Scott* decision upholding slavery). In *Ex parte Merryman*, Taney, writing for the Court, held that only Congress could suspend the writ of habeas corpus.[46] Lincoln ignored the opinion. In 1863, Congress passed a statute authorizing Lincoln to suspend the writ.[47]

Obviously, President Bush hasn't imprisoned or exiled members of Congress or state legislators who oppose his handling of the war on terrorism. Indeed, he hasn't taken any actions to silence his critics. The Bush administration has detained only two U.S. citizens, and then only for overt acts of war.[48]

On February 19, 1942, during World War II, President Franklin Roosevelt issued Executive Order 9066, which directed military commanders to designate areas "from which any or all persons may be excluded."[49] While the order didn't apply specifically to a particular ethnic group, its effect was clear. Tens of thousands of Japanese Americans and Americans of Japanese ancestry were systematically removed from their homes in western coastal regions and forced into internment camps—not because of any evidence of criminal or disloyal behavior, but because of their race.

The president has not issued an edict rounding up, say, law-abiding Islamic and Arab Americans, or Americans of Arab ancestry, forcing them into guarded camps where the government could watch over them. In fact, the administration is loath to give special scrutiny to aliens who travel to the United States even from countries known to harbor or tolerate terrorists, including the home countries of the September 11, 2001, terrorists. For the Supreme Court to intervene in the *Hamdi* and *Rasul* cases, and use them as vehicles to usurp the commander in chief's role despite the president's restraint, is indefensible as a matter of law and policy. Thanks to the Supreme Court's ruling, in July 2004, the detainees at Guantanamo Bay were informed they could use American courts "to contest their detention."[50]

It is difficult to win a war when the enemy is armed not only with rifles and rocket propelled grenades, but also with subpoenas, affidavits, and lawyers. And it's difficult to maintain a republic when the judiciary abuses its constitutional authority. These cases illustrate perhaps more than any others just how dangerous and reckless an unbridled judiciary can be, not only to the Constitution, but to our national security.[51]

CHAPTER NINE

SOCIALISM FROM THE BENCH

"Freedom in economic arrangements is itself a component of freedom broadly
understood, so economic freedom is an end in itself. . . . Economic freedom is
also an indispensable means toward the achievement of political freedom."

Milton Friedman, 1962[1]

Have you ever wondered how a federal government that is supposed
to have limited power can now involve itself in essentially any
aspect of our society? The answer comes down to two words: commerce clause. The Constitution gives Congress the power, under Article I,
Section 8, "to regulate commerce with foreign nations and among the several
States."[2] Under the Articles of Confederation, each state had been free to issue
its own currency and set its own tariffs.[3] The purpose of the commerce clause
was to promote commerce and trade by breaking down these barriers. But
over the years, the Supreme Court has adopted an expansive definition of
"commerce" to justify virtually unfettered federal intrusion into the conduct
of state and local governments, and to defend the establishment of massive
bureaucracies and their imposition of seemingly endless regulations on private enterprise. As a result, the government has become increasingly centralized, and the economy is lurching toward socialism.

In addition to contravening the proscribed and specified powers the Constitution confers on the federal government, an expansive use of the commerce clause violates the Tenth Amendment, which underscores the limited role intended for the federal government. It states, "The powers not delegated to the United States by the Constitution, nor prohibited by it to the States, are reserved to the States respectively, or to the people."[4]

Steven Calabresi, professor of law at Northwestern University School of Law, has eloquently credited federalism with being an essential part of the genius of the American system:

> [I]t prevents violence and war. It prevents religious warfare, it prevents racial warfare. It is part of the reason why democratic majoritarianism in the United States has not produced violence or secession for 130 years, unlike the situations for example, in England, France, Germany, Russia, Czechoslovakia, Yugoslavia, Cyprus, or Spain. There is nothing in the U.S. Constitution that is more important or that has done more to promote peace, prosperity, and freedom than the federal structure of that great document. There is nothing in the U.S. Constitution that should absorb more completely the attention of the U.S. Supreme Court.[5]

Unfortunately, federalism has absorbed the attention of the Supreme Court only to the extent of overruling it.

The seminal case involving congressional regulation of interstate commerce is the 1824 decision in *Gibbons v. Ogden*, in which the Supreme Court affirmed that Congress could regulate interstate commerce.[6] But Chief Justice John Marshall, writing for the Court, emphasized that the power to regulate interstate commerce did not extend to the regulation of any other commerce between individuals and within states. He wrote that the power to regulate interstate commerce "is not intended to say that these words comprehend that commerce, which is completely internal, which is carried on between man and man in a State, or between different parts of the same State, and which does not extend to or affect other States. Such power would be inconvenient, and is certainly unnecessary."[7]

Gibbons outlined the basic tenets of congressional regulation of interstate commerce. Over the next 110 years, Congress was relatively careful to limit its use of the commerce clause as a pretext to enact new laws. As Justice Clarence Thomas has noted:

> From the time of the ratification of the Constitution to the mid-1930s, it was widely understood that the Constitution granted Congress only limited powers, notwithstanding the Commerce Clause. Moreover, there was no question that activities wholly separated from business, such as gun possession, were beyond the reach of the commerce power. If anything, the "wrong turn" was the Court's dramatic departure in the 1930s from a century and a half of precedent.[8]

The "dramatic departure" Thomas referred to was President Franklin Roosevelt's New Deal. During the first half of the 1930s, Congress enacted a number of laws that were purportedly intended to revive the American economy. The Supreme Court, however, routinely struck down these laws because they went far beyond the commerce clause of the Constitution. For example, in 1934 Congress passed the Railroad Retirement Act, which established compulsory retirement plans for railroad workers.[9] The Supreme Court invalidated it in 1935 because Congress had no constitutional authority to regulate a business relationship between employer and employee. "We feel bound to hold that a pension plan thus imposed," the Court wrote, "is in no proper sense a regulation of the activity of interstate transportation. It is an attempt for social ends to impose by sheer fiat non-contractual incidents upon the relation of employer and employee, not as a rule or regulation of commerce and transportation between the States, but as a means of assuring a particular class of employees against old age dependency."[10]

Later that same month, the Supreme Court ruled that sections of the National Industrial Recovery Act of 1933 were unconstitutional. In *Schechter Poultry Corp. v. United States*, frequently referred to as the "sick chicken" case, a unanimous Court determined that the commerce clause did not give Congress the power to enact a law that set the wages and hours of poultry slaughterhouse workers in Brooklyn, New York.[11] The Court stated, "Defendants held the poultry at their slaughterhouse markets for slaughter and local sale to retail dealers and butchers who in turn sold directly to consumers. Neither the slaughtering nor the sales by defendants were transactions in interstate commerce."[12] Consequently, Congress did not have the power to regulate such business. The Court added:

> So far as the poultry here in question is concerned, the flow in interstate commerce had ceased. The poultry had come to a permanent rest within the State. It was held, used or sold by defendants in relation to any further transaction in interstate commerce and was not destined for transportation to other States.[13]

The Supreme Court also underscored the "well established" test used for determining whether a law violated the commerce clause. If an intrastate transaction (a transaction within a state) "directly" affected interstate commerce, then Congress could regulate that type of transaction.[14] Importantly, the unanimous Court also noted, "If the commerce clause were construed to reach all enterprises and transactions which could be said to have an indirect effect upon interstate commerce, the federal authority would embrace practically all the activities of the people."[15]

In 1936, in *Carter v. Carter Coal Company*, the Supreme Court ruled that another piece of New Deal legislation, the Bituminous Coal Conservation Act of 1935, was unconstitutional.[16] The act created a national coal commission, coal districts, and "the fixing of all prices for bituminous coal, [including the fixing] of the wages, hours and working conditions of the miners throughout the country."[17] The Court again ruled that Congress did not have the power to regulate the relationship between employer and employee:

> Much stress is put upon the evils which come from the struggle between employers and employees over the matter of wages, working conditions, the right of collective bargaining, etc., and the resulting strikes, curtailment and irregularity of production and effect on prices; and it is insisted that interstate commerce is greatly affected thereby. But, in addition to what has just been said, the conclusive answer is that the evils are all local evils over which the federal government has no legislative control.[18]

In these rulings, the Supreme Court was merely upholding the Constitution and preserving the constitutional balance of power between the federal government and the states. This was about to change. At a press conference, an unhappy Roosevelt said, "For the benefit of those of you who haven't read through [the Supreme Court's decision striking down the National Industrial Act of 1934] I think I can put it this way: The implications of this decision are much more important than almost certainly any decision of my lifetime or yours, more important than any decision probably since the *Dred Scott* case, because they bring the country as a whole up against a very practical question."[19]

Comparing the Supreme Court's decision in the *Schechter* case with the judicial abomination that was *Dred Scott* was outrageous, but effective, politics against the Court. Roosevelt threatened to pack the Court by adding five new justices to its nine members. That threat, and the eventual turnover of the Court's membership, led to the Supreme Court's capitulation.

In 1937, in *NLRB* (National Labor Relations Board) *v. Jones & Laughlin Steel Corporation*, the Supreme Court ruled that "intrastate activities that 'have such a close and substantial relation to interstate commerce that their control is essential or appropriate to protect that commerce from burdens and obstructions' are within Congress' power to regulate."[20] The legal stage was now set for a massive expansion of the commerce clause and federal government control over the marketplace.

In 1942, the Court used *Wickard v. Filburn* for that very purpose.[21] Roscoe Filburn owned and operated a small dairy farm in Ohio. Every year he would use a section of his land to grow wheat. A portion of the wheat was sold, a portion was fed to livestock (which were also sold), a portion was used to make flour, and the rest was used for seeding the following year. In every respect, Filburn's sale or use of his wheat occurred *within* the state of Ohio. In 1941, Filburn was assessed a penalty of $117.11 for exceeding the marketing quota established for his farm.[22] It was part of the federal Agricultural Adjustment Act of 1938.[23] Filburn challenged the penalty in court and the case reached the Supreme Court.

Incredibly, Justice Robert Jackson, writing for a unanimous Court, ruled that Congress could regulate the amount of wheat that a farmer grew on his farm. The Court reasoned that Filburn's wheat affected interstate commerce—*even though none of it ever left the state of Ohio*. The Court's rationale was that: (1) Filburn grew excess wheat on his farm, as determined by a marketing quota established by the federal Agricultural Adjustment Act of 1938; (2) Filburn used that excess wheat to feed his livestock; (3) because of the excess wheat, Filburn would not have to purchase wheat on the open market; (4) by not purchasing wheat on the open market, Filburn was affecting interstate commerce. The Court wrote:

> It can hardly be denied that a factor of such volume and variability as home-consumed wheat would have a substantial influence on price and market conditions. This may arise because being in marketable condition such wheat overhangs the market and if induced by rising prices tends to flow into the market and check price increases. But if we assume that it is never marketed, it supplies a need of the man who grew it which would otherwise be

reflected by purchases in the open market. Home-grown wheat in this sense competes with wheat in commerce. The stimulation of commerce is a use of the regulatory function quite as definitely as prohibitions or restrictions thereon.[24]

Richard Epstein, professor of law at the University of Chicago, noted that though the "decision cannot pass the 'giggle test,'" under its logic "just about anything" can be covered by the commerce clause.[25] And for the next fifty years, the Supreme Court used the commerce clause as legal justification to uphold federal intrusion into "just about anything." For example, in 1968, in *Maryland v. Wirtz*, the Court ruled that the federal Fair Labor Standards Act applied to state-run hospitals, nursing care facilities, and schools[26] because "labor conditions in schools and hospitals can affect commerce."[27] It concluded that if Congress had a "rational basis" for enacting the law, the Court (and by fiat all lower courts) would uphold it.[28]

Again, Epstein noted that the "rational basis test" is a "de facto death knell to a constitutional challenge that seeks to vindicate individual rights against government regulation" because all regulations passed by a legislature almost by definition must "have at least some benefits to commend them." [29]

In 1971, in *Perez v. United States*, the Supreme Court upheld certain sections of the Consumer Credit Protection Act, making loan sharking a federal offense despite the fact that these activities were purely intrastate.[30] In a vain and lone dissent, Justice Potter Stewart argued:

> But under the statute before us, a man can be convicted without any proof of interstate movement, of the use of the facilities of interstate commerce, or of facts showing that his conduct affected interstate commerce. I think the Framers of the Constitution never intended that the National Government might define as a crime and prosecute such wholly local activity through the enactment of federal criminal laws.[31]

The benefits of retaining power at the state and local level and its implications for protecting individual liberties are considerable. As Professor
Michael McConnell, now a federal judge, wrote:

> Assume there are only two states, with equal populations of 100
> each. Assume further that 70 percent of State A, and only 40 per-
> cent of State B, wish to outlaw smoking in public buildings. The
> others are opposed. If the decision is made on a national basis by
> a majority rule, 110 people will be pleased, and 90 displeased. If
> a separate decision is made by majorities in each state, 130 will be
> pleased, and only 70 displeased. The level of satisfaction will be
> still greater if some smokers in State A decide to move to State B,
> and some anti-smokers in State B decide to move to State A.[32]

State power also allows for societal solutions best suited to satisfy a given
locality and permits experimentation with different public policy initiatives.
The framers understood that the best way to address the wide variety of
issues faced by any culture was not from the top down, but at the grassroots
level.

There have been recent but rare acknowledgments by a bare majority of
the Supreme Court that it has strayed badly from the Constitution.

In 1995, in *United States v. Lopez*, the Supreme Court considered whether
it was constitutional to make possessing a firearm near a school zone a federal crime.[33] In a glimmer of sanity, the Court struck down the law. Chief Justice William Rehnquist, writing for the majority, stated the obvious: "The
possession of a gun in a local school zone is in no sense an economic activity that might, through repetition elsewhere, substantially affect any sort of
interstate commerce."[34] No kidding. But it's the Court's past rulings that have
made this an issue.

Justice Stephen Breyer's dissent is a perfect example of how activist judges
don't see their role as simply applying the Constitution, but promoting policies that they personally favor. Breyer wrote:

For one thing, reports, hearings, and other readily available literature make clear that the problem of guns in and around schools is widespread and extremely serious. These materials report, for example, that four percent of American high school students (and six percent of inner-city high school students) carry a gun to school at least occasionally; that 12 percent of urban high school students have had guns fired at them; that 20 percent of those students have been threatened with guns; and that in any 6-month period, several hundred thousand schoolchildren are victims of violent crimes in or near their schools. Based on reports such as these, Congress obviously could have thought that guns and learning are mutually exclusive. Congress could therefore have found a substantial educational problem—teachers unable to teach, students unable to learn—and concluded that guns near schools contribute substantially to the size and scope of that problem.

Having found that guns in schools significantly undermine the quality of education in our Nation's classrooms, Congress could also have found, given the effect of education upon interstate and foreign commerce, that gun-related violence in and around schools is a commercial, as well as a human, problem. Education, although far more than a matter of economics, has long been inextricably intertwined with the Nation's economy.[35]

Breyer's position is, in essence, that the commerce clause empowers Congress to supersede the Constitution's limits on federal power without limitation. Keep in mind, state and local representatives have the power to outlaw gun possession near schools, and many have. They are more likely to reflect the viewpoints and desires of their communities. In some rural areas, it's not unusual, for example, for parents or teachers to possess firearms near or on school property. But Breyer (and a majority of Congress) believes his policy preferences should be imposed on every state and local elected body in the nation.

In 2000, in *United States v. Morrison*, the Supreme Court had another opportunity to reverse course. It was asked whether the Violence Against Women Act of 1994, which allowed victims of gender-based violence to sue in federal civil court, was constitutional based on the commerce clause.[36]

Again, Rehnquist authored the majority's decision and determined that "Gender-motivated crimes of violence are not, in any sense of the phrase, economic activity"[37] of the sort Congress is authorized to regulate. Rehnquist added that if the link between gender-based violence and interstate commerce was upheld in this case, then as a practical matter, the Court would have to affirm that all crime is federal crime.[38]

These two baby steps for judicial responsibility, however, have not established precedents beyond their specific cases, nor have they overturned the other Supreme Court rulings that have given the federal government a degree of power the founders rejected.

The federal budget today exceeds $2.3 trillion a year—and that doesn't factor in the continuing cost of federal regulations, statutes, and rules on individuals and businesses.[39] Milton Friedman, the Nobel Prize–winning economist, has estimated that in addition to the 40 percent of our income that is taken and spent by government at all levels, we and American businesses spend an additional 10 percent of our income on government rules and mandates.[40] A common barometer of this ever-increasing regulatory maze is the size of the Federal Register, the official compendium of federal rules. The Federal Register issued in 2002 set a new record at 75,606 pages, nearly a 9 percent increase over the previous year.[41] This increase even tops the previous record set in 2000, the year Bill Clinton was pushing through "midnight regulations" in the last days of his presidency.[42] In dollar terms, the Cato Institute, a libertarian think tank, has estimated that the cost of regulatory compliance to our economy is $860 billion a year. To put this number in perspective, that's 8.2 percent of our gross domestic product,[43] and exceeds the economic output of some entire countries, like Canada and Mexico.[44]

Rather than upholding the Constitution, the Supreme Court has energetically helped Congress use the commerce clause to accumulate power at the expense of state and local authority, in direct violation of the Constitution. The framers wanted to increase commerce between the states and trade between their citizens. But the Court has turned the commerce clause into precisely the opposite—and worse: a vehicle to strengthen federal power, deny authority to the states, and deny liberty to the American people.

CHAPTER TEN

Silencing Political Debate

"If men are to be precluded from offering their sentiments on a matter which may involve the most serious and alarming consequences that can invite the consideration of mankind, reason is of no use to us; the freedom of speech may be taken away, and dumb and silent we may be led, like sheep to the slaughter."

George Washington[1]

W hat was once unthinkable is now law. Your right to free speech—especially political speech—is being suppressed with the active support of the courts. So absurd and dangerous has the Supreme Court's view of free speech become that it struck down an anti–virtual child pornography statute as a violation of the First Amendment, but upheld prohibitions against running a political ad during the month before a federal general election as criminal.[2] Indeed, you can burn an American flag as a form of protest,[3] but you can't distribute pro-life leaflets within one hundred feet of an abortion clinic.[4] When students wear armbands to school, they are engaging in protected speech,[5] but mentioning God at a commencement ceremony is unconstitutional.[6] The illogic of these rulings, and the extent to which the justices are willing to split hairs and manufacture various standards when interpreting the First Amendment's free speech clause, is mind-boggling.

Here's what the First Amendment says about free speech: "Congress shall make no law...abridging the freedom of speech."[7] That's it, all of it. The framers could not have been clearer about what they meant or about their intentions. Ten simple and straightforward words. Yet our most cherished form of speech, political speech, is not so free anymore.

The Supreme Court used to understand this. In 1966 it noted that "[w]hatever differences may exist about interpretations of the First Amendment, there is practically universal agreement that a major purpose of that Amendment was to protect the free discussion of governmental affairs."[8]

I'd like to think that it's beyond argument that open and free political debate is central to our freedoms, but according to the Supreme Court, I'm wrong. I'm wrong because Senators John McCain of Arizona and Russ Feingold of Wisconsin drafted a bill, passed by Congress, and signed into law by the president, which uses words like "reform," "corruption," and "special interests" to justify restricting and even criminalizing political speech under the guise of "campaign reform."

But who, exactly, is being "corrupted" by our political system? Don't ask McCain. While he's quick to make the charge, he seems unable to back it up. During a key debate on the Senate floor with Senator Mitch McConnell of Kentucky, the Senate's leading opponent of McCain-Feingold, McConnell challenged McCain for evidence:

> McConnell: I am just interested in engaging in some discussion here about what specifically—which specific senators he believes have been engaged in corruption. I know he [McCain] said from time to time the process is corrupt. But I think it is important to note, for there to be corruption, someone must be corrupt. Someone must be corrupt for there to be corruption. So I just ask my friend from Arizona what he has in mind here, in suggesting corruption is permeating our body and listing these [spending] projects for the benefit of several states as examples.[9]

After McCain gave a long and unresponsive reply, McConnell persisted.

McConnell: I ask the Senator from Arizona, how can it be corruption if no one is corrupt? That is like saying the gang is corrupt but none of the gangsters are. If there is corruption, someone must be corrupt.... I repeat my question to the Senator from Arizona. Who is corrupt?[10]

McCain: First of all, I have already responded to the senator that I will not get into people's names.[11]

The McCain-Feingold Act, signed into law in 2002, ignores the clear wording of the free speech clause and imposes draconian limits on political speech. The act, among other things, bans contributions to political parties from corporations, labor unions, and other groups, and prohibits certain forms of political advertising in the crucial days leading up to elections.[12]

The McCain-Feingold Act is obviously unconstitutional. The First Amendment specifically protects the right of the people to influence their representatives. It states, in part, that "Congress shall make no law... abridging the right of the people... to petition the government for a redress of grievances."[13] If that isn't clear enough, the Supreme Court ruled in 1976 in *Buckley v. Valeo* that giving money to support political campaigns was protected by the First Amendment.[14] While limits on contributions to campaigns were permissible in order to prevent corruption or the appearance of corruption, individuals or groups were permitted to spend as much money as they desired in running advertisements that supported a particular issue rather than a specific candidate.[15] The Court also ruled that individuals and groups could make unlimited financial contributions to political parties.[16]

There are aspects of *Buckley v. Valeo* that I believe violate the First Amendment, but it's a bulwark of constitutionality compared with the Supreme Court's 2003 opinion upholding most parts of the McCain-Feingold bill in *McConnell v. Federal Election Commission.*[17]

The Court stamped its approval on prohibiting national parties from raising or spending so-called "soft money" (money *not* spent in direct support of a specified candidate); regulating how state political parties can spend soft money in federal elections;[18] banning federal officeholders or candidates from raising or spending soft money; prohibiting political parties from transferring or soliciting soft money for politically active tax-exempt groups; banning state candidates from spending soft money on public communications that promote or attack federal candidates; defining "electioneering communication" as a broadcast advertisement mentioning a federal candidate, targeted at their electorate, and aired within thirty days of a primary or sixty days of a general election; requiring corporations and unions to use only "hard money" (money that *is* spent in direct support of a specified candidate) to pay for electioneering communication; requiring that individuals disclose their spending on electioneering communications to the Federal Election Commission (FEC); requiring that "coordinated" electioneering communications be treated as contributions to candidates and parties; defining "coordination" as "Congress has always treated expenditure made after a wink or nod as coordinated"; and affirming the new FEC requirements for candidate disclosure.[19]

Confusing? Do the terms "soft money," "hard money," and "coordination" mean anything to you? Probably not. They are all inventions of the federal government. Remember, the Constitution's free speech clause states: "Congress shall make no law...abridging the freedom of speech." Yet McCain-Feingold creates an environment in which anyone who dares to enter the political arena, and hopes to have a real influence on the outcome of an election, will risk fines or even imprisonment if he runs afoul of this law while merely trying to exercise his free speech. He'll need a team of election-law experts to help steer him through this legal minefield. Even then, he can't be certain he'll escape allegations of wrongdoing.

Now, you might think that the members of Congress who voted for this law would have read it and understood it before passing it. You might think that McCain-Feingold supporters, who insisted that this law was critical to cleaning up rampant corruption in politics, would have had some idea before supporting it as to how it would supposedly eradicate that corruption. But, for the most part, you'd be wrong.

In February 2003, the *New York Times* reported how McCain-Feingold was confounding even members of Congress and quoted Robert F. Bauer, a lawyer for the Democrats' House and Senate campaign committees who gives seminars on the law, as saying: "We sometimes leave our audiences in a state of complete shock," with the congressmen expressing a "sort of slack-jawed amazement at how far this thing reached," followed by "a lot of very anxious questions." The article goes on:

> The new chairman of the Democratic Congressional Campaign Committee, Representative Robert T. Matsui...who voted for McCain-Feingold, says he has been surprised by its fine print.
>
> "[I] didn't realize what all was in it," Matsui said. "We have cautioned members: 'You have to really understand this law. And if you have any ambiguity, err on the side of caution.'"[20]

The confusion surrounding McCain-Feingold involves virtually every aspect of what used to be considered perfectly legitimate, legal, and even important politicking:

> For example, members of Congress have been informed that while they can attend annual state party dinners back home, they cannot permit their names to appear on the invitation as members of the host committee, since most state parties are permitted to raise money in excess of the $2,000 hard-money limit embodied in the federal law.
>
> And, while the lawmakers are allowed at least to show up, socialize, and speak at those state party dinners, the law may be less forgiving when it comes to their attendance at bread-and-butter fund-raisers held by candidates running for state and local

office. Some party lawyers have concluded that a member of Congress can attend and even speak at a fund-raising dinner for a local politician, but others argue that the question is open to interpretation, involving everything from what the candidate says to the maximum level of contributions at the dinner.

Those are among the issues that will surely be litigated in the months to come. Given the confusion in the meantime, party officials are urging members of Congress to consult their lawyers about every political invitation.[21]

Of course, the courts will now decide all nuances involving myriad political issues, no matter how intricate. The slippery slope has been greased by the Supreme Court itself. Rather than striking down McCain-Feingold as blatantly unconstitutional, it has unleashed what will be never-ending litigation and court oversight of the political process, something the framers never would have sanctioned.

Nor could the framers ever have envisioned prohibiting groups from running advertisements about a candidate's positions thirty days before a primary election and sixty days before a general election. As Justice Anthony Kennedy said in his partial dissent:

> The majority permits a new and serious intrusion on speech when it ... prohibits corporations and labor unions from using money from their general treasury to fund electioneering communications. [The majority] silences political speech central to the civic discourse that sustains and informs our democratic processes. Unions and corporations, including nonprofit corporations, now face severe criminal penalties for broadcasting advocacy messages that "refer to a clearly identified candidate."[22]

During the debates leading to the enactment of McCain-Feingold, Congressman Steve Chabot noted how the media was exempted from anti-corruption campaign reforms: "[Campaign finance] would ban corporations, labor unions, social welfare groups and political groups from advocating issues important to them during specific times in campaigns, subjecting them to not only new speech restrictions, but also increased penalties beyond those imposed by current law. At the same time, [McCain-Feingold] exempts the media."[23]

And so it does. The media is not regulated by campaign finance law—not that it should be, of course. Besides specifically protecting free speech, peaceable assembly, and petitioning the government, the First Amendment also singles out freedom of the press for protection. But interestingly, this is the only First Amendment right entirely exempt from McCain-Feingold's reach. It's troubling to note that, with its own freedom preserved, much of the press rushed to embrace McCain-Feingold.

The reaction of the *New York Times* editorial page was typical of the mainstream media:

> The Supreme Court delivered a stunning victory for political reform yesterday, upholding the McCain-Feingold campaign finance law virtually in its entirety. The court rejected claims that the law violates the First Amendment, making it clear that Congress has broad authority in acting against the corrupting power of money in politics. The ruling is cause for celebration, but it should also spur Congress to do more to clean up our political system.[24]

On Sunday, October 17, 2004, a mere sixteen days before the 2004 presidential election, the *New York Times*—well within the sixty-day prohibition against the broadcasting of political advocacy advertisements—continued its long practice of endorsing Democrat nominees for president with an editorial titled "John Kerry for President."[25]

The *Washington Post* called the Court's McCain-Feingold decision "one of its most important decisions in a generation."[26] It would be more accurate to call it one of its worst.

But more is on the way. The Court acknowledged as much in its McCain-Feingold decision when it said, "We are under no illusion that [the law] will be the last congressional statement on the matter. Money, like water, will always find an outlet."[27]

Indeed, one of the unintended but entirely predictable consequences of McCain-Feingold's maze of regulations has been the growth of groups known as 527s (after the section in the Internal Revenue Code under which they are organized). They can raise as much unregulated soft money contributions as they want. These organizations, run by a handful of individuals unaccountable to any political institutions, have become extremely influential.

Since the Democrat Party is and has always been less successful at raising funds from small contributors, some of its wealthy donors have discovered they can simply divert their contributions to these 527 groups, which can in turn use the money to help Democrat candidates. And that's exactly what has happened. For example, billionaire financier George Soros has committed tens of millions of dollars to Democrat-related groups. The *Washington Post* reported, "Soros's contributions are filling a gap in Democratic Party finances that opened after the restrictions in the 2002 McCain-Feingold law took effect. In the past, political parties paid a large share of television and get-out-the-vote costs with unregulated 'soft money' contributions from corporations, unions and rich individuals. The parties are now barred from accepting such money. But non-party groups in both camps are stepping in, accepting soft money and taking over voter mobilization."[28]

According to the Center for Public Integrity, between August 2000 and November 2004, Soros's contributions to 527 groups included:

America Coming Together—Nonfederal Account	$7,500,000
Joint Victory Campaign 2004	$12,050,000
MoveOn.org Voter Fund	$2,500,000
Campaign for a Progressive Future	$500,000
Campaign for America's Future (Labor)	$300,000
Democracy for America—Nonfederal	$250,000
DASHPAC—Nonfederal Account	$20,000[29]

Soros isn't alone. Among the biggest of the Democrat 527 groups' financial backers is Peter Lewis, who has also poured tens of millions of dollars into several of these organizations. The Center for Public Integrity reported that, as of November 1, 2004, Lewis had contributed the following amounts to Democrat-related organizations:

Joint Victory Campaign 2004	$16,000,000
America Coming Together—Nonfederal Account	$2,995,000
MoveOn.org Voter Fund	$2,500,000
Marijuana Policy Project Political Fund	$485,000
Young Democrats of America	$650,000
Punk Voter Inc.	$50,000[30]

The Democrats have been far more successful in funding these organizations than the Republicans. The vast majority of the top fifty 527 groups support Democrat causes. As of December 2, 2004, here are the top fifty 527 groups in receipts and expenditures:

Committee Name	Receipts	Expenditures
Joint Victory Campaign 2004	$65,553,751	$59,222,983
America Coming Together	$61,832,339	$55,135,924
Media Fund	$51,655,183	$46,653,162
Progress for America	$37,897,201	$28,808,577
Service Employees International Union	$28,762,575	$30,850,034
American Federation of State/County/ Municipal Employees	$20,493,101	$19,965,342
MoveOn.org	$12,075,952	$20,383,124
Swift Vets and POWs for Truth	$11,836,949	$13,766,664
New Democrat Network	$10,848,380	$10,691,349
Club for Growth	$10,116,855	$12,275,112
Sierra Club	$6,811,875	$5,405,139
College Republican National Committee	$6,372,843	$8,207,393

Committee Name	Receipts	Expenditures
EMILY's List	$6,274,978	$6,362,021
Voices for Working Families	$5,946,461	$5,115,582
AFL-CIO	$5,058,057	$4,971,382
League of Conservation Voters	$4,253,000	$1,170,183
Democratic Victory 2004	$3,953,070	$2,594,645
National Association of Realtors	$3,215,263	$2,093,134
Laborers Union	$3,175,349	$2,790,785
Citizens for a Strong Senate	$3,145,030	$2,502,485
Partnership for America's Families	$3,071,211	$2,874,538
November Fund	$3,053,995	$2,620,314
Communications Workers of America	$2,515,692	$2,095,733
Grassroots Democrats	$2,404,728	$1,792,594
America Votes	$2,383,686	$1,997,660
Democrats 2000	$2,161,395	$747,414
Coalition to Defend the American Dream	$1,825,754	$1,561,838
Sheet Metal Workers Union	$1,767,405	$1,706,040
International Brotherhood of Electrical Workers	$1,724,823	$4,566,925
GOPAC	$1,705,862	$2,147,424
Stronger America Now	$1,607,000	$1,167,310
California Republican Convention Delegation	$1,600,750	$1,468,748
Music for America	$1,567,820	$1,460,861
Americans for Progress and Opportunity	$1,306,092	$1,305,667
Republican Leadership Coalition	$1,267,700	$1,270,903
Gay & Lesbian Victory Fund	$1,063,419	$1,010,332
Environment 2004	$1,060,187	$1,008,352
Natural Resources Defense Council	$1,048,907	$761,497
National Federation of Republican Women	$1,031,553	$3,196,806
Young Democrats of America	$1,009,286	$$560,279
America's PAC	$1,001,700	$960,443
Americans for Jobs, Healthcare & Values	$1,000,000	$994,137

Committee Name	Receipts	Expenditures
Ironworkers Union	$899,919	$896,227
Americans for Better Government	$882,965	$669,586
Public Campaign Action Fund	$830,236	$670,754
Revolutionary Women	$799,640	$935,267
Republican Leadership Council	$743,303	$767,625
American Dental Association	$730,499	$335,372
Americans United to Preserve Marriage	$679,720	$618,889
American Federation of Teachers	$643,975	$630,687[31]

Many prominent Democrats either run, are affiliated with, or fund these 527 organizations. They've argued for McCain-Feingold and provided most of the votes in Congress for its passage. And these are the same people who for years have proselytized against the undue influence of wealthy, fat-cat Republicans in the political process (though Republicans raise more money from small donors than do the Democrats). Without the millions contributed by Soros, Lewis, and other liberal billionaires and millionaires, the Democratic Party would be at a serious fund-raising disadvantage.

Don't get me wrong. These organizations should be free to collect money and influence the political process. But so, too, should any other group or person. There's no reason the political parties should be prohibited from accepting large contributions. There's no reason individual donors should be limited in the amount they can contribute to candidates. These are all artificial limitations that are intended to control the influence of the electorate over the elected. And I have no doubt that the day is near when these 527 groups will either be regulated out of business or have their voices severely weakened.

Beyond limiting political speech, McCain-Feingold criminalizes unauthorized political participation to an extent that should frighten every citizen. As explained by election law experts Jan Witold Baran and Barbara Van Gelder:

Prior to... [McCain-Feingold], the Justice Department rarely initiated criminal prosecutions under the Federal Election Campaign Act of 1971. Accordingly, most enforcement actions occurred under the Federal Election Commission's civil authority to seek fines.

The [McCain-Feingold law] increases the number of campaign finance violations that may be charged as felonies and boosts maximum penalties to two years of incarceration for even the least serious offenses and five years for more serious offenses. [Its] broad sweep offers criminal penalties to prosecutors for violations involving the making, receiving or reporting of any prohibited contribution, donation or expenditure. The [law] sets the maximum penalty for aggregate violations exceeding $25,000 during a calendar year at five years of imprisonment. Campaign finance violations aggregating between $2,000 and $25,000 during a calendar year carry a maximum penalty of one year in jail.... [Under certain circumstances, these penalties can be increased.][32]

In essence, people may wind up in federal prison for speaking too much about a particular candidate or campaign.

The Supreme Court's approach to free speech in general is bizarre. For example, the Court was recently more deferential to commercial speech (advertisements) than political speech (the manner in which we select our representatives). Ostensibly, a law that regulates political speech would be upheld only in very narrow situations, while lawmakers would have more latitude to regulate commercial speech. However, in 2001, in *Lorillard Tobacco v. Reilly*, the Supreme Court overturned a Massachusetts law that attempted to regulate commercial speech.[33] The Court struck down several provisions of the Massachusetts law that would have banned tobacco advertising close to playgrounds and schools. The Supreme Court stated, "The First Amendment also constrains state efforts to limit advertising of tobacco products, because as long as the sale and use of tobacco is lawful for adults, the tobacco industry has a protected interest in communicating information about its products and adult customers have an interest in receiving that information."[34]

The Court also stated that "[p]rotecting children does not justify an unnecessarily broad suppression of speech addressed to adults."[35] It concluded that, "A careful calculation of the costs of a speech regulation does not mean that a State must demonstrate that there is no incursion on legitimate speech interests, but a speech regulation cannot unduly impinge on the speaker's ability to propose a commercial transaction and the adult listener's opportunity to obtain information about products."[36]

But if a state cannot restrict commercial speech in the name of protecting children, how can Congress, with the approval of the Supreme Court, put such restrictive limits on free political speech?[37] Make sense? It wouldn't have to the framers.

The Supreme Court has gone so far as to grant constitutional protection for the distribution of virtual child pornography. In 2002, in *Ashcroft v. Free Speech Coalition*, the Court held sections of the Child Pornography Prevention Act of 1996 (CPPA) unconstitutional, specifically the prohibition on material that involved "any visual depiction, including any photograph, film, video, picture, or computer or computer-generated image or picture" that "is, or appears to be, of a minor engaging in sexually explicit conduct."[38] Writing for the Court, Justice Kennedy stated, "Virtual child pornography is not 'intrinsically related' to the sexual abuse of children.... While the Government asserts that the images can lead to actual instances of child abuse, the causal link is contingent and indirect. The harm does not necessarily follow from the speech, but depends upon some unquantified potential for subsequent criminal acts."[39]

The Court added, "The possible harm to society in permitting some unprotected speech to go unpunished is outweighed by the possibility that protected speech of others may be muted. The overbreadth doctrine prohibits the Government from banning unprotected speech if a substantial amount of protected speech is prohibited or chilled in the process."[40]

The Supreme Court found the link between virtual child pornography and instances of child abuse too weak to justify a ban. Yet the mere assertion of "corruption" is enough to reject the First Amendment's protection of political speech in McCain-Feingold.

In 1989, in *Texas v. Johnson*, the Court also determined that flag burning was a constitutionally protected act of expression.[41] Justice William Brennan, writing for the majority, stated, "We are tempted to say, in fact, that the flag's deservedly cherished place in our community will be strengthened, not weakened, by our holding today. Our decision is a reaffirmation of the principles of freedom and inclusiveness that the flag best reflects, and of the conviction that our toleration of criticism such as Johnson's [flag burning] is a sign and source of our strength."[42]

So conduct like flag burning is protected speech, but running an ad on television criticizing a candidate within sixty days of a general election is not.

President Bush had an opportunity to veto the McCain-Feingold bill. Instead, he signed it into law, thereby passing the buck to the Supreme Court. In a statement released at the time, the president said:

> [T]he bill does have flaws. Certain provisions present serious constitutional concerns. In particular, [McCain-Feingold] goes farther than I originally proposed by preventing all individuals, not just unions and corporations, from making donations to political parties in connection with federal elections.
>
> I also have reservations about the constitutionality of the broad ban on issue advertising, which restrains the speech of a wide variety of groups on issues of public import in the months closest to an election. I expect that the courts will resolve these legitimate legal questions as appropriate under the law.[43]

By signing this law, the president committed his Justice Department to defending it against all legal challenges, which it did, including in *McConnell v. FEC*.

The executive branch's responsibility to uphold the Constitution is no less vital than that of the Supreme Court. The president should not cede such authority to the Court. President Bush gambled that he could avoid the slings and arrows of the campaign finance reformers and their media cheerleaders by signing the McCain-Feingold bill and leaving it to the Court to strike down its most constitutionally offensive aspects. He was wrong. The Court, these days, is no reliable guardian of the Constitution. And as a result of the Supreme Court's decision, Americans enjoy less liberty today than they did yesterday. The framers would be appalled. These laws are passed by the very incumbent politicians who benefit from silencing their opponents. A representative republic cannot remain a republic for long when its representatives become increasingly immune from public scrutiny and criticism.

CHAPTER ELEVEN

THE COURT COUNTS THE BALLOTS

"We will take to the streets right now, we will delegitimize Bush, discredit him, do whatever it takes, but never accept him."

Jesse Jackson,
speaking outside the Supreme Court, December 11, 2000[1]

The 2000 presidential election spawned a historic and egregious example of judicial recklessness. The Florida Supreme Court's rogue rewriting of state election law—in a bold attempt to micromanage an election in real time—and the U.S. Supreme Court's unprecedented intervention to restrain that court will reverberate ominously for years to come. Now defeated "win-at-all-costs" candidates and professional party operatives have an open invitation to try to influence the outcome in close elections—or even attempt to overturn the results—with the help of unelected judges.

The controversy demonstrated how the courts can plunge themselves directly into politics and how politicians can use the courts. And sadly, none of this was necessary. Well established, time-tested statutory and constitutional mechanisms were already in place to resolve challenges to the presidential election results and determine the outcome in a clear and unassailable manner. And George W. Bush would have been elected president despite everything the Florida Supreme Court did to deliver the state's electoral votes to Al Gore. By acting as they did in the weeks after the election, both supreme courts inserted judges into one of the last bastions of democratic—and non-judicial—authority: how we, the people, elect our president and vice president. Because the U.S. Supreme Court selected a constitutional sword to strike down the Florida Supreme Court's blatantly lawless intervention, our presidential elections may never be the same. Consider what the courts have wrought.

Elections in America are conducted by local authorities—county, city, and state governments—within certain broadly defined federal requirements. In 2000, Florida's election laws required that any electoral contest in which the margin of victory was half of 1 percent or less be subject to an automatic recount of the machine tallies of votes cast.[2] Florida statutes also allowed any candidate for elective office, or any political party on the ballot, to request a manual recount of votes cast in an election.[3] These provisions detailed procedures and standards under which recounts should be conducted, including specific requirements that the recount be held in public view[4] and that specific county election board representatives actually conduct the recount.[5]

Florida law imposed certain deadlines for when candidates could request recounts[6] and for when final election returns had to be submitted to the Florida Department of State.[7] Federal law required that the procedures for resolving recounts and other disputes surrounding a presidential election be in place and a final determination made six days before members of the electoral college were to meet and vote.[8] The same federal statutes placed a deadline on when states had to submit their electoral college ballots to the archivist of the United States, who is the official recipient of the electoral college ballots, and to Congress.[9] The statutory deadlines ensured that all electoral college ballots would be physically present and that all reasonable disputes concerning the selection of electors would be resolved by the time Congress assembled to open and count them under the provisions of the Constitution.[10]

The Florida Supreme Court, however, disregarded these laws in favor of a desired outcome: the election of Al Gore. The U.S. Supreme Court intervened to bring an end to the Florida Supreme Court's obvious manipulation of the ballot-counting process.

Florida's initial vote tabulation showed that Bush had won the state by more than 1,700 votes.[11] Florida law mandated an automatic machine recount,[12] which was immediately conducted. Following that recount, Bush was still the winner.[13] The recount gave Bush a margin of 327 votes out of almost six million cast.[14]

Florida law provided that either candidate could request a manual recount in any county.[15] When such a request is made, the county's canvassing board could then, in its discretion, conduct a manual recount of 1 percent of the county's total votes in at least three precincts. If that 1 percent sampling dictated "an error in vote tabulation which could affect the outcome of the election," the board was required to correct the error and recount the other precincts with the vote tabulation system, request the Department of State to verify the tabulation software, or conduct a full manual recount.[16] In other words, only if the initial selective recount indicated a vote tabulation error could the county canvassing board begin a full manual recount of *all* the ballots. No one—even on the Gore team—argued that there were any machine errors. Consequently, there was no statutory authority for the four counties to conduct full manual recounts of all the votes.

Nevertheless, within two days after the election, Gore called for a manual recount in four Florida counties—Palm Beach, Miami-Dade, Broward, and Volusia.[17] Gore apparently believed a recount in these overwhelmingly Democratic counties would reverse the state's election results. On November 12, the Palm Beach and Volusia county boards of election started hand recounts, while Bush's attorneys went to federal court to prevent manual recounts as not being authorized under the statutes—which they weren't.[18] Other lawsuits were filed on behalf of both political parties, boards of elections, the Bush and Gore campaigns, and individual voters to both stop or require manual recounts, and to include or exclude certain absentee ballots.[19]

A deadline was looming. According to Florida law, if a county's returns are not received by the secretary of state by 5 p.m. on the seventh day following the election, the secretary of state shall ignore that county's votes.[20] Florida law also directed that the secretary of state can, but is not required to, ignore late-filed ballots.[21] The "shall ignore" statute spelled out the secretary of state's specific duties. The "may ignore" statute merely provided notice to the county canvassing board members of what the secretary of state could do if deadlines for the vote tallies weren't met.

Florida Secretary of State Katherine Harris, an elected Republican, showed unusual courage throughout the process, for which she would be personally vilified and disparaged. On November 13, she announced that Florida law would be enforced, and that the sixty-seven counties that composed her state would have until 5 p.m. November 14, 2000, to deliver their certified vote totals to her office.[22]

Harris had no discretion to extend or waive the deadline imposed by Florida law, which provided, in part: "If the county returns are not received by the Department of State by 5 p.m. of the seventh day following an election, all missing counties *shall* be ignored, and the results shown by the returns on file shall be certified."[23] (Emphasis added.)

The statute was unambiguous, and the challenges against it by Gore's legal team should have been dismissed. The effect of this statute, and its strict adherence to a specific date and time, is to ensure that counties don't manipulate vote returns after electoral winners and losers are announced. In other words, it prevents the kind of endless vote counting that was under way in heavily Democratic counties. All states impose deadlines on vote tallying.

By November 15, when the deadline passed for counties to submit certified election returns to Harris, she announced that she would not accept additional recount returns. Harris also asked the Florida Supreme Court to stop manual recounts under way in various counties.[24] This was consistent with Florida law. On November 16, Gore filed a motion in a Florida circuit court to force Harris to accept amended vote returns after the deadline.[25] Judge Terry Lewis ruled that Harris was not required to enforce the deadline, but acted within her proper discretion in doing so.[26]

On November 17, 2000, the Florida Supreme Court, on its own motion, issued a temporary stay against Harris, stopping her from certifying the election results on the day and time provided by law, pending a full hearing before the court.[27] Meanwhile, on November 17, the Eleventh U.S. Circuit Court of Appeals in Atlanta denied the Bush camp's motion to stop manual recounts.[28] Bush's lawyers had argued that recounts in only heavily Democratic counties violated the Fourteenth Amendment's equal protection clause, which provides that no state shall deny its citizens equal protection under the law. They essentially claimed that giving special attention to ballots in certain counties violated the equal protection of citizens in other counties. The court, in rejecting the Bush team's argument, correctly (and painfully, for Bush supporters like me) stated, "After expeditious but thorough and careful review, we conclude that the Emergency Motion for Injunction Pending Appeal should be denied without prejudice. Several factors lead us to this conclusion. Both the Constitution of the United States and [federal statutes] indicate that states have the primary authority to determine the manner of appointing Presidential Electors and to resolve most controversies concerning the appointment of Electors."[29]

On November 21, the Florida Supreme Court ordered that manual recounts could continue, but must be completed within five days. The Florida Supreme Court held that Harris abused her discretion in enforcing the statutory deadline. The court completely ignored existing Florida law governing deadlines and recounts, and imposed its own new deadline out of thin air—November 26.[30] Three days later, the U.S. Supreme Court agreed to hear arguments about whether the Florida Supreme Court's order was constitutional.[31]

Broward County, one of the four counties subject to a manual recount, had completed its recount inside of the November 26 deadline.[32] But Broward County changed its counting rules in midstream to include dimpled ballots—even chads with barely discernible indentations—ensuring that Gore received more votes. Moreover, at least one Democratic canvassing board member was caught bending ballots so that light could peek through an otherwise unpricked Gore chad.[33]

Another Gore-targeted county, Palm Beach, kept shifting its standards for counting votes. Dimpled ballots had not been counted at first, but eventually they were. Virtually every other kind of marked chad was also counted.[34] Palm Beach County canvassing board members were unable to complete their recount within the extended deadline, however. Harris refused to grant another extension for the late filing beyond the second deadline and the results were not included in her submission to Florida governor Jeb Bush. Nonetheless, Palm Beach County continued counting past the deadline.[35]

A third county, Miami-Dade, concluded that it could not meet the Florida Supreme Court's extended deadline and decided not to conduct a full manual recount. This was within the county's discretion.[36]

On November 26, the deadline set by the Florida Supreme Court passed. Harris's submission to Governor Jeb Bush was consistent with the Florida Supreme Court's decision of November 21. Harris was legally obligated to certify the results of the popular vote and submit those results to Governor Bush, which she did. Bush then carried out his legal duty and signed a "certificate of ascertainment" appointing George W. Bush's slate of electors to the electoral college. He then forwarded the results to the archivist of the United States.[37] At this point, the election was over. But this momentous fact was missed or ignored by the courts, both legal teams, and the press.

Despite Harris's and Jeb Bush's actions, the court haggling continued. On November 27, Gore's attorneys challenged the voting results in a Tallahassee state circuit court.[38] On November 30, the Republican-controlled state legislature voted to convene a special session of the legislature to appoint electors if the matter was not resolved through other means by December 12, the deadline under federal law when states must certify their slates of electors.[39]

On December 1, the U.S. Supreme Court heard oral arguments on the issue of whether the Florida Supreme Court acted unconstitutionally when it ordered Harris to include manual recounts submitted after the statutory deadline.[40] Three days later (during which Gore's challenge to the returns in Palm Beach and Miami-Dade counties in state circuit court was denied), the

U.S. Supreme Court set aside the Florida Supreme Court's decision to extend manual recounts, pending an explanation for its action.[41]

But the worst was yet to come. December 8 saw the Florida Supreme Court commit a flagrant act of judicial abuse. Basing its actions on no constitutional, legal, or judicial precedent, it ordered manual recounts in every Florida county that had significant numbers of "undervotes."[42] Undervotes are ballots in which no vote for president is recorded or detectable by machine tabulation. Ballots on which votes are cast for more than one candidate for president are called "overvotes."[43] The court stated, "[W]e agree with the appellees that the ultimate relief would require a counting of the legal votes contained within the undervotes in all counties where the undervote has not been subjected to a manual tabulation."[44] The court set aside its own November 26 deadline and ordered additional recounts.[45]

But the court didn't provide a deadline for completing a manual recount. This problem was raised in a dissent by Justice Major Harding:

> While this Court must be ever mindful of the Legislature's plenary power to appoint presidential electors [under Article II, Section 1, Clause 2 of the U.S. Constitution], I am more concerned that the majority is departing from the essential requirements of the law by providing a remedy which is impossible to achieve and which will ultimately lead to chaos.
>
> Even if by some miracle a portion of the statewide recount is completed by December 12, a partial recount is not acceptable. The uncertainty of the outcome of this election will be greater under the remedy afforded by the majority than the uncertainty that now exists.[46]

Another problem was that the court failed to provide a standard for recounting ballots. The question of whether a dimpled chad, a hanging chad, or a "swinging door" chad constituted a vote was left unanswered.

Chief Justice Charles T. Wells's dissent recognized that his colleagues on the Florida Supreme Court were doing great harm to the U.S. Constitution and the rule of law. He wrote, in part:

> [T]he majority's decision cannot withstand the scrutiny which will certainly immediately follow under the United States Constitution.
>
> Importantly to me, I have a deep and abiding concern that the prolonging of judicial process in this counting contest propels this country and this state into an unprecedented and unnecessary constitutional crisis. I have to conclude that there is a real and present likelihood that this constitutional crisis will do substantial damage to our country, our state, and to this Court as an institution.
>
> Judicial restraint in respect to elections is absolutely necessary because the health of our democracy depends on elections being decided by voters—not by judges. We must have the self-discipline not to be embroiled in political contests whenever a judicial majority subjectively concludes to do so because the majority perceives it is "the right thing to do." Elections involve the other branches of government. A lack of self-discipline in being involved in elections, especially by a court of last resort, always has the potential of leading to a crisis with other branches of government and raises serious separation of powers concerns.[47]

And Wells warned that continual delays imposed by the court raised the "very real possibility" of Florida missing the federal electoral college election deadlines, thus "disenfranchising those nearly six million voters who are able to correctly cast their ballots on election day."[48]

As Wells predicted, the following day, the U.S. Supreme Court voted 5–4 to halt the manual recounts ordered by the Florida court.[49] On December 11, the Supreme Court held a hearing on the Florida court's latest action.[50]

On December 12, by another 5–4 margin, the Supreme Court held that the Florida court had violated the equal protection clause of the U.S. Constitution by ordering statewide manual recounts with different standards in the various counties.[51]

In its decision in *Bush v. Gore*, the Supreme Court stated, "The right to vote is protected in more than the initial allocation of the franchise. Equal protection applies as well to the manner of its exercise. Having once granted the right to vote on equal terms, the State may not, by later arbitrary and disparate treatment, value one person's vote over that of another."[52] The Court continued, "The recount process, in its features here described, is inconsistent with the minimum procedures necessary to protect the fundamental right of each voter in the special instance of a statewide recount under the authority of a single state judicial officer.... When a court orders a statewide remedy, there must be at least some assurance that the rudimentary requirements of equal treatment and fundamental fairness are satisfied."[53]

The manual recounts were halted and the frenzy of litigation initiated by Gore was ended. Gore made his long-delayed concession speech the day following the U.S. Supreme Court's ruling.[54]

It is clear that the three judicial originalists on the U.S. Supreme Court, Chief Justice Rehnquist and Justices Antonin Scalia and Clarence Thomas, were not able to assemble a majority of the Court on the straightforward question of whether the Florida Supreme Court usurped the authority of the Florida legislature in ordering standardless manual recounts past the federal deadline. Article II, Section 1, Clause 2 of the United States Constitution specifically empowers state legislatures to determine how electors are chosen. "Each State shall appoint, in such Manner as the Legislature thereof may direct," electors to the electoral college.[55] The Florida Supreme Court's repeated manipulation of state election law procedures and rules supplanted the legislature's authority under the federal Constitution.

Nevertheless, the actions of the Florida Supreme Court were so egregious that a majority of the U.S. Supreme Court believed something had to be done to address it. While five justices signed on to the U.S. Supreme Court's decision based on equal protection clause violations, two additional justices actually embraced the equal protection argument even though they voted in the minority for other reasons.[56] I believe Rehnquist, Scalia, and Thomas obviously tried to make the best of a bad situation, unable to convince Justices Sandra Day O'Connor and Anthony Kennedy to overturn the Florida Supreme Court on Article II grounds alone. Still, the best decision would have been no decision. While the U.S. Supreme Court's motive was understandable—reining in a lawless Florida Supreme Court—it may well have unleashed future election challenges based on the equal protection clause involving voting mechanisms, voting procedures, the tabulation of votes, the qualification of candidates, and so forth.

As I wrote in *National Review Online* back in December 2000, the question now is: What has the high court wrought? For example, does a federal cause of action exist if different ballots are used throughout a state, if different methods of voting are used in different counties, or if different methods of voting are used in different localities within a county? Does a federal cause of action exist if older voting machines are used in poor areas and newer machines are used in affluent areas? Where once federal courts were loath to get involved in elections—based on lack of standing and/or the separation of powers/political question doctrine—federal judicial intervention in state and federal elections may now become commonplace. Litigants will attempt to use the courts to overturn the results of elections.[57]

The effects of the Supreme Court's ruling in *Bush v. Gore* were felt in 2002 when Senator Robert Torricelli, a Democrat from New Jersey, withdrew from his Senate race. State law provided that a political party could not replace one candidate with another within fifty-one days of an election. Torricelli announced his withdrawal thirty-six days before the election.[58] Rather than upholding the law and keeping Torricelli's name on the ballot, the New Jersey Supreme Court, in a unanimous decision, said that the Democratic Party could replace Torricelli with former senator Frank Lautenberg. The New Jersey Supreme Court said that election law should be broadly interpreted to "allow parties to put their candidates on the ballot, and most importantly, to allow the voters a choice on Election Day."[59] While the New Jersey court did not rely on the federal equal protection clause for its ruling, its heavy-handed intrusion into the election process may well have been encouraged by the recent precedent set by the U.S. Supreme Court.

The federal equal protection argument was raised in 2003 when the ACLU attempted to delay the 2003 recall election for governor of California. The ACLU filed a lawsuit based on federal equal protection grounds alleging that voters in at least six counties would be disenfranchised "because voters in counties that use punch-card machines will have a comparatively lesser chance of having their votes counted than voters in counties that use other technologies."[60] At first, a panel of the Ninth U.S. Circuit Court of Appeals agreed with the ACLU and ordered a halt to the recall election. It was then reversed by the full court.[61] But the stage has been set for additional challenges in future elections.

Even before the first vote was cast in the 2004 presidential election, numerous lawsuits were filed—especially in battleground states—with the intention of influencing the election. The suits challenged everything from alleged equal protection violations affecting minorities, ballot access for prisoners, disenfranchisement of overseas voters (including military personnel), accuracy of voter registration rolls, absentee ballot requirements, provisional ballots, and certain paperless voting technologies. There were thousands of lawyers poised to file additional suits had the election been close.[62]

• • •

There are several significant questions about the 2000 presidential election that are raised frequently but rarely answered.

Could the Florida legislature have intervened and chosen the state's presidential electors itself?

Yes. Article II, Section 1, Clause 2 of the U.S. Constitution provides that "Each State shall appoint, in such Manner as the Legislature thereof may direct, a Number of Electors, equal to the whole number of Senators and

Representatives to which the State may be entitled in the Congress: but no Senator or Representative, or Person holding an Office of Trust or Profit under the United States, shall be appointed an Elector."[63]

The Florida legislature could have (and, in fact, was preparing) to intervene and name a slate of electors if the Florida Supreme Court continued to interfere with the election.[64] The legislature, which was controlled by the Republican Party in 2000, had absolute authority under the Constitution to choose Florida's members of the electoral college. This is another reason why Gore's litigation strategy was never going to succeed in winning him the Florida electoral votes he needed to become president.

Was it necessary—or appropriate—for the U.S. Supreme Court to enter the controversy?

I believe that the U.S. Supreme Court intervened in the 2000 election not to choose a winner, but rather to rein in the Florida Supreme Court, which was intent on allowing county election boards to recount returns under increasingly flawed standards until the desired result had been achieved—a victory for Gore. But it was not necessary for the Court to become involved at all. The issue would have been resolved—under the explicit language of the Constitution—by the Florida legislature and ultimately by Congress.

Is there any scenario under which Gore could have won?

Both practically and constitutionally, no. There are three basic reasons for this. First, on November 26, 2000, after Florida's returns had been certified by Katherine Harris, Governor Bush sent a certificate of ascertainment to the archivist of the United States certifying the election of the Republican slate of electors to the electoral college, as required by federal statute.[65] Once Bush had done so, no authority—state or federal, legislative or judicial—could force him to withdraw his certification. Certainly, his certification could have been challenged in Congress when the electoral college votes were counted,[66] but federal law recognizes no other authority who could actually certify Florida's electors or the votes of those electors.[67]

Second, once the electoral college votes were counted in Congress, a challenge of the Florida votes would have required a majority vote in each house to reject Florida's electoral vote, an unlikely scenario as the Republicans controlled the House of Representatives.[68] Even if this hurdle had been jumped, the House would then have chosen the president by a vote of the majority of state delegations.[69] Since Republicans outnumbered Democrats in a majority of the state delegations, the Republicans controlled a majority of those delegations. I have no doubt they would have voted to uphold the election of George W. Bush. (A very unlikely but technically possible scenario of a Democrat winning would have involved the vice presidency, not the presidency. Had a challenge been made, the Senate, which was split 50–50 along party lines, would have selected the vice president by the vote of individual senators. Since Gore was still serving as vice president, and therefore president of the Senate, he could have cast the tie-breaking vote for Joe Lieberman.)

Third, since Article II, Section 1, Clause 2 of the Constitution gave the Florida legislature ultimate authority over the state's selection of electors, it was clear at the time that the Republican-controlled legislature was preparing to do just that, had the U.S. Supreme Court not intervened to stop the Florida court's rewriting of state election law.[70]

In my view, Gore's litigation efforts were never going to grant him the presidency, the Florida Supreme Court's lawlessness on Gore's behalf was for naught, and the U.S. Supreme Court's decision to rein in the Florida Supreme Court had no effect on the ultimate outcome of the election.

What should have happened in 2000?

The canvassing boards in the various Florida counties should have performed their duties under Florida law and certified their returns.[71] The boards should have followed the specific standards for hand recounts as prescribed by Florida law.[72] Those returns should have been sent within the required deadline to the Florida department of state,[73] and then Governor Jeb Bush should have certified the appointment of electors to the archivist of the United States.[74] Once Florida's electors met in Tallahassee on December 18, they should have certified their ballots and forwarded them to the president of the Senate, the Florida secretary of state, the archivist of the United States, and the local federal district judge where the electors met—all as required by federal law.[75]

Florida's circuit courts should have considered only whether the state's election laws were being observed by the election boards, and should have refused to hear the spate of challenges offered by the political parties, by the candidates, and by individual Florida voters. In other words, the state courts should have limited the cases before them to the question of whether the election was conducted in accordance with the clear wishes of the state legislature, as expressed in the state's election statutes.[76]

The Florida Supreme Court should have recognized the very limited role courts have in the electoral process and refused to consider most of the issues raised before it. And it certainly should not have ordered manual recounts to proceed past the statutory deadlines. The Florida Supreme Court should have deferred to the Florida legislature over the selection of electors, as required by the Constitution. Instead, it sought to rewrite Florida's election laws and to use the judiciary as a political vehicle to achieve a partisan electoral victory.

The Gore campaign should not have asked the Florida Supreme Court to act in contravention of both state and federal election law in its demands for multiple manual recounts, the exclusion of absentee ballots from military personnel, changes in the standards by which votes in many counties were tabulated, and other issues the campaign raised in state court. Gore should have respected the dictates of the Constitution and appreciated the dangerous precedent his efforts could set for judicial intervention in future elections.

In short, Gore should have put the needs of our constitutional system of government before his personal political ambitions. If he didn't win through the constitutional mechanisms available to him, he should have gracefully accepted defeat. After all, he was twice elected vice president under the same procedures he sought to overturn in 2000. And despite false allegations that the U.S. Supreme Court selected Bush as president, it was Gore who first went to court, and he would have been perfectly happy had the Florida Supreme Court succeeded in handing him the presidency.

By the same token, Bush's campaign also set a very dangerous precedent by raising the equal protection issue in its challenges in federal court. Since equal protection had never been successfully raised previously in connection with ballot tabulation issues, the door has now been opened wide for future courts to interfere in close elections, at both the state and federal levels.

The U.S. Supreme Court did not select Bush as president. Instead, it stopped a rogue state supreme court from violating the rule of law. But it should not have invoked the equal protection issue to halt manual recounts. Chief Justice Rehnquist and Justices Scalia and Thomas were correct in their concurring opinion that the selection of state electors should have been the exclusive prerogative of the state legislature.

The ultimate arbiter of the outcome of the 2000 presidential election, like all presidential elections, was Congress. The candidates and the courts should have respected a process that has served us so well for so long.

CHAPTER TWELVE

LIBERALS STACK THE BENCH

"Every judge I appoint will be a person who clearly understands the role
of a judge is to interpret the law, not to legislate from the bench.
To paraphrase the third occupant of this house, James Madison, the courts
exist to exercise not the will of men, but the judgment of law.
My judicial nominees will know the difference."

President George W. Bush[1]

So committed is the Left to changing our country through judicial fiat that it has now embarked on a brazen and unconstitutional strategy to pack the federal judiciary from top to bottom with activist judges. The Left has been very successful in advancing its big-government agenda and social goals through the least democratic of our institutions—the court— because it cannot achieve its ends through the ballot box. Indeed, over the decades, a kind of symbiotic relationship has developed between the Left and the judiciary. The Left brings cases alleging some purported constitutional abuse requiring judicial intervention, and the judiciary uses the occasion of such cases to expand its own power.

This relationship is threatened by the nomination of would-be jurists who don't share the activist approach to lawmaking and constitutional tampering from the bench.

When George W. Bush was running for president in 2000, he made clear his intention to appoint originalist judges. He said, "Voters should assume that I have no litmus on [the] issue [of abortion] or any other issue. The voters will know I'll put competent judges on the bench, people who will strictly interpret the Constitution and will not use the bench to write social policy. I believe in strict constructionists."[2]

After he took office, President Bush did the unthinkable—he reversed a decades-old White House practice of referring judicial candidates to the American Bar Association (ABA) for qualification ratings before sending their nominations to the Senate for consideration. The president's reasoning was simple: The ABA had stopped vetting judicial nominees based on professional credentials alone, because it had evolved from a traditional professional association into a liberal advocacy group advancing the Left's agenda. It opposes the death penalty and favors abortion. When officials in the Reagan and Bush administrations were the targets of independent counsel investigations, the ABA supported the Independent Counsel Act. When Bill Clinton became the target of an independent counsel, the ABA opposed the act.

Perhaps the ABA's most controversial and disgraceful behavior occurred when President Ronald Reagan nominated Judge Robert Bork, one of America's finest legal minds, to the Supreme Court. In 1987, in an act of transparent partisanship, the ABA's judicial review committee helped to undercut Bork's nomination. While a majority of committee members rated Bork "well qualified," four members actually rated him "not qualified" to serve on the Court. Keep in mind, Bork had been solicitor general of the United States (the government's top litigator), a judge on the U.S. Court of Appeals for the D.C. Circuit, and a longtime professor of law at Yale. The politically and ideologically skewed ABA rating was used by Bork's opponents to unleash a campaign of character assassination against him, which ultimately defeated his nomination.

President Bush's decision to end the ABA's formal participation in the vetting process outraged two of the most liberal members of the Senate, Patrick Leahy of Vermont (the top Democrat on the Senate Judiciary Committee) and Charles Schumer of New York. They insisted that Senate Democrats would involve the ABA in the judicial selection process, regardless of the president's decision. Leahy and Schumer said at the time: "We are extremely disappointed that the President... [has] decided to downgrade and delay the American Bar Association's role in evaluating prospective nominees for the federal bench. Now that the White House has eliminated the ABA's initial role in the nomination process, we will work to ensure they play a role in the Senate confirmation process."[3]

Having deluded themselves about the 2000 presidential election by claiming that somehow Al Gore had really won, these Democrats were now committed to stopping the president from making his mark on the federal judiciary. The *Boston Globe* unabashedly urged political payback via judicial nominees, writing, "The Senate will have the right and the duty to examine any Bush nominee to the Supreme Court through the lens of the Court's *Bush v. Gore* decision." It continued, "The Senate should not allow the five-member conservative majority on the Court to perpetuate its ideology through such a contrived political decision."[4] Increasingly extreme contentions and demands were openly advocated by the likes of Yale law professor Bruce Ackerman:

> This is the first time in American history that the majority of the Supreme Court has the potential to arrange for its own succession. By intervening in the last presidential election, the conservative majority removed the American people's check on a runaway court. It is one thing for the justices, who are not elected, to exercise the sovereign power of judicial review. It is quite another for them to insulate themselves yet further from popular control by putting their man in the White House.
>
> This unprecedented situation *requires the Senate to ask new questions and draw new lines. The first step should be a moratorium on Supreme Court appointments until the American people return to the polls in 2004. Under present rules, it only takes forty senators to block any appointment to the Court. Senators should use this*

power to force President Bush to demonstrate that he can win reelec-
tion in 2004 without the court's assistance.[5] [Emphasis added.]

The Senate Democrats then hatched a plan to circumvent the Constitution and delay—and, where possible, defeat—the president's judicial nominations. They decided to turn the judicial confirmation process on its
head—first by obstructing confirmation hearings to delay consideration of
judicial nominees, and then by threatening and instituting unprecedented
filibusters of judicial nominations.

To implement this plan, Democrats on the Senate Judiciary Committee—
who are among the most liberal in the Senate—have mounted a highly partisan and destructive campaign to defeat judicial nominees for the federal
bench, especially appellate nominees.[6] If a candidate does not follow the liberal activist approach to the law, he is labeled "right-wing" or "extreme," and
his nomination is denied a vote on the Senate floor. It doesn't matter whether
these nominees have distinguished records as federal or state judges or are
respected legal scholars or successful attorneys.

These Democratic senators work very closely with extreme left-wing
groups committed to the appointment of only the most activist candidates
to the courts. Until now, most of their work took place in the shadows, out
of public view. But thanks to the uncovering of explosive memoranda in
2003, we now know how they collaborate and coordinate their efforts. The
memoranda refute the public perception that senators on the Judiciary Committee vet judicial nominees on merit, focusing on the nominee's ability to
be a capable judge. Rather, the memoranda show that Senators Ted Kennedy
of Massachusetts, Schumer, Leahy, Tom Daschle of South Dakota, and Dick
Durbin of Illinois regularly meet with the ideological leaders of these outside
groups that have the express goal of defeating President Bush's nominees to
the federal bench. In almost every case, these groups oppose a nominee
because they believe he does not meet the litmus test of their own radical
activist agenda.

When these memoranda became public, the senators succeeded in making the release of the memoranda a more important issue than their contents. They demanded investigations to determine who released the memoranda and how they got them. Senator Orrin Hatch of Utah, the Republican chairman of the Senate Judiciary Committee, ordered an immediate investigation. An investigation was conducted by the Senate's sergeant at arms and certain Republican staffers were forced to resign. However, the shocking substance of the memoranda—revealed in the Appendix—has never received the attention it deserves. The memoranda reveal that within the U.S. Senate, a small cabal of senators has conspired to undermine the Constitution and judicial selection.

Consider the following, a memorandum purportedly written to Senator Kennedy by a staffer, dated April 17, 2002. It states, in part:

> Elaine Jones of the NAACP Legal Defense Fund (LDF) tried to call you today to ask that the Judiciary Committee consider scheduling Julia Scott Gibbons, the uncontroversial nominee to the 6th Circuit at a later date, rather than at a hearing next Thursday, April 25. As you know, Chairman [of the Senate Judiciary Committee] Leahy would like to schedule a hearing next Thursday on a 6th Circuit nominee because the Circuit has only 9 active judges, rather than the authorized 16. (These vacancies are, as you know, the result of Republican inaction on Clinton nominees). Senator Leahy would also like to move a Southern nominee, and wants to do a favor for Senator Thompson.
>
> *Elaine would like the Committee to hold off on any 6th Circuit nominees until the University of Michigan case regarding the constitutionality of affirmative action in higher education is decided by the en banc 6th Circuit.* This case is considered the affirmative action case most likely to go to the Supreme Court. Rumors have been circulating that the case will be decided in the next few weeks. The thinking is that the current 6th Circuit will sustain the

affirmative action program but if a new judge with conservative views is confirmed before the case is decided, that new judge will be able, under 6th Circuit rules, to review the case and vote on it.

LDF asked Senator Leahy's staff yesterday to schedule Richard Clifton, an uncontroversial nominee to the 9th Circuit, before moving Gibbons, but they apparently refused. The decision has to [be] made today (or by early Thursday morning) since the hearing will be noticed on Thursday.

[Name redacted] and I are a little concerned about the propriety of scheduling hearings based on the resolution of a particular case. *We are also aware that the 6th Circuit is in dire need of additional judges. Nevertheless we recommend that Gibbons be scheduled for a later hearing.*[7] [Emphasis added.]

This memo tells us a great deal. These groups are obviously deeply involved in the judicial confirmation process, and even go so far as to suggest when Kennedy should schedule a vote on a judicial nominee. They are also trying to influence the outcome of a judicial decision by encouraging Kennedy to hold back the nominee until a hoped-for favorable opinion can be issued on affirmative action by the court—even though there was a "dire" need for more judges on this court. Indeed, seven of sixteen authorized slots for judges on this court—the Sixth U.S. Circuit Court of Appeals—were vacant. This is court tampering, plain and simple.

A June 4, 2002, memorandum, written to Senator Kennedy by a staffer, states, in part:

As you know, the meeting with the groups to discuss the strategy on judicial nominations is scheduled for tomorrow at 11:50. Both Senator Schumer and Senator Durbin will be able to attend. The six principals who will attend are: (1) Wade Henderson [of the Leadership Conference on Civil Rights], (2) Ralph Neas [President of People for the American Way], (3) Leslie Proll of the

NAACP LDF [Legal Defense Fund], (4) Nancy Zirkin [Deputy Director, Leadership Conference on Civil Rights], (5) Nan Aron [President, Alliance for Justice], and (6) Kate Michelman [President, NARAL Pro-Choice America].[8]

These individuals appear throughout the memoranda as pivotal power players in marshalling and orchestrating the Democratic opposition to President Bush's judicial nominees. They run radical organizations that seek to utilize the court system to advance a left-wing agenda. For example, People for the American Way, founded by Hollywood millionaire Norman Lear, advocates the defeat of school voucher programs, the legalization of gay marriage, and the defeat of the USA Patriot Act.[9] NARAL Pro-Choice America has worked extensively to defeat the bans on partial-birth abortions.[10] The other groups pursue similar agendas.

The elevation of any originalist—a nominee who believes in applying and interpreting the Constitution—to a federal court is a direct threat to the policies these groups seek to impose on the nation through an activist judiciary. And the Left is hell-bent on stopping them.

The memoranda reveal some of the tactics these groups use to defeat President Bush's judicial nominees. For example, regarding the nomination of Priscilla Owen to the federal appellate bench, a June 4, 2002, memorandum states, in part:

Our Next Big Fight

The current thinking from Senator Leahy is that Judge Owen will be our next big fight, after the July 4th recess. We agree that she is the right choice—she has a bad record on labor, personal injury, and choice issues, and a broad range of national and local Texas groups are ready to oppose her. The groups seem to be in agreement with the decision to move Owen in July.

Recommendation: Move Owen in July.[11]

Justice Owen, who currently serves on the Texas Supreme Court, was nominated by President Bush for a seat on the U.S. Fifth Circuit Court of Appeals on May 9, 2001.[12] Despite serving with distinction since 1994, and even having received a "well qualified" rating from the American Bar Association, Owen's nomination to the federal bench has been blocked for years. She was voted out of the Senate Judiciary Committee on March 23, 2003, yet enough Senate Democrats joined in a filibuster to prevent an "up or down" vote on her nomination by the full Senate. Four attempts to invoke cloture (to get the sixty votes necessary to break the filibuster) have all failed. The Owen nomination remains in limbo.

In November 2001, Kennedy met with representatives from self-described civil rights groups. A resulting memorandum, directed to Senator Dick Durbin of Illinois, stated, in part:

> Due to the floor activity last night, you missed a meeting with Senator Kennedy and representatives of various civil rights groups. This was intended to follow-up a meeting in Senator Kennedy's office in mid-October, when the groups expressed serious concern with the quick hearing for Charles Pickering and the pace of judicial nominations generally.
>
> Yesterday's meeting accomplished two objectives. First the groups advocated for some procedural ground rules. These include: (1) only one hearing per month; (2) no more than three judges per hearing; (3) giving Committee Democrats and the public more advance notice of scheduled nominees; (4) no recess hearings; and (5) a commitment that nominees voted down in Committee will not get a floor vote. Earlier yesterday, Senator Leahy's staff committed to the third item in principle.
>
> Second, yesterday's meeting focused on identifying the most controversial and/or vulnerable judicial nominees and a strategy for targeting them. The groups singled out three—Jeffery Sutton (6th Circuit); Priscilla Owen (5th Circuit); and Caroline Kuhl

(9th Circuit)—as a potential nominee for a contentious hearing early next year, with an eye to voting him or her down in Committee. They also identified Miguel Estrada (D.C. Circuit) as especially dangerous, because he has a minimal paper trail, he is Latino and the White House seems to be grooming him for a Supreme Court appointment. They want to hold Estrada off as long as possible.[13]

This shocking memorandum establishes that these outside radical groups are setting the nation's agenda for the confirmation of judges nominated by the president. Seven memoranda also classified nineteen nominees for the federal appellate bench into three categories: "Good," "Bad," and "Ugly." Charles Pickering was assigned to the "Bad" category. Priscilla Owen, Michael McConnell, Miguel Estrada, and Caroline Kuhl were all rated "Ugly." (Estrada has since withdrawn his nomination, Kuhl remains in limbo, and McConnell won a rare confirmation.)

But the Alliance for Justice even opposed McConnell's nomination, despite widespread support for him:

> President Bush has nominated Michael W. McConnell to a seat on the United States Court of Appeals for the Tenth Circuit in an attempt to continue to pack the circuit courts with judges prepared to carry out his administration's anti-choice, anti-consumer, anti-civil rights, anti-labor and anti-environment agenda. Through his numerous academic articles, Professor McConnell promotes a jurisprudence of "originalism," a method of interpreting the Constitution that calls for analyzing how its framers would have decided an issue at the time that the relevant part of the Constitution was adopted. If confirmed to a lifetime seat on the federal appellate bench, Professor McConnell would be in a position to apply his academic theories, as well as the extremist ideas he propounds in non-academic publications, to

further roll back protections for well-established Constitutional rights, including civil rights and reproductive freedoms.[14]

The Alliance for Justice didn't oppose McConnell's nomination because of his qualifications or character, but because of his fidelity to the Constitution!

It is also becoming increasingly clear that if you are a traditional Catholic you will have a very difficult time becoming a federal judge. Columnist Byron York has reported that Republican Senate staffers circulated a series of quotations from Senate Judiciary Committee Democrats that suggest an anti-Catholic bias. The quotes included, from New York Democrat Charles Schumer: "In Attorney General Pryor's case his beliefs are so well known, so deeply held, that it is very hard to believe, very hard to believe, that they are not going to deeply influence the way he comes about saying, 'I will follow the law....'" and "Based on the comments Attorney General Pryor has made on this subject [abortion], I have got some real concerns that he cannot [judge fairly on abortion-related issues] because he feels these views so deeply and so passionately."

From California Democrat Dianne Feinstein: "Virtually in every area you have extraordinarily strong views which continue and come out in a number of different ways. Your comments about *Roe* make one believe, could he really, suddenly, move away from those comments and be a judge?"[15]

Besides being extraordinarily offensive and discriminatory (plus, these comments have received barely any attention), the notion that individuals who hold traditional religious beliefs are now prevented from serving in the judiciary because of these beliefs is a major perversion of the Senate's "advise and consent" role.

As these memoranda prove, the Alliance for Justice and other liberal groups now have enormous influence over the confirmation process and regularly strategize with Democratic senators. Consider a memorandum to Senator Durbin, written by a Kennedy staffer:

Senator Kennedy has invited you and Senator Schumer to attend a meeting with civil rights leaders to discuss their priorities as the Judiciary Committee considers judicial nominees in the coming months...

This meeting is intended to follow-up your meetings in Senators [sic] Kennedy's office last fall. The guest list will be the same: Kate Michelman (NARAL), Nan Aron (Alliance for Justice), Wade Henderson (Leadership Conference on Civil Rights), Ralph Neas (People for the American Way), Nancy Zirkin (American Association of University Women), Marcia Greenberger (National Women's Law Center), and Judy Lichtman (National Partnership).[16]

Another memorandum, dated November 6, 2001, was addressed to Durbin and stated, in part:

Today's meeting [with these groups] is likely to touch on a number of related issues. The primary focus will be on identifying the most controversial and/or vulnerable judicial nominees. The groups would like to postpone action on these nominees until next year, when (presumably) the public will be more tolerant of partisan dissent. They would also like to develop a strategy for moving these nominees. Among their priorities: (1) they want to ensure that they receive adequate notice before controversial nominees are scheduled for hearings; (2) they think Senator Leahy should use controversial nominees as bargaining chips, just as the Republicans did; and (3) they are opposed to holding hearings during [Congressional] recess.[17]

This remarkable memorandum, detailing the bill of particulars these extreme groups presented to their Senate Democrat backers, was written in late 2001, when the Democrats still retained a slim majority in the Senate and controlled the Senate Judiciary Committee.

After the 2002 midterm elections, the Republicans won the Senate majority, including most of the seats on the Senate Judiciary Committee. They could now schedule hearings and votes on the president's judicial nominees. But the Senate Democrats still had an arrow left in their quiver—the unconstitutional and unprecedented filibuster of judicial nominees. A filibuster is a procedural tactic in which a single senator, or a small number of senators, can extend debate on the Senate floor in order to delay or prevent consideration or a vote on a particular piece of legislation.

For a judicial nominee to be confirmed by the full Senate, there must be a vote on his nomination with a majority of senators present voting to confirm. For example, if all the senators are present, a nominee will be confirmed if fifty-one or more senators vote for the nominee (the vice president can always cast the tie-breaking vote). By using a filibuster, or even threatening to invoke the filibuster procedure against a judicial nominee, a small group of senators can prevent a vote for confirmation from ever taking place. The only way to defeat a filibuster and end the delay tactic is by a super-majority of sixty senators voting to cut off debate (this is called a cloture vote). Consequently, only forty-one senators are needed to block a Senate vote on the confirmation of a judicial nominee.

Additional memoranda from Democrats on the Senate Judiciary Committee described the plan for using the filibuster this way:

> This afternoon, Democratic members of the Judiciary Committee met with Leader Daschle and Assistant Leader [Harry] Reid to discuss [judicial nominee] Miguel Estrada. In addition to Daschle and Reid, Senators Leahy, Durbin, Edwards, Kennedy, Feinstein, and Schumer attended.
>
> All in attendance agreed to attempt to filibuster the nomination of Miguel Estrada, if they have the votes to defeat cloture.

They also agreed that, if they do not have the votes to defeat cloture, a contested loss would be worse than no contest.

All in attendance, including Senators Daschle and Reid, voiced the view that the Estrada nomination should be stopped because: 1) Not to do so would set a precedent, permitting the Republicans to force through all future controversial nominees without answering Senators' questions or providing important information; 2) Estrada is likely to be a Supreme Court nominee, and it will be much harder to defeat him in a Supreme Court setting if he is confirmed easily now; 3) The process must be slowed down and the Republicans' attempt to set up an automatic "assembly line" of controversial nominees thwarted; and 4) The Democratic base is particularly energized over this issue.[18]

A copy of talking points on the nomination of Miguel Estrada prepared for the Democratic Caucus stated, in part:

> We must filibuster Miguel Estrada's nomination. He is clearly an intelligent lawyer, but being a judge requires more. He must demonstrate his commitment to core constitutional values, and he has to prove that he has the ability to be fair and impartial.
>
> The D.C. Circuit is far too important to appoint someone about whom we have so many questions. Key labor, civil rights, environmental, and administrative law cases are decided there, and we know it is a "feeder" circuit for the Supreme Court. The White House is almost telling us that they plan to nominate him to the Supreme Court. We can't repeat the mistake we made with Clarence Thomas.[19]

Estrada was a primary target of these radical groups and Democrat senators *because* he was such an outstanding candidate. He immigrated to the

United States from Honduras as a teenager. He attended Columbia University and went on to attend Harvard Law School. After law school, Estrada served in the Department of Justice as an assistant U.S. attorney and then as deputy chief of the appellate section of the U.S. Attorney's Office in New York. Later, he served in the Department of Justice's Solicitor General's Office. At the time of his nomination, Estrada was a partner at a distinguished Washington, D.C., law firm, where he specialized in constitutional law.[20] Estrada had also argued several cases before the Supreme Court and was endorsed by top lawyers of both parties. But Estrada's main offense in the eyes of his opponents was that he would not be an activist judge. He believed in following the Constitution. And neither these groups nor their Democrat supporters in the Senate could tolerate even the possibility that an originalist like Estrada might one day become the first Hispanic American to ever serve on the U.S. Supreme Court.

I have reiterated that filibustering judicial nominees is unconstitutional because the framers assigned specific duties and powers to the president and the Senate regarding judicial nominations:

> [The President] shall have Power, by and with the Advice and Consent of the Senate, to make Treaties, provided two thirds of the Senators present concur; and he shall nominate, and by and with the Advice and Consent of the Senate, shall appoint Ambassadors, other public Ministers and Consuls, Judges of the supreme Court, and all other Officers of the United States, whose Appointments are not herein otherwise provided for.[21]

As Alexander Hamilton wrote in *Federalist* 66:

> It will be the Office of the President to nominate, and, with the advice and consent of the Senate, to appoint. There will, of course, be no exertion of choice on the part of the Senate. They

may defeat one choice of the Executive, and oblige him to make another; but they cannot themselves choose—they can only ratify or reject the choice he may have made.[22]

And the framers intended that the Senate exercise its "advise and consent" power with great deference to the president. As Professor John O. McGinnis of Northwestern University explains:

> The Framers thought the Senate should only reject nominees for weighty and publicly compelling reasons. They well understood that, by concentrating the power of nomination in a single person who has a mandate of national scope and including within that power the ability to make successive nominations, the Appointments Clause generally gives a substantial political advantage to the President over a diffuse legislative body like the Senate in a disagreement over appointments. Because of this institutional balance of power, the Senate, regardless of which party controls it, will generally be forced to find compelling reasons for rejection.[23]
>
> The Framers did not, however, expect the Senate to exercise an independent choice that it would rival the President in determining the nature of appointments.... [T]he Framers contrasted the role of the President, who was given a role of plenary choice in the appointments process, with that of the Senate, which was given only the power of rejection. Given that the Senate was not to exercise choice itself, it appeared to Alexander Hamilton that a nominee should be rejected only for "special and strong reasons." Moreover, according to the *Federalist*, the Senate must persuade the public that its reasons compelled rejection, for otherwise the "censure of rejecting a good [nomination] would lie entirely at the Senate." Thus, the original understanding of the Appointments

Clause does not contemplate rejections for reasons of partisanship, disagreement over the nominee's likely vote in a single case, because these reasons would be neither special or strong.[24]

Democratic legal scholar Michael Gerhardt wrote, "By requiring only a simple majority of the Senate to approve a nominee, the Constitution sets a low threshold for confirmation relative to virtually all other significant legislative action, which must satisfy much stiffer procedural requirements...." He added, "As a practical matter, the requirement of a bare majority of the Senate for confirmation means that smaller factions cannot thwart a presidential nomination in the absence of special Senate procedures empowering individual senators, or some special subset, with the necessary authority."[25]

Clearly the framers did not intend for a small cadre of senators, at the command of a handful of radical groups, to hold sway over the nation's judicial confirmation process. And they certainly didn't intend for a filibuster to be used to block a president's judicial appointments. Indeed, the Constitution provides only a few specific instances in which a super-majority vote is required:

- "The Concurrence of two thirds" of either the House or the Senate is required to expel a member of Congress under Article I, Section 5.
- "No Person shall be convicted" by the Senate in an impeachment trial "without the Concurrence of two thirds of the Members present," according to Article I, Section 3.
- Legislation can be enacted over presidential veto if "two thirds" of each House approves, pursuant to Article I, Section 7.
- The president is authorized to ratify treaties only if "two thirds of the Senators present concur," under Article II, Section 2.
- Congress may propose amendments to the Constitution "whenever two thirds of both Houses shall deem it necessary," according to Article V.

- Under the Fourteenth Amendment, Congress is authorized, "by a vote of two-thirds of each House," to restore the right of federal service to rebels who, having previously sworn allegiance to the United States as a federal or state officer, subsequently supported the Confederacy during the Civil War.
- Under the Twenty-fifth Amendment, Congress may determine "by two-thirds vote of both Houses" that "the President is unable to discharge the powers and duties of his office."[26]

Past Senates, regardless of which party was in the majority, have understood the framers' intent. The Senate occasionally rejected nominees, but senators held enough respect for the Constitution that to resort to a filibuster—especially as a repeated tactic, as Democrats use it today—would have been unimaginable.

The president can counter Democrats' efforts by appointing judges when the Senate is not in session. By doing so, he would be exercising his power under Article II of the Constitution to make recess appointments. Article II provides, in part, "The president shall have power to fill up all vacancies that may happen during the recess of the Senate, by granting commissions which shall expire at the end of their next session." The purpose of the recess appointments clause is to ensure that the government can function smoothly even when Congress is not in session. The terms of recess-appointed judges are only temporary—they serve for one year—but the president is free to make subsequent recess appointments. Recess appointments to the federal judiciary are not unprecedented. According to a recent federal court, there have been more than 300 recess appointments to the federal judiciary.[27]

In fact, President Bush recently used this authority to counter Democratic stonewalling. He appointed William Pryor to the Eleventh U.S. Circuit Court of Appeals and Charles Pickering to the Fifth U.S. Circuit Court of Appeals when the Senate was not in session. Shortly thereafter, Pryor's recess appointment was challenged in the Eleventh U.S. Circuit Court of Appeals by, among others, Ted Kennedy. It ruled that the president had acted within his constitutional authority.[28] The court stated, "We are not persuaded that the President exceeded his constitutional authority in a way that causes Judge Pryor's judicial appointment to be invalid. We conclude that Judge Pryor may sit with this Court lawfully and act with all the powers of a United States Circuit Judge during his term of office."[29]

If Senate Democrats continue to use the filibuster to obstruct the president's judicial nominees, he should make more aggressive use of the recess appointment power to defeat this unconstitutional strategy.

The Republican majority in the Senate can also utilize what has been described by its critics as the so-called "nuclear" option. As described by Capitol Hill columnist Byron York, "The [nuclear scenario] envisions Republicans using parliamentary maneuvers either to declare the Democratic filibusters...unconstitutional, or to decide that the Senate rules forbid the minority party from using the filibuster in cases of judicial nominations. In either case, the scenario goes, a simple majority of 51 votes could then be held to uphold the parliamentary ruling. Then, the Senate could move on to a final confirmation vote for both nominees."[30]

To his credit, President Bush has repeatedly criticized the filibuster attack:

> Highly qualified judicial nominees are waiting years to get an up-or-down vote from the United States Senate. They wait for years while partisans search in vain for reasons to reject them. The obstructionist tactics of a small group of senators are setting a pattern that threatens judicial independence. Meanwhile, vacancies on the bench and overcrowded court dockets are causing delays for citizens seeking justice. The judicial confirmation process is broken, and it must be fixed for the good of the country.[31]

President Bush has also stated that, "[A] minority of senators continued to filibuster highly qualified judicial nominees who enjoy the support of a majority of senators. These obstructionist tactics are unprecedented, unfair, and unfaithful to the Senate's constitutional responsibility to vote on judicial nominees."[32] He has called upon the Senate to abandon these devices: "Every judicial nominee should receive an up-or-down vote in the full Senate, no matter who is President or which party controls the Senate. It is time to move past the partisan politics of the past, and do what is right for the American legal system and the American people."[33]

The fiercest battle will come if President Bush has the opportunity to nominate someone to the Supreme Court. Court observers expect at least one of the current justices of the Supreme Court to retire, and it's likely to be Chief Justice William Rehnquist, due to his unfortunate struggle with thyroid cancer. Radical outside groups such as the Alliance for Justice, People for the American Way, and NARAL will vehemently oppose any originalist—or anyone who doesn't embrace their activist agenda—nominated to the Supreme Court. This battle will make all past judicial confirmation battles pale in comparison. And the reason is simple: The extreme left has scored few victories at the ballot box. They must rely on the tyranny of an activist judiciary to advance their policy agenda.

CHAPTER THIRTEEN

RESTORING THE CONSTITUTION

"There is in all a strong disposition to believe that anything lawful is also legitimate. This belief is so widespread that many persons have erroneously held that things are 'just' because the law makes them so."

Frédéric Bastiat, 1850[1]

The Supreme Court is abusing and subverting its constitutional role. It has chosen to become the unelected, unassailable social engineer of American society. The sad truth is that the other branches of government have been complicit in the Court's power grab.

Article III of the Constitution gives Congress the authority to create lower courts under the Supreme Court. Congress also has the authority to determine the original and appellate jurisdiction of the lower courts and, within limits, the original and appellate jurisdiction of the Supreme Court.[2] The president has the authority to nominate candidates to the federal bench who take office with the advice and consent of the Senate.[3] The House of Representatives can impeach judges and the Senate can try and remove them, including Supreme Court justices.[4] The elected branches can use these constitutional powers to correct the imbalance created by a federal judiciary that has used "judicial review" to undermine the Constitution and the framework of our government.

The last serious effort to rein in the Supreme Court—President Franklin Roosevelt's "court packing" scheme of the 1930s—was an attempt to change the Court's direction by expanding its size. Since the Constitution is silent about the number of justices who serve on the Court, its membership is determined by federal legislation. Congress set the original number at six, and after some fluctuation, the Court has been made up of nine justices since 1869. Roosevelt, whose New Deal agenda had been stymied by the Supreme Court, wanted the power to name additional justices who would be sympathetic to his proposals. This blatantly political effort had mixed results.

In March 1937, shortly after the start of his second term, Roosevelt used his ninth "fireside chat" from the White House to rouse the public against the Supreme Court. He told his listeners:

> The Court, in addition to the proper use of its judicial functions, has improperly set itself up as a third house of Congress—a super-legislature, as one of the justices has called it—reading into the Constitution words and implications which are not there, and which were never intended to be there.
>
> We have therefore reached the point as a nation where we must take action to save the Constitution from the Court and the Court from itself. We must find a way to take an appeal from the Supreme Court to the Constitution itself. We want a Supreme Court which will do justice under the Constitution and not over it. In our courts we want a government of laws and not of men.[5]

The president added that the Supreme Court and the lower federal courts were blocking his New Deal legislation because so many of the justices and judges were old and feeble. Roosevelt proposed legislation giving the president power to appoint new justices for every justice who stayed on past the age of seventy, up to a total of six new justices. The president could also add judges to lower federal courts if the judges didn't retire at seventy.[6]

Nevertheless, Congress and the American public were skeptical. Roosevelt's own vice president, John Nance Garner, a former speaker of the House and longtime member from Texas, broke with the president over the plan and worked actively against it.[7] Chief Justice Charles Evans Hughes even wrote to Senator Burton K. Wheeler (a liberal Democrat and a leading opponent of the plan) to contradict the president's claims that the Court was overburdened and that additional justices would alleviate that condition. "An increase in the number of justices of the Supreme Court . . . would not promote the efficiency of the court. It is believed that it would impair the efficiency so long as the court acts as a unit. There would be more judges to hear, more judges to confer, more judges to discuss, more judges to be convinced and more judges to deride."[8]

The otherwise loyal Democrat leadership in both houses rejected the president's rationale for "fixing" the court, and ultimately the legislation never made it through either the House or the Senate. Roosevelt's personal prestige was seriously damaged by his attempt to "reform" the Supreme Court.

In the long run, however, Roosevelt got what he wanted: One of the four "conservative" justices[9] (Willis Van Devanter) announced his retirement, and the two swing votes on the Court (Charles Evans Hughes and Owen Roberts) began to vote in favor of the New Deal legislation that came before the Court. When he died in office on April 12, 1945, Roosevelt had appointed a total of eight Supreme Court justices.[10]

In the framers' perspective, the chief method for controlling judges was impeachment. Article II, Section 4 of the Constitution provides for the removal of the president, vice president, and "civil Officers" such as justices "on Impeachment for, and Conviction of, Treason, Bribery, or other high Crimes and Misdemeanors."[11] There have been sixteen impeachments to date—one associate justice of the Supreme Court (Samuel Chase, 1804, acquitted, a precedent that has discouraged further impeachment proceedings against Supreme Court justices), eleven federal judges,[12] one senator (William Blount, charges dismissed, 1799), one Cabinet official (Secretary of

War William Belknap, acquitted, 1868), and two presidents (Andrew Johnson, 1868, acquitted; Bill Clinton, 1999, acquitted).

Chase's case resulted in a fundamental redefinition of the constitutional mechanism of impeachment. The Jeffersonian Republicans (swept into power in 1800) charged Chase, a federalist appointed by President John Adams, with numerous abuses of discretion in his conduct of a treason trial[13] and in the trial of publisher James Callendar, who had allegedly violated the Sedition Act.[14] Charges were brought by the House after the Republicans, under the leadership of Thomas Jefferson, gained power as a result of the election of 1800.[15]

With regard to the treason trial, Chase was charged with conducting "himself in a manner highly arbitrary, oppressive, and unjust."[16] He was accused of "delivering a written legal opinion tending to prejudice the jury against the defendant before defense counsel had been heard"[17] and denying the defense counsel the right to cite English common-law authorities and U.S. statutes.[18] It was further claimed that Chase prevented the defendant's counsel from addressing the jury concerning applicable federal law and violated Virginia law in his rulings during the trial.[19] In the Callendar case, Chase allegedly seated an individual on the jury who had already declared his determination that the defendant was guilty.[20]

The trial in the Senate—presided over by Vice President Aaron Burr—was considered one of the first "show" trials in the nation, with Jefferson applying behind-the-scenes pressure for Chase's conviction. Nonetheless, Chase was acquitted of all charges.[21] According to Chief Justice William Rehnquist, in his account of the trial:

> The acquittal of Samuel Chase by the Senate had a profound effect on the American Judiciary. First, it assured the independence of federal judges from congressional oversight of the decisions they made in the cases that came before them. Second, by assuring that impeachment would not be used in the future as a method to remove members of the Supreme Court for their

judicial opinions, it helped to safeguard the independence of that body.[22]

As a result of Chase's acquittal, the limited and extraordinary power of Congress to impeach and remove a judge from his post has been denuded to the point where a judge or a justice must act in a flagrantly illegal fashion before that conduct would be considered beyond the Constitution's "good behavior" standard as it is currently interpreted. But I believe the framers intended impeachment to be a practical limitation on the scope of judicial conduct (as well as, of course, the conduct of all "federal officers" who abuse the authority of their office or fail to follow the dictates of the Constitution). We don't necessarily have to carry it to the point made by Representative (and later president) Gerald Ford, when he declared, during debate on the prospective impeachment of Justice William O. Douglas, that "an impeachable offense is whatever a majority of the House of Representatives say it is."[23] But there is considerable merit in recognizing that it would not compromise the independence of the federal judiciary to treat egregious abuse of judicial authority as a "high crime" worthy of impeachment and removal from office. Knowingly doing harm to the Constitution, in my view, is not the sort of "good behavior" the framers envisioned justifying continuance in office.

Congress also possesses the constitutional authority to change the methods by which judges are disciplined, short of impeachment and removal. In 1980, Congress enacted a law that created a process for removing and/or substituting new federal judges because of disability or misconduct.[24] The act allowed the chief justice of the United States and a majority of the members of the judicial council in a given federal circuit to attest to a specific judge's inability to perform his duties. If the president agrees with the findings, he can appoint an additional judge to that circuit. When the original judge dies, retires, or is removed from office, the original judge's position is not filled.

The same law also created a procedure for the filing of complaints of misconduct, short of impeachment, against the judges who sit on lower federal courts. The chief judge can investigate the complaint or appoint a judicial committee to do so. The committee reports to the judicial council of the circuit, which can then either ask the accused judge to voluntarily retire, direct the chief judge to not assign cases to him, censure or reprimand him, or inform the Judicial Conference of the United States.[25] The Judicial Conference either takes action on its own or recommends to the House of Representatives that the judge in question be impeached.[26]

There are several problems with this judicial discipline system, especially from a public-accountability viewpoint. There is no transparency to the process. Complaints against judges are not published anywhere, nor is there any requirement that records of any evidence gathered to evaluate a complaint be published, nor are there set standards or procedures for handling complaints. Each federal judicial district establishes its own procedural rules, and the standards differ in each district.[27] Judicial councils and the Judicial Conference are not required to conduct public hearings on a complaint.[28] There is also no requirement that judges, judicial councils, or the Judicial Conference report to any governmental body about the results of investigations or deliberations.

Furthermore, as a practical matter, these methods for removing judges are ill-suited for a systemic reform of the judiciary. If impeachment by Congress has failed as a method to curb the judiciary's power grab, it is foolish to think that a process initiated and controlled by judges would effect anything other than minor changes.[29]

Probably more potent and practical than the removal of individual judges and justices is Congress's power to limit the Supreme Court's jurisdiction. In 1996, for instance, Congress enacted the Illegal Immigration Reform and Immigrant Responsibility Act. This act gave exclusive authority to the Immigration and Naturalization Service (INS) to determine whether an immigrant will be granted asylum, without the right to appeal to the courts.[30]

There have been other recent cases of Congress enacting limitations on judicial review. The judiciary's ability to alter prison conditions was restricted in the 1996 Prison Litigation Reform Act.[31] The Antiterrorism and Effective Death Penalty Act limits the number of habeas corpus petitions inmates can make to federal courts.[32] And in July 2004, the House of Representatives passed the Marriage Protection Act, which, if enacted, would limit the judiciary's jurisdiction in determining the constitutionality of the Defense of Marriage Act.[33] The practical problem of limiting judicial review is that it requires appropriate language to be included in each piece of legislation, and the courts themselves must be willing to abide limitations on their power.

This concern is a real one. The case of the late Representative Adam Clayton Powell is an egregious example of the Court inserting itself into a dispute that, under the clear mandate of the Constitution, should have been left exclusively to Congress. Article I, Section 5 of the Constitution empowers each house of Congress to determine the qualifications of its members.[34] Yet, in 1969, the Supreme Court ruled that the House could not exclude Powell as a member.[35] The House had found that Powell had falsified financial information, causing fraudulent expense and payroll payments to be made to himself, several of his employees, and his wife.[36] Chief Justice Earl Warren, writing for the majority, declared, "Our system of government requires that federal courts on occasion interpret the Constitution in a manner at variance with the construction given the document by another branch. The alleged conflict that such adjudication may cause cannot justify the courts avoiding their constitutional responsibility."[37]

Impeachment, lesser forms of discipline, and legislative limits on judicial jurisdiction are not, however, systemic solutions to judicial abuse. I believe the independence of the judiciary to legitimately exercise its constitutional role can be preserved, and the unconstitutional influence of the federal courts somewhat curtailed, if the Constitution were amended to limit judges to fixed terms of office.

Associate justices of the Supreme Court serve an average of nearly seventeen years. Chief justices serve an average of just over thirteen years. The longest serving justice, William O. Douglas, sat for thirty-six years. Eleven other justices served thirty years or more. Perhaps Supreme Court justices should be appointed to fixed, staggered terms of twelve years, with three years intervening between terms.[38]

Moreover, sitting judges and justices could be renominated and subject to a new confirmation process. This way, outstanding jurists could remain on the bench for a lifetime, pending congressional approval. And clearly defined terms of office would limit the influence of any single Congress in controlling the ideological bent of the Court. These changes would add accountability to the federal bench.

The most meaningful step Congress could take would be a constitutional amendment limiting the Supreme Court's judicial review power by establishing a legislative veto over Court decisions—perhaps a two-thirds vote of both houses. The rationale is the same one the framers used when creating the congressional override of a presidential veto as a check on the president's power. The framers worried that a president might amass too much authority. Today, the problem is an oligarchical Court, not a presidential monarchy, supplanting the constitutional authority of the other branches.

In the meantime, we face a liberal cabal of hard-left Democratic senators when it comes to confirming nominees to the Supreme Court. Their voices have grown louder and more shrill following the results of the 2004 election, in which President Bush won a decisive popular and electoral victory and led Republicans to an even larger majority of fifty-five in the Senate. Nevertheless, the Senate Democrats continue to threaten to use the filibuster to block the president's best nominees.[39] The prospect has taken on a new sense of urgency with Chief Justice Rehnquist's serious illness.

But the president is not without a potent short-term weapon to beat back the obstructionist minority. As the Constitution makes clear, "The President shall have Power to fill up all Vacancies that may happen during the Recess of the Senate, by granting Commissions which shall expire at the End of their next Session." Presidents have used their recess appointment power to fill twelve vacancies on the U.S. Supreme Court.[40] Indeed, in recent times Chief Justice Earl Warren and Justices William Brennan and Potter Stewart were each recess appointments to the Supreme Court.[41] President Bush has used this authority to appoint judges to the U.S. circuit courts of appeal.[42] President Clinton did the same.[43] If the president were to make a recess appointment to the Supreme Court after January 1, 2005, the new justice would serve until the end of the second session of the new Congress in late 2006[44]— enough time for both the Court's 2004–05 term and 2005–06 term to be completed. This approach would also place the issue squarely before voters for the 2006 and 2008 Senate elections, and it might cause a few fence-sitting senators to remember Senate Minority Leader Tom Daschle's fate—rejection by the people of South Dakota, in part for his obstructionist conduct with regard to judges.

As Thomas Jefferson said, "I know of no safe depository of the ultimate powers of the society but the people themselves; and if we think them not enlightened enough to exercise their control with a wholesome discretion, the remedy is not to take it from them, but to inform their discretion."[45]

Jefferson is right.

OPPOSING TYRANNY

Since I was a teenager, I've been fascinated with America's founding fathers. I was fortunate to live just outside Philadelphia. My buddy Eric Christensen and I would frequently take the train to the city to visit Independence Hall, which is now a national park. The history within only a few blocks of that small building is beyond description.

Independence Hall—specifically, the Pennsylvania Assembly Room—is where the Second Continental Congress met, where the Declaration of Independence was debated and ratified, and where the Articles of Confederation were drafted and ratified. This is also where the Constitutional Convention was held, and where the Constitution was drafted and adopted.

Later, the Federal Congress met in Congress Hall—adjacent to Independence Hall—from 1790 until 1800, when Philadelphia was the capital of the United States. The Supreme Court also established chambers in Independence Hall for several years. Washington's second inauguration and John Adams's only presidential oath took place there as well.

On each visit, my friend and I roamed these buildings for hours at a time. We examined every desk, quill pen and ink well, and spittoon in the rooms where such great men as George Washington, James Madison, Alexander Hamilton, Benjamin Franklin, and George Mason met to consider the new Constitution. We spent hours listening to tour guides recount the debates. Over the years, each guide had new and unique details to tell us as we grilled them with more and more questions. We walked the grounds around Independence Hall, speculating about the trails the framers might have traveled during breaks in their sessions. And we marveled at the brilliance, foresight, and courage of these men, who risked everything to form the most successful and just experiment in governance in history.

Around the dinner table and between debates about sports, school, and current events, my family would discuss American history, particularly the nation's founding. My parents, Jack and Norma, and my brothers, Doug and Rob, were all history buffs. Indeed, most of what I learned about America's founding occurred outside the formal classroom.

I have spent a lifetime studying, debating, and thinking about what made our founders so special. What drove these men? What inspired them? What made the government they created so different from those that existed before? The answer is not complicated. We need not research the nation's libraries to find it. It's in the Declaration of Independence, our founding document, which states, in part:

> When in the Course of human Events, it becomes necessary for one People to dissolve the Political Bands which have connected them with another, and to assume among the Powers of the Earth, *the separate and equal Station to which the Laws of Nature and of Nature's God entitle them,* a decent Respect to the Opinions of Mankind requires that they should declare the causes which impel them to Separation.... *We hold these Truths to be self-evident, that all Men are created equal, that they are endowed by their Creator with certain unalienable Rights, that among these are*

Life, Liberty, and the Pursuit of Happiness—That to secure these Rights, Governments are instituted among Men, deriving their just Powers from the Consent of the Governed. [Emphasis added.]

This is what makes America different from other nations, past and present. We recognize a greater, higher authority than the government as the source of our rights. When the framers met to rewrite the Articles of Confederation, they decided to replace it with the Constitution. The Constitution wasn't drafted to conflict with or replace the founding principles in the Declaration. Rather, it was intended to establish a more workable federal governing system.

During the Constitutional Convention, the framers were struggling constantly with ways to ensure that the federal government they were establishing would not threaten the principles they fought for during the Revolutionary War. They took extraordinary steps to protect those principles by dividing the federal government into three equal branches and assigning them specific, enumerated powers. They would later adopt ten amendments, known as the Bill of Rights. The Ninth Amendment underscored that we, the people, possess unalienable rights which the Constitution, our governing document, was not intended to usurp. The Tenth Amendment highlighted the framers' intent to limit federal authority to that which was spelled out in the Constitution.

But look at where we are today. It's difficult to find any aspect of society where the federal government doesn't have some role or influence. And the Supreme Court, more than any other branch or entity of government, is the most radical and aggressive practitioner of unrestrained power. The purpose in creating a branch of government not subject to election, and whose members are appointed for life, was to ensure that it would undertake its responsibility to interpret the Constitution and arbitrate disputes in an almost ministerial fashion. There was no expectation the courts would assume the functions of the legislative or executive branches.

This is exactly the kind of unchecked centralized decision-making—by a mere nine justices—that the framers hoped the Constitution would deter.

Their fear that our founding principles would be subjugated to the will of a handful of government officials is a growing reality today.

Over and over again, dispirited and alarmed callers to my radio show ask me why so many of our nation's great issues are decided by the federal courts. They question whether elections matter each time the Supreme Court hands down a decision that's so outside the norm of American life. And they want to know what can be done to regain control of our governmental process.

I wrote *Men in Black* to address these concerns and because I believe it's time for a serious national debate about the role of the judiciary in modern America. I hope this book will encourage it. For too long the courts have grabbed ever more authority over the course of our society, and the elected branches of government at the federal and state levels have been unwilling to do anything about it. If we're to remain a great republic—where the people "are endowed by their Creator with certain unalienable Rights"—we must not quietly accept the fate the courts have in store for us. We must oppose tyranny, whatever its form.

AFTERWORD

BY EDWIN MEESE III

T he Constitution of the United States has been described as "the most wonderful work ever struck off at a given time by the brain and purpose of man." But the Constitution can fulfill that promise only if it is faithfully interpreted by those responsible for its application to our legal system. When the federal judiciary usurps the authority of the legislative and executive branches, and when judges substitute their personal prejudices and policy preferences for what the Constitution actually says, it creates a potential crisis for our democratic republic. Such a situation has occurred continuously over the past half-century, as this important book, *Men in Black*, documents.

Mark Levin served as my chief of staff when I was attorney general of the United States under President Ronald Reagan. He has been my close and loyal friend for twenty years. He's also one of the most exceptional lawyers I've known. Mark's extensive knowledge of American history, especially the nation's founding, is second to none, as displayed in this outstanding book.

Men in Black is one of the finest books on the Constitution and the judiciary I've read in a very long time. It combines history, law, and current events in an extremely interesting, insightful, and compelling examination of a dire problem—the intensifying assault on our constitutional process and governmental structure by a relentlessly power-hungry judiciary. *Men in Black* is a clarion call to those who care about the manner in which we, the people, are governed. This is an issue near and dear to my heart. It was an issue that greatly concerned President Reagan. As attorney general, I spoke repeatedly about the judiciary's alarming disregard for its limited constitutional role. Unfortunately, the situation has only worsened.

As the Declaration of Independence states, governments are legitimate only when they represent the consent of the governed. The reason for the original founding of the United States was to gain independence from an oppressive government that was neither selected by nor responsive to those under its authority. Today we face a similar situation in which the "consent of the governed" is frequently frustrated by special interest groups that seek to obtain their policy desires through litigation and decisions of judges, rather than through the elected representatives of the people. They seek such judicial decisions because no legislator (at least none who would like to be reelected) would vote in favor of such proposals.

Not a single participant at the Constitutional Convention, not a single legislator of the ratifying states, and not a single leading political theorist at the time argued that the judiciary should be the branch of government to hold sway over the others. As *Men in Black* makes clear, the framers had no intention of trading one form of tyranny for another. They had no intention of creating a government where a mere handful of unelected officials, appointed for life, would dictate policy to Congress, the states, and ultimately the people. The purpose of the judiciary was straightforward: to decide cases and controversies and interpret—narrowly—the Constitution. It was not granted broad authority to sculpt a new constitution, negate legislation at will, or advance political causes through judicial opinions.

Men in Black describes how federal courts, and the Supreme Court in particular, treads recklessly on virtually every avenue of modern life and governance. Even in areas such as the political process and electing a president, over which the framers gave exclusive authority to Congress and the states, judges and justices have interjected themselves and twisted fundamental constitutional precepts—such as free speech and equal protection—into dangerous weapons.

Perhaps nothing troubles me more than justices who invoke international law and the decisions of international tribunals in interpreting the Constitution. As *Men in Black* makes patently clear, foreign laws and foreign courts are not legitimate guideposts for interpreting the Constitution. And when justices rely on them, they're violating their oaths to uphold our own Constitution.

Men in Black cogently explores the rationale for the judiciary's relentless quest for primacy over the other branches. It details how the Supreme Court has become the de facto driving force for social engineering in the twenty-first century, through its convoluted immersion into issues such as same-sex marriage and abortion—areas that should be largely beyond its purview. It matters very little to many of the men and women on the bench today that the will of the people—expressed repeatedly in election after election and poll after poll—rejects the radicalization of our social institutions. The courts increasingly abolish, alter, and substitute the foundational principles of our republic for their own preferences.

The judiciary was not established to divorce the power and reach of the public sector from the people it is supposed to serve. Nor was it intended to strip the state governments—the entities most responsive to the people, from whom sovereignty flows—of the authority to act as those governments generally choose, as long as they don't violate the federal powers and rights specifically enumerated in the Constitution.

James Madison, whom many credit as the "father of the Constitution," proclaimed that the combination of the judiciary's powers with those of the executive and legislative was "the very definition of tyranny."

Men in Black not only discusses the background and current threat of judicial tyranny, it also points to several innovative approaches for addressing it, including term limits for Supreme Court justices. They're both serious and thought-provoking.

It is well past time for a thorough examination of this gathering constitutional crisis. This is a debate we must have, and a topic the American public must begin to understand—lest the country we bequeath to our children barely resemble that which the framers established for us. And there is no better source for understanding and grasping the seriousness of this issue than *Men in Black*.

APPENDIX

The following memoranda show the shocking influence radical left-wing groups hold over Democrats in Congress. These Democrats and their allies on the Left desire to subvert the judicial selection process and thwart the president's constitutional power to appoint judges.

Why have a hearing at all.'

Memorandum   June 21, 2002

TO   :   Senators Kennedy, Schumer, Durbin, and Cantwell

FROM   :   ████████████

SUBJECT :   Strategy on Judges

___

In advance of the Judiciary Democrats' meeting on Tuesday at 2:15, below is the strategy regarding judges that we recommend that you suggest to Senator Leahy.

1.   **Cancel or Reschedule Deborah Cook, 6ᵗʰ Circuit nominee.** Senator Leahy is suggesting that a hearing for Deborah Cook be scheduled for August 1ˢᵗ, and, Senator Leahy may have promised Senator DeWine that he will hold a hearing for Cook this year. Cook is extremely controversial on labor, employee rights, and right to jury issues and should not have a hearing this year. If Senator Leahy has indeed promised DeWine a Cook hearing, we suggest that he schedule Cook for _after_ the November elections. Given our schedule of controversial nominees (see below), it will be difficult to mount any effective challenge to Cook if she is scheduled for early August. We recommend that Reena Raggi (2ⁿᵈ Circuit) be scheduled for early August instead of Deborah Cook.

2.   **Limit the Number of Hearings**
Senator Leahy has promised hearings for Priscilla Owen, Miguel Estrada, and Michael McConnell. Other than these nominees, and the two remaining non-controversial nominees Reena Raggi (2ⁿᵈ Circuit) and Jay Bybee (9ᵗʰ Circuit), no additional judges should be scheduled.

3.   **Timing of Hearings**
•   Owen. The consensus is to make Priscilla Owen the big fight for July 18ᵗʰ, as Senator Leahy has suggested, with the hope that we will succeed in defeating her.
•   Estrada. Miguel Estrada will be more difficult to defeat given the sparseness of his record. We agree with Senator Leahy that Estrada should be scheduled for September 19ᵗʰ. This will give the groups time to complete their research and the Committee time to collect additional information, including Estrada's Solicitor General memos (see below).
•   McConnell. McConnell will also be difficult to defeat. While he has a clear anti-choice record, he has the strong support of some Democrats and progressives. McConnell's clear anti-choice record, however, makes him a good nominee to bring up before the November elections. While Senator Leahy has suggested that a hearing for McConnell be scheduled on October 3ʳᵈ, we would suggest October 10ᵗʰ, to provide enough time for preparation after the difficult Estrada

hearing.

Suggested Schedule:

July 18th:	Priscilla Owen -5th Circuit
August 1st:	Reena Raggi – 2nd Circuit (non-controversial) –instead of Cook.
September 5th:	Jay Bybee – 9th Circuit (supported by Reid)
September 19th:	Miguel Estrada – D.C. Circuit
October 10th:	Michael McConnell - 10th Circuit

4. **Obtaining Estrada's Solicitor General's Memos**

Senator Leahy took the important first step of asking for Memoranda that Estrada produced while working at the Solicitor General's Office. Unfortunately, the Department of Justice has refused to turn over the memos, and Senator Leahy has been harshly criticized for this in the Press (two pieces in the Washington Post alone). We expect the Administration will continue to fight any attempt to turn these over, but there is precedent for getting these Memos—It was done for the Bork nomination and three other lower court nominations. We suggest that you encourage Senator Leahy to continue fighting the Administration for these Memos and, if possible, that one of you help him in this fight.

U. Michigan scandal

Bag

Memorandum

April 17, 2002

TO : SENATOR *(Kennedy)*

FROM : ███████

SUBJECT : Call from Elaine Jones re Scheduling of 6th Circuit Nominees

Elaine Jones of the NAACP Legal Defense Fund (LDF) tried to call you today to ask that the Judiciary Committee consider scheduling Julia Scott Gibbons, the uncontroversial nominee to the 6th Circuit at a later date, rather than at a hearing next Thursday, April 25th. As you know, Chairman Leahy would like to schedule a hearing next Thursday on a 6th Circuit nominee because the Circuit has only 9 active judges, rather than the authorized 16. (These vacancies are, as you know, the result of Republican inaction on Clinton nominees). Senator Leahy would also like to move a Southern nominee, and wants to do a favor for Senator Thompson. *Talk about political!!*

Elaine would like the Committee to hold off on any 6th Circuit nominees until the University of Michigan case regarding the constitutionality of affirmative action in higher education is decided by the *en banc* 6th Circuit. This case is considered the affirmative action case most likely to go to the Supreme Court. Rumors have been circulating that the case will be decided in the next few weeks. The thinking is that the current 6th Circuit will sustain the affirmative action program, but if a new judge with conservative views is confirmed before the case is decided, that new judge will be able, under 6th Circuit rules, to review the case and vote on it.

LDF asked Senator Leahy's staff yesterday to schedule Richard Clifton, an uncontroversial nominee to the 9th Circuit, before moving Gibbons, but they apparently refused. The decision has to be made today (or by early Thursday morning) since the hearing will be noticed on Thursday.

███████ and I are a little concerned about the propriety of scheduling hearings based on the resolution of a particular case. We are also aware that the 6th Circuit is in dire need of additional judges. Nevertheless we recommend that Gibbons be scheduled for a later hearing: the Michigan case is important, and there is little damage that we can foresee in moving Clifton first. (It should be noted that Clifton was nominated three months before Gibbons and that Clifton's seat, and not Gibbons', has been designated a judicial emergency.) Elaine will ask that no 6th Circuit nominee be scheduled until after the Michigan case is decided. This may be too much to promise: we only have three uncontroversial circuit court nominees left and two of these are from the 6th Circuit.

Recommendation: Let Elaine know that we will ask Senator Leahy to schedule Gibbons after Clifton. Given the dearth of uncontroversial nominees, however, the Committee will probably have to hold a hearing for Gibbons on May 9th even if there's yet no decision in the Michigan case.

Influence of special interests

BAG

June 4ᵗʰ, 2002

Memorandum

TO   :   SENATOR (Kennedy)

FROM   :   ████████ and ████

SUBJECT   :   Meeting with Groups on Judges – Wednesday, 11:50am

---

As you know, the meeting with the groups to discuss the strategy on judicial nominations is scheduled for tomorrow at 11:50. Both Senator Schumer and Senator Durbin will be able to attend. The six principals who will attend are: (1) Wade Henderson, (2) Ralph Neas, (3) Leslie Proll of the NAACP LDF, (4) Nancy Zirkin, (5) Nan Aron, and (6) Kate Michelman. It turns out that neither Marcia nor Judy can make it tomorrow – Marcia has a board meeting and Judy, a family emergency.

We expect that the agenda will include a discussion of: (1) delaying a hearing for Dennis Shedd, a nominee to the Fourth Circuit, who Sen. Leahy would like to schedule on June 27ᵗʰ; (2) which circuit court nominees should be scheduled prior to adjournment; and, (3) our next big fight.

Schedule

At present, there is only one noncontroversial circuit court nominee (with a complete file and blue slips) who has not already been scheduled for a hearing. This nominee is John Rogers (6ᵗʰ Circuit), who Senator Leahy will likely schedule for a hearing on June 13ᵗʰ. In addition, there have been two recent nominees to the 2ⁿᵈ Circuit and to the Ninth Circuit, whose records are now being researched, and who may prove to be noncontroversial.

Senator Leahy would then like to schedule Dennis Shedd on June 27ᵗʰ, Judge Priscilla Owen after the July 4ᵗʰ recess, and Miguel Estrada in September.

The groups should be encouraged to propose some specific nominees who can be moved forward before adjournment. Clearly, there are few nominees who are noncontroversial, but the groups should be pushed on whether they would agree on a hearing for some controversial nominees such as Steele, Tymkovich, or Michael McConnell (for whom Leahy has already promised a hearing), on the theory that these nominees are less problematic than others.

Shedd

Senator Leahy has told the groups that he would like to have a hearing on Dennis Shedd this month. Senator Hollings is supportive of Dennis Shedd's nomination and is, reportedly, pressuring Senator Leahy to move forward on a hearing. The groups have strong concerns about Shedd. He is quite bad on civil rights and federalism issues, and he has hundreds of unpublished opinions that have not yet been reviewed. The groups are opposed to having a hearing on him this month in part because they do not believe that they will be able to do an adequate review of his extensive record by June 27th, particularly given that they are gearing up to oppose Judge Owen.

We believe that you should hear the groups' concerns regarding Shedd, but that you should strongly encourage the groups to work with South Carolina groups and individuals to apply pressure on Senator Hollings. We know that some of the groups, including LCCR and the NAACP will meet with Sen. Hollings on Thursday regarding Shedd, but more pressure will likely need to be applied because Sen. Hollings is quite committed to moving Shedd this month.

Recommendation: Encourage groups to work with South Carolina groups to influence Sen. Hollings.

<u>Our Next Big Fight</u>
The current thinking from Senator Leahy is that Judge Owen will be our next big fight, after July 4th recess. We agree that she is the right choice – she has a bad record on labor, personal injury, and choice issues, and a broad range of national and local Texas groups are ready to oppose her. The groups seem to be in agreement with the decision to move Owen in July.

Recommendation: Move Owen in July.

cc:

MEMORANDUM

To: Senator Durbin
From: ▓▓▓▓▓▓▓▓
Date: June 5, 2002
Re: **Meeting with Civil Rights Leaders to Discuss Judicial Nominations Strategy**
        Thursday, June 6, 5:30pm, Russell 317

Senator Kennedy has invited you and Senator Schumer to attend a meeting with civil rights leaders to discuss their priorities as the Judiciary Committee considers judicial nominees in the coming months. This meeting was originally scheduled for late Wednesday morning.

This meeting is intended to follow-up your meetings in Senators Kennedy's office last fall. The guest list will be the same: Kate Michelman (NARAL), Nan Aron (Alliance for Justice), Wade Henderson (Leadership Conference on Civil Rights), Ralph Neas (People For the American Way), Nancy Zirkin (American Association of University Women), Marcia Greenberger (National Women's Law Center), and Judy Lichtman (National Partnership).

The meeting is likely to touch upon the following topics:

• Their floor strategy for opposing D. Brooks Smith, who was voted out of Committee 12-7.

• Their concerns with **Dennis Shedd**, a controversial 4th Circuit nominee from South Carolina. Under pressure from Senator Hollings — who apparently is backing Shedd because the trial lawyers want him off the district court bench — Chairman Leahy is planning to hold a hearing in late June. The groups would like more time to read through Shedd's many unpublished opinions, which were only recently provided to the Committee, and to request court transcripts. Based on a preliminary review, this nominee poses a number of problems: he has narrowly interpreted Congress's power under the 14th Amendment (in one instance, he was unanimously reversed by the Supreme Court); he has a long track record of dismissing civil rights claims; he once revoked indigent status for a litigant who used her mother's computer and fax machine to file pleadings; and he has made insensitive comments about the Confederate flag.

• The Judiciary Committee's schedule for the summer and fall. In spite of the White House's intransigence, the Committee continues to schedule hearings at a rapid pace — every two weeks through the end of the session. Bruce Cohen has outlined the following schedule:
    June: Rogers (6th Circuit–KY); Shedd (4th Circuit–SC)
    July: Owen (5th Circuit–TX); Raagi (2d Circuit–NY)
    Sept: Estrada (DC Circuit); possibly Bybce (9th Circuit–NV) (backed by Reid)
    Oct: McConnell (10th Circuit–UT)
Leahy has effectively promised that Owen, Estrada, and McConnell would get hearings this year. Like Shedd, these three will generate significant opposition and controversy. The groups feel that Owen is vulnerable to defeat, but Estrada and McConnell will be hard to vote down in Committee.

• The White House's unwillingness to compromise. On NPR this week, White House Counsel Alberto Gonzales said:

> I'm not sure this [judges] is an area where there should be a great deal of compromise on principle. Regrettably, . . . we may have to be patient and wait to see what happens in the November election. And that may be viewed as a sort of crass political assessment but that is in fact true. One way to get this thing moving is to take back the Senate so that we can at least get our judges onto the full Senate floor.

At the moment, a number of Democrats — Edwards, Graham, Nelson (FL), Levin, Stabenow — are in stalled negotiations with the White House over judges.

MEMORANDUM   June 12, 2002

TO   :   SENATOR (Kennedy)

FROM   :   ███████████████

SUBJECT   :   Judges – Schedule for the Year & Chairing A Hearing

I.   Schedule for the Year and the Shedd and Cook Problems

As you know, during your meeting with the groups, you and Schumer discussed
approaching Leahy regarding the Shedd hearing. You proposed telling him that because of the
number of unpublished opinions and the divisiveness of the nomination (angering the African
American community prior to the election), you think we should refrain from having a hearing on
Shedd in June. Based on the groups recommendation, you were also going to propose an end-of-
June hearing on another nominee. The following has happened in the interim:

-     Lott approached Daschle with an unreasonable request for nominations hearings before
      the July 4th recess. Daschle told him "no" but approached Leahy to discuss a more
      aggressive hearing schedule. The proposed schedule is as follows:

      -     June 13th   Rogers (6th Circuit)
      -     June 27th   Shedd (4th Circuit)
      -     July 18th   Owen (5th Circuit)
      -     August 1st   Cook (6th Circuit)
      -     September 5th   Raggi (2nd Circuit)
      -     September 19th   Estrada (DC Circuit)
      -     October 3rd   McConnell (10th Circuit)

-     The August 1st Cook hearing is a surprise to us, and it will be a *huge* problem for the
      judges coalition. For many, many months they have told us that Cook is highly
      problematic – particularly for labor. Cook is consistently bad on labor/workplace injury
      cases, right to jury trial issues, civil rights and rights of criminal defendants cases. Her
      frequent dissents (from the moderate majority) show a pattern at least as egregious as
      Pickering. We must press Leahy not to schedule Cook (Cook is strongly supported by
      DeWine, but how many times did Hatch disregard your request to move DC Circuit
      nominee Alan Snyder?).   → Daschle's Counsel

-     Regarding Shedd, Wade Henderson spoke with Mark Childress, and Childress is going to
      speak with Hollings' staff director. But, because we feel Leahy will not cancel the Shedd
      hearing unless Hollings' backs off (and because several of the outside groups believe the
      same), we don't think you should expend a great deal of effort trying to change Leahy's
      mind about the Shedd hearing.

-     Instead, you should speak with Schumer, and the two of you should bring Durbin up to speed (since he couldn't attend the meeting in your hideaway). The three of you should approach Leahy as soon as possible and tell Leahy that:

- You are very concerned about Shedd because he has numerous unpublished opinions and because his nomination will infuriate the African American community before the SC election, but you understand the Hollings problem. If Hollings can be moved, you propose postponing the Shedd hearing.

- You understand he is contemplating a more aggressive hearing schedule that includes a hearing for Debbie Cook for the 6th Circuit, and you believe she should not get a hearing this year. For months, labor and other groups have told us that she is highly problematic, and we should send her nomination back to the White House. We won't suffer publically if we don't have a nomination hearing for her.

- Ultimately, if Leahy _insists_ on having an August hearing, <u>it appears that the groups are willing to let Tymkovich go through (the core of the coalition made that decision last night, but they are checking with the gay rights groups).</u>

Given this information, do you want to talk to Schumer – and Durbin – about having this conversation with Leahy and then speak with Leahy? We strongly recommend that you have these conversations, and we believe Leahy must be approached quickly.

DECISION:

Yes, I will talk to Schumer and Durbin; the three of us will go to Leahy   ____

No, I will not speak with Schumer and Durbin or Leahy   ____

II.   Chairing A Hearing

As you know, Senator Leahy asked that you chair the last nominations hearing, but given your schedule, you could not. His staff is now asking us to choose the hearing you would like to chair (see the schedule above).

▆▆▆ and I propose that you chair the Owen hearing on July 18th . As you know, Owen will probably be our next big fight . The grassroots organizations are organized in Texas, and the national groups are prepared, as well. In addition, Judiciary Democrats expect to fight her, hearing attendance should be good, and the issues are clear – Enron/pro-business and choice.

You should know, the Leahy staff (and the Schumer staff) propose that you chair the Estrada hearing. ▆▆▆ and I disagree. Although other staffers see Estrada as a civil rights problem, because he has no record, there isn't civil rights ammunition. We don't believe Estrada is "your kind of fight." We think Durbin or Schumer might be better for the Estrada hearing (and, at least on the staff level, there's interest from the Schumer office).

DECISION:	I will chair a hearing on	Shedd (6/27)		
		Owen (7/18)	___	
		Cook (8/1)	___	(we want this to go away)
		Raggi (9/5)	___	
		Estrada (9/19)	___	
		McConnell (10/3)	___	

cc: ▆▆▆▆▆▆▆▆▆▆▆▆▆▆▆▆

2001- 2002 - Durbin : Kennedy memos showing role of special interest groups

MEMORANDUM

To: Senator Durbin
From:
Date: October 15, 2001
Re: Meeting with Civil Rights Leaders, Tuesday, October 16, 2001 at 5:30 p.m.

You are scheduled to meet with leaders of several civil rights organizations to discuss their serious concerns with the judicial nomination process. The leaders will include: Ralph Neas (People For the American Way), Kate Michelman (NARAL), Nan Aron (Alliance for Justice), Wade Henderson (Leadership Conference on Civil Rights), Leslie Proll (NAACP Legal Defense & Education Fund), Nancy Zirkin (American Association of University Women), Marcia Greenberger (National Women's Law Center), Judy Lichtman (National Partnership), and a representative from the AFL-CIO. The meeting will take place in 317 Russell, with Senators Kennedy and (possibly) Schumer also present.

The immediate catalyst for Tuesday's meeting was the announcement last Thursday that the Judiciary Committee would hold a hearing in one week on district court judge Charles W. Pickering, Sr., a highly controversial nominee for the Fifth Circuit. The interest groups have two objections: (1) in light of the terrorist attacks, it was their understanding that no controversial judicial nominees would be moved this fall; and (2) they were given assurances that they would receive plenty of notice to prepare for any controversial nominee.

Judge Pickering, you will recall, has a checkered past: he wrote a law review student note recommending that the Mississippi legislature restore its miscegenation law; as a state legislator, he opposed the Equal Rights Amendment and voted to seal the records of the infamous sovereignty commission; and as a Republican activist, he promoted an anti-abortion plank to the national party platform. He has written some controversial opinions while serving on the district court, criticizing prisoner access to the courts and the "one person-one vote" principle. The interest groups believe that a high percentage of Pickering's opinions are unpublished. one reason why they object to the lack of time to prepare for his hearing.

Recognizing that Thursday's hearing is likely to go forward, the groups are asking that the Committee hold a second hearing on Pickering in a few weeks, when they will have had adequate time to research him fully. The decision to schedule Pickering's hearing was made by Senator Leahy himself, not his staff. so the groups are likely to ask you to intercede personally. They will also seek assurances that they will receive adequate warning of future controversial nominees.

MEMORANDUM

To: Senator Durbin
From: ████████
Date: November 6, 2001
Re: Meeting with Civil Rights Leaders, Tuesday, November 6, at 5:00 p.m.
       317 Russell

Following up on a meeting in mid-October, you are scheduled to meet with leaders of several civil rights organizations to discuss their serious concerns with the judicial nomination process. The leaders will likely include: Ralph Neas (People For the American Way), Kate Michelman (NARAL), Nan Aron (Alliance for Justice), Wade Henderson (Leadership Conference on Civil Rights), Leslie Proll (NAACP Legal Defense & Education Fund), Nancy Zirkin (American Association of University Women), Marcia Greenberger (National Women's Law Center), and Judy Lichtman (National Partnership). The meeting will take place in 317 Russell, with Senators Kennedy and Schumer also present.

Today's meeting is likely to touch on a number of related issues. The primary focus will be on identifying the most controversial and/or vulnerable judicial nominees. The groups would like to postpone action on these nominees until next year, when (presumably) the public will be more tolerant of partisan dissent. They would also like to develop a strategy for moving these nominees. Among their priorities: (1) they want to ensure that they receive adequate notice before controversial nominees are scheduled for hearings; (2) they think Senator Leahy should use controversial nominees as bargaining chips, just as the Republicans did; and (3) they are opposed to holding hearings during recess. Although Senator Leahy has resisted these moves so far, they are reasonable requests in our estimation. *Is Leahy in charge?*

There will likely be a discussion about how to respond effectively to recent Republican charges that the pace of judicial nominations is too slow. The Republicans have continued to hold-up the appropriations bills. As of Friday, it was their intention to launch a new campaign this week, charging the Democrats with hindering the war effort by not confirming judges who are needed to approve wire taps and search warrants. This claim is deeply flawed, because the Committee has been especially quick to move along district court judges and the White House has not nominated people to fill more than half of the current vacancies.

MEMORANDUM

To: Senator Durbin
From: ████████
Date: November 7, 2001
Re: Meeting with Civil Rights Leaders Yesterday to Discuss Judges

---

Due to the floor activity last night, you missed a meeting with Senator Kennedy and representatives of various civil rights groups. This was intended to follow-up a meeting in Senator Kennedy's office in mid-October, when the groups expressed serious concern with the quick hearing for Charles Pickering and the pace of judicial nominations generally.

Yesterday's meeting accomplished two objectives. First, the groups advocated for some procedural ground rules. These include: (1) only one hearing per month; (2) no more than three judges per hearing; (3) giving Committee Democrats and the public more advance notice of scheduled nominees; (4) no recess hearings; and (5) a commitment that nominees voted down in Committee will not get a floor vote. Earlier yesterday, Senator Leahy's staff committed to the third item in principle.

Second, yesterday's meeting focused on identifying the most controversial and/or vulnerable judicial nominees, and a strategy for targeting them. The groups singled out three — Jeffrey Sutton (6th Circuit); Priscilla Owen (5th Circuit); and Caroline Kuhl (9th Circuit) — as a potential nominee for a contentious hearing early next year, with a eye to voting him or her down in Committee. They also identified Miguel Estrada (D.C. Circuit) as especially dangerous, because he has a minimal paper trail, he is Latino and the White House seems to be grooming him for a Supreme Court appointment. They want to hold Estrada off as long as possible.

Attached is a table that I compiled, evaluating the 19 Court of Appeals nominees and a few of the controversial district court nominees. Based on input from the groups, I would place the appellate nominees in the categories below. Asterisks indicate that a Senator has placed a hold on the nominee.

Good	Bad	Ugly
Clifton (9th Cir.)*	Shedd (4th Cir.)	Boyle (4th Cir.)*
Melloy (8th Cir.)	Roberts (D.C. Cir.)	Owen (5th Cir.)
O'Brien (10th Cir.)	L. Smith (8th Cir.)	Sutton (6th Cir.)*
Howard (1st Cir.)	Pickering (5th Cir.)	Cook (6th Cir.)*
B. Smith (3rd Cir.)	Tymkovich (10th Cir.)	McConnell (10th Cir.)
	Gibbons (6th Cir.)	Estrada (D.C. Cir.)
	Steele (11th Cir.)	Kuhl (9th Cir.)*

EMK

MEMORANDUM

TO   :   SENATOR (*Kennedy*)

FROM   :   ██████████

SUBJECT :   Judges and the Latino Community

DATE   :   February 28, 2002

Ralph Neas called to let us know that he had lunch with Andy Stern of SEIU. Andy wants to be helpful as we move forward on judges, and he has great contacts with Latino media outlets – Univision and others. Ralph told Andy that you are anxious to develop a strategy for the Supreme Court and a strategy for dealing with conservative Latino Circuit Court nominees that are hostile to constitutional and civil rights. Ralph and Andy discussed the possibility of a relatively small meeting to discuss media strategy, and Andy believes there are several Latino media leaders who share our concerns and would like to meet with you. Ralph proposes that you meet with key Latino media leaders, Raul, Antonia, Wade, and Ralph. ████ and I think this is a very good idea.

Would you like to have such a meeting to discuss media strategy and the Latino community? If so, Ralph and Andy will take the lead in getting everyone to DC.

DECISION:

Yes, I want to meet with them ____   No, I don't want to meet ____

cc: ████████████████████████████

MEMORANDUM

To: Senator Durbin
From: ████████
Date: June 3, 2002
Re: **Meeting with Civil Rights Leaders to Discuss Judicial Nominations Strategy**

Senator Kennedy has invited you and Senator Schumer to attend a meeting with civil rights leaders to discuss their priorities as the Judiciary Committee considers judicial nominees in the coming months. For example, they believe that the Committee's current pace for nominations hearings (every two weeks) is too quick; and they need more time to consider the record of Judge Dennis Shedd, a controversial 4th Circuit nominee whom Senator Hollings is backing.

This meeting is intended to follow-up your meetings in Senators Kennedy's office last fall. The guest list will be the same: Kate Michelman (NARAL), Nan Aron (Alliance for Justice), Wade Henderson (Leadership Conference on Civil Rights), Ralph Neas (People For the American Way), Nancy Zirkin (American Association of University Women), Marcia Greenberger (National Women's Law Center), and Judy Lichtman (National Partnership). The meeting has been tentatively scheduled for late Wednesday morning.

Assuming your schedule permits, do you want to accept Kennedy's invitation and attend the meeting?

EMK

MEMORANDUM

BAG

September 27, 2002

TO: SENATOR (*Kennedy*)

From: ▪▪▪▪▪▪▪▪▪▪▪▪▪▪▪▪▪▪

Re: Members Meeting on Judges—Monday or Tuesday, Place TBA

There will be a judiciary members' meeting early next week. We are trying to schedule the meeting for Monday, after the 5:30 vote, though Leahy has proposed after the Caucus lunch on Tuesday, which would conflict with your schedule. Sen. Leahy is calling this meeting at the request of several members, and, we recommend that the following items be discussed: (1) Delaying a hearing for Cook; (2) Putting off a vote on McConnell or Estrada until after the recess; and (3) next Thursday's vote on Shedd.

Cook

As you know, Debbie Cook—who currently sits on the Ohio Supreme Court—is a nominee to the 6th Circuit who is fiercely opposed by labor and civil rights groups in Ohio. Sen. Leahy wants to schedule Cook for a hearing on October 9th or 10th, because he feels he has made a promise to DeWine to do so.

While we haven't finished reviewing Cook's record, Justice Cook—like Justice Owen—seems terrible in cases involving workers and consumers. She is the most prolific dissenter on the moderate Ohio Supreme Court. In her judicial campaigns—Ohio, like Texas, elects its judges—she has received more money than any other justice from manufacturing and business, and has received no money from labor unions. The Ohio Chamber Commerce has given her its highest ratings for her decisions in employment law, insurance, and medical malpractice cases. On the other hand, the Ohio Academy of Trial Lawyers has written the committee that Cook is "willing to disregard precedent, misinterpret legislative intent and ignore constitutional mandates in an effort to achieve a result that favors business over consumers." Ohio NOW and the Ohio Employment Lawyers' Association have written that Cook's "anti-worker record is becoming legendary in Ohio" and that her opinions seek to undermine the enforcement of state and federal civil rights laws. She is known for adopting strained or extreme legal propositions to deny relief for workers, and is seen as "heartless" and indifferent.

Sen. Leahy has asked whether you would be willing to chair a hearing for Cook on October 9th or 10th. We believe that you should agree to chair her hearing, but that you should push back against scheduling this hearing before the elections. The Committee has held hearings on too many controversial nominees in a row. Not only would preparing for Cook's hearing be a challenge, but it would demoralize Democrats' key constituents—in particular, labor—to have a hearing for her before the election.

AFL-CIO has weighed in with Daschle and Reed (as well as Leahy) about delaying Cook, and Reed and Daschle have said they will discuss Cook with Leahy. Sen. Levin, who is opposed to moving any additional 6th Circuit nominee given that the White House is not cooperating with him regarding nominees to that circuit, will likely be approaching Democratic members about delaying Cook.

Recommendation: Agree to chair a hearing for Cook, but _after_ the election in the lame duck session.

McConnell and Estrada

Sen. Leahy might want to schedule a Committee vote on McConnell and Estrada before the recess. We think this is a terrible idea and that voting on (and for) these nominees would be demoralizing to our base before the election. McConnell likely has sufficient votes to go through the Committee, but members have not yet submitted follow-up questions to him regarding contradictory statements he made at the hearing about his views on abortion, the Bob Jones case, and the constitutionality of the FACE Act. As for Estrada, he just had his hearing and we certainly should not move him forward without resolving the matter concerning the SG memos.

Recommendation: Do not schedule a vote on McConnell and Estrada until after the election.

Shedd

Shedd--the nominee to the Fourth Circuit who has terrible record in cases involving civil rights, women's rights, disability and federalism and who is fiercely opposed by Southern Civil Rights groups (see attached article)-- is scheduled for next Thursday's Exec. We do not know how other members will vote regarding Shedd. We have heard that Sen. Edwards and Sen. Durbin are leaning against Shedd.

It is likely that Leahy will voice vote Shedd and we suggest that you record a "no" vote on him. Particularly given the high percentage of African-Americans on the Fourth Circuit and the Republicans' resistance to placing Clinton nominees on that Court, it seems necessary to resist a judge with such a dismal record on core civil rights and constitutional issues. While Shedd doesn't have the "cross-burning" case of Pickering to disqualify him, he is as bad--perhaps worse--on the core substantive issues.

cc: ███████████████████████

Buildup to Owen & Estrada, filibusters

Senator Must See By 1/30
Senator Has Seen _____

MEMORANDUM

TO: ▉▉▉▉▉▉▉▉▉▉▉
FROM: ▉▉▉▉▉▉▉▉▉▉▉▉▉▉▉▉▉▉
CC:
RE: **Members Meeting with Leader Daschle**
DATE: **January 30, 2003**

This afternoon, Democratic members of the Judiciary
Committee met with Leader Daschle and Assistant Leader Reid to
discuss Miguel Estrada. In addition to Daschle and Reid, Senators
Leahy, Durbin, Edwards, Kennedy, Feinstein and Schumer attended.

<u>**All in attendance agreed to attempt to filibuster the
nomination of Miguel Estrada, if they have the votes to defeat
cloture. They also agreed that, if they do not have the votes to
defeat cloture, a contested loss would be worse than no contest**</u>.

All in attendance, including Senators Daschle and Reid, voiced
the view that the Estrada nomination should be stopped because: 1)
Not to do so would set a precedent, permitting the Republicans to
force through all future controversial nominees without answering
Senators' questions or providing important information; 2) <u>Estrada is
likely to be a Supreme Court nominee, and it will be much harder to
defeat him in a Supreme Court setting if he is confirmed easily now</u>;
3) The process must be slowed down and the Republicans' attempt
to set up an automatic "assembly line" of controversial nominees
thwarted; and 4) The Democratic base is particularly energized over
this issue.

It is expected that a motion to proceed to the nomination will be
brought to the floor on Monday. The Democrats do not intend to
oppose that motion <u>A motion for cloture could be voted on as
early as Wednesday</u>.

Leader Daschle asked all Democratic members of the
Committee to spend the time between now and Tuesday speaking to
Senators who have questions about Estrada, and to attempt to recruit
votes to oppose cloture. The topic may also be discussed at the
Democratic Senators' retreat tomorrow. On Tuesday, Senator
Daschle intends to raise it at the policy lunch, and presumably
conduct a vote count.

Everyone also agreed to keep this matter confidential.

MEMORANDUM   February 4, 2003

TO   :   SENATOR *(Kennedy)*

FROM   :   ██████████

SUBJECT   :   Judges, Judiciary Issues, Meeting with Civil Rights Leaders

Estrada

The Senator-to-Senator conversations continue and things appear to be going well. That being said, we've heard that Breaux will support Estrada. Landrieu is a problem, but many are focused on her. Bayh is also on the fence. Edwards spoke with him without much luck, and Senator Bayh, Sr. is going to speak with him, too. *Would you be willing to speak with him, as well?* I understand he has some substantive questions that we've been trying to answer through his staff, but he's also concerned because he doesn't want to be like the Republicans or part of a witch hunt. I think you – speaking from 40+ years of experience -- can help him understand how the process has changed and why it's important to focus on Estrada (he refuses to answer questions, we know of his temperament/ideological problems, he'll fly to the Supreme Court and we won't be able to stop him). *Do you want to speak with Bayh?*

You should also know that Wade spoke with Kerry and told him that they want him to take a leadership role on this issue. Kerry agreed but wants to speak with you. I think you should encourage Kerry to speak on the floor. *Do you agree?*

Judiciary Hearing (Wednesday/9:30 a.m.) & Exec (Thursday/9:30 a.m.)

Hearing. As you know, there will be a nominations hearing on Wednesday at 9:30 a.m. ████ put a memo in the bag on Monday evening – the nominee is Jay Bybee (9th Cir.). Not surprisingly, Bybee is an awful nominee. As the memo outlines, he has serious immigration, gun control, tribunal/detainee problems. We believe you should attend the hearing and ask him questions. I know that the Powell speech begins at 10:30 and there will be press associated with it. But, if you could drop by the hearing for 15 minutes (@11:30) to ask Bybee questions, it would be very, very helpful. We know this is a marathon and not a sprint and that we have to choose our battles, but we also feel that it's important to ask the bad nominees questions at the hearing. Bybee shouldn't get a complete pass and at this point, only 2 or 3 Democrats can attend the hearing.

Exec. There will be a Judiciary Exec on Thursday at 9:30. I don't think you need to attend, but you should know that (a) we expect Sutton, Roberts, and Cook to be on the schedule and held over and (b) the nasty conceal/carry gun bill (the one you fought at the end of last year) will also be on the schedule. We'll have it held over, but this means we should discuss your strategy for next week.

Conversation with Daschle – Estrada and Beyond

- Tom, thanks so much for your hard work on the Estrada nomination. You have done a terrific job rallying the caucus. Because of you, I think we will be successful.

- I know this is hard work, and it's difficult getting the caucus to stick together around the issue of judicial nominations. Accordingly, I hope we can develop a long-term strategy that acknowledges the importance of the issue and the problems associated with a filibuster strategy.

- Given Bush's plan to pack the courts, there are many bad nominations coming down the track. I know we can't fight all of them, but we should have a short list of consensus nominees that we agree to filibuster.

- I'm concerned that after this fight, several in our caucus won't be willing to filibuster again, and Bush will fill the courts with conservatives. If we develop a long-term strategy, we can let members vote for many nominees because we've all agreed that from time to time, we have to stick together. What do you think?

EMK

Talking Points on Estrada for Caucus

- We must filibuster Miguel Estrada's nomination. He is clearly an intelligent lawyer, but being a judge requires more. He must demonstrate his commitment to core constitutional values, and he has to prove that he has the ability to be fair and impartial. By design, we know very little about Mr. Estrada, but the burden is on him to prove to us that he is fit for a life-time appointment. He simply hasn't done that.

- He has serious temperament problems. He's been criticized by his direct supervisor in the Solicitor General's Office as too ideological to be a judge. Members of the Hispanic Caucus and other Latino leaders have described him as not being "even-tempered" and as having a "short fuse."

- As Pat and Chuck have described, Estrada has virtually no paper trail, and he has refused to answer the most basic questions about his views. Over and over again, the Justice Department refuses to provide us with the documents from Estrada's time in government practice. That's simply unacceptable.

- I've been here for 40 years and I've worked with Republican and Democratic Administrations in the confirmation process. This Administration is the worst. They are applying a litmus test at 1600 Pennsylvania Avenue and then they dare us to prevent them from packing the courts of appeals with ideologues. As ███ and ███████ can attest, any attempt to work with them is rebuffed.

- If we allow them to place a stealth, right-wing zealot on this court, we have only ourselves to blame. Although a few Hispanic groups support Estrada, we have the support of many of the largest, oldest Hispanic organizations, including dozens of Hispanic labor leaders across the country, MALDEF, the Puerto Rican Legal Defense Fund, and the Congressional Hispanic Caucus.

- These groups are taking their message and their concerns about Estrada to mainstream and to Spanish-language press. The Republican claim that we are anti-Hispanic won't stick. We have too much support, and their record is hostile to the interests of that community.

- The D.C. Circuit is far too important to appoint someone about whom we have so many questions. Key labor, civil rights, environmental, and administrative law cases are decided there, and we know it is a "feeder" circuit for the Supreme Court. The White House is almost telling us that they plan to nominate him to the Supreme Court. We can't repeat the mistake we made with Clarence Thomas.

EMK

OWEN TALKING POINTS FOR CAUCUS

- Maria and others have highlighted how Owen has distorted the law in the Jane Doe parental notification cases. What these cases show is that Owen will disregard the clear language of a statute to put forward her own view. That's why then-Judge Gonzalez called her reading "unconscionable judicial activism"

- The sad thing is that women's rights are not the only area of concern. She is to the far-right of the right-wing Texas Supreme Court. She has racked up more dissents in cases involving workers, consumers, victims of personal injury than any other Judge on the Texas Supreme Court except one. She is criticized by her colleagues for distorting the law not only in the Jane Doe cases but in these cases involving the rights of victims as well.

- The 5th Circuit was traditionally a bastion of fairness and justice even in the toughest of times. It has already been turned into one of the least fair and least just circuit courts. We have an obligation to make sure it doesn't get any worse.

- I think it's important that people look through the material on Owen, consider these arguments, and listen to the debate on the floor before making up their mind on how to vote.

- I know there is some concern that we have a lot of bad judges in the pike and we do have others (such as Sutton, who is ready for floor action). But Owen, is clearly one of our worst. She had nine votes against her in Committee. Even if, at the end of the day, we don't defeat Owen's nomination, we have to mount a fight to make clear to the public what's at stake with judges, and to dissuade the White House from sending us such controversial nominees.

Memorandum

BAG

April 7, 2003

TO   :   SENATOR *(Kennedy)*

FROM   :   ▓▓▓▓

SUBJECT :   **OWEN—ON FLOOR**

We have heard that the Republicans will move to a vote on Owen's nomination this afternoon. Leadership plans to withhold consent to a time agreement, and we imagine that the debate could begin as early as tonight and continue at least through tomorrow. ▓▓ is talking to leadership about the possibility of convening a meeting with Judiciary Dems. Owen will be discussed in Caucus tomorrow, and we will provide you talking points. We have also heard that Sen. Feinstein is convening a meeting of the women Senators today after the floor vote.

We have heard that several Democratic Senators have expressed concern about any filibuster of a judicial nominee that is based on substance, as opposed to process. The Senators that may be wavering or opposed to an extended debate are: Lincoln, Pryor, Carper, Graham, Nelson (Fl), Nelson (NE), Bayh, Landrieu, Breaux, Dorgan, Conrad, Baucus, Hollings, Byrd and Miller.

They got over this after Estrada.

It would be helpful, if during the floor vote, you spoke to some of these Members. The key points are:

- Owen is extremely bad on choice issues, worker's rights, civil rights, environmental protection. She is clearly one of the worst of Bush's nominees.
- She is to the far-right of a very right-wing court, is criticized by her colleagues for her extreme dissents, including by White House counsel Justice Gonzalez when he was on the Court. A very broad coalition of Texas-based women, labor, civil rights, worker's right groups oppose her, as well as all the major Washington groups.
- It is important that Democrats keep their powder dry until the Caucus and Leadership have decided how best to proceed on her nomination.

cc: ▓▓▓▓▓▓▓▓▓▓▓▓▓▓▓▓▓

From: Allison Herwitt [AHERWITT@prochoiceamerica.org]
Sent: Wednesday, April 02, 2003 11:04 AM
Cc: ▮▮▮▮▮▮
Subject: Owen floor vote

At any time, Senate leaders may bring the nomination of Priscilla Owen to the Fifth Circuit Court to the floor for a full Senate vote. *NARAL Pro-Choice America strongly opposes this nomination and will score this vote in the 2003 Congressional Record on Choice.*

This is how they enforce discipline:

Last year the Judiciary Committee rejected nominations of both Priscilla Owen and Charles Pickering - both based on the nominees' records of hostility to constitutional freedoms and civil rights. In spite of this, President Bush renominated both individuals. Last week the Judiciary Committee, now under anti-choice control, reversed course and approved the Owen nomination, sending it to the floor in spite of its earlier defeat. The Owen nomination represents a grave threat to a woman's right to choose; pro-choice senators should not approve this lifetime appointment to the federal bench.

- Priscilla Owen is a dedicated conservative judicial activist whose record on the Texas Supreme Court clearly indicates her willingness - indeed, her eagerness - to restrict freedom of choice and undermine *Roe v. Wade*. Owen was a regular dissenter to an already conservative court on the issue of reproductive rights. Her writing in one case led former Texas Supreme Court justice, now White House counsel, Alberto Gonzales, to characterize her dissent as "an unconscionable act of judicial activism."
- Owen has repeatedly attempted to legislate from the bench to create impossibly high barriers - nowhere found in Texas law - to prevent a young woman from exercising her right to choose. She inappropriately and unconstitutionally wanted the Court to force young women to consider religious issues in the decision of whether to have an abortion. She wanted the Court to require young women to demonstrate that they understand "that many women experience emotional and psychological" harm from abortion, even though this claim is not medically supported. She even tried to legislate from the bench and create a new barrier, not in the state statute, forcing a young woman to prove to a public official that she considered the impact of abortion on the fetus.

Clearly, these are actions of a judicial activist intent on using her power to influence and rewrite - not fairly interpret - the law. Were she confirmed to a lifetime appointment to the Fifth Circuit, her decisions could affect women's reproductive freedom for a generation to come.

Many of President Bush's judicial nominees, including Priscilla Owen, have sought to reassure the Senate about their views on a woman's right to choose by claiming they will follow "settled law." This is a simplistic and facile response to a legitimate concern. In the 1992 case *Planned Parenthood of Southeastern Pennsylvania v. Casey*, the Supreme Court relaxed the standard by which laws restricting abortion were to be judged. The test for such laws was no longer "strict scrutiny", but merely whether such laws imposed an "undue burden" on a woman's right to choose. This lower standard has given the green light to anti-choice advocates and state legislators, and indeed, many new restrictions on reproductive rights have been enacted post-*Casey*. State laws abridging freedom of choice are evaluated by judges who use their own discretion in deciding whether an anti-choice law imposes an "undue burden." Yet when one is hostile to the right in the first instance, it is questionable whether one would ever find the burden undue. Indeed, NARAL Pro-Choice America's analysis of 32 court of appeals cases applying *Casey* shows that only 18 of these cases were decided by unanimous panels. That is, more than half the time, judges viewing the same facts and law reached different conclusions. In other words, in this post-*Casey* era, "settled law" is actually in turmoil.

Finally, in understanding the potential consequences of the Owen nomination, and others like it, one must consider the importance of circuit courts overall. While Supreme Court nominations receive the most public attention, circuit courts can have just as much or more effect on the law as the Supreme Court. The Supreme Court typically hears lower than 100 cases a year; the federal courts of appeal, the courts immediately below the Supreme Court, decide almost 30,000 cases a year. Thus, for most Americans, these are the courts of last resort. Conservative activists realized this long ago, and set out on a patient but relentless effort to capture the courts. Patrick Buchanan summed up the right-wing's plan: "[Our conservative judicial appointment strategy] could do more to advance the social agenda – school prayer, anti-pornography, anti-busing, right-to-life and quotas in employment – than anything Congress can accomplish in 20 years."

President Bush and anti-choice advocates and lawmakers are continuing to implement this strategy, and nominations like Priscilla Owen's are critical to their success. NARAL Pro-Choice America urges senators to vote "no" on the Owen nomination.

Attached are important materials on Priscilla Owen's work to undermine reproductive rights. We hope you find this information helpful and, as always, invite you to call Allison Herwitt at 973-3003 or Donna Crane at 973-3047 with any questions.

<<Owen Hearing Analysis FINAL.doc>> <<Owen Report FINAL 7-15-02.doc>>

****

Allison Herwitt
Director, Government Relations
NARAL Pro-Choice America
1156 15th Street, NW
Suite 700
Washington, D.C. 20005
(202) 973-3003
(202) 973-3070 (fax)
aherwitt@ProChoiceAmerica.org
www.ProChoiceAmerica.org

All memos were taken from:

http://fairjudiciary.canpsol.com/cfj_contents/press/judges.pdf

ACKNOWLEDGMENTS

en in Black was nine months in the making. In addition to the honor of running the finest conservative legal foundation in the nation—Landmark Legal Foundation—and hosting a nightly talk radio program on WABC (770 AM) in New York City, I spent endless hours late into the night and on weekends researching and writing this book. My most important responsibilities, however, are as husband and father. But for the love, support, and patience of my wife, Kendall, and our kids, Lauren and Chase—who make me proud and happy every day—I simply could not have undertaken this project. I adore them and am truly blessed.

My parents, Norma and Jack, have always been my biggest fans. They encouraged me from a young age to pursue my dreams and sacrificed both their time and limited resources to support my numerous journeys. And most of all, by example and word, they instilled in their three boys love of country and family. Whatever character I have I owe to them. I am forever grateful for their unconditional love.

I also can't say enough about my older brother, Doug, and my younger brother, Rob. Their friendship, selflessness, and integrity are inspirational. Even though we've always stood shoulder-to-shoulder, I've always looked up to them. They're the very best.

Like most authors, I could not have written *Men in Black* without the support of an outstanding team of exceptionally talented individuals. David Limbaugh is not only my friend and agent, he's also a superlative lawyer and author. His guidance and wise counsel throughout this process, as well as his editing assistance, was crucial. I am indebted to him.

My friend since childhood, Eric Christensen, is an extraordinary person. He has an encyclopedic knowledge of American history, which he used to help with research and editing. He also was an indispensable sounding board, for which I am extremely thankful.

Mike O'Neill and Matt Forys are two of the sharpest young lawyers practicing today. Their superb research and legal analysis were essential to the book. I can't thank them enough for their friendship, hard work, and significant contributions.

John Richardson, my close confidant and friend from our days together in the Reagan White House and the Meese Justice Department, provided a critical eye and insightful advice in the final stages of writing, making the book much better. He has my gratitude and admiration.

Pete Hutchison is a lawyer's lawyer and my right-hand man. His support and friendship made it possible for me to undertake this project. It has been an honor to work with him at Landmark for over a decade.

The folks at Regnery Publishing were wonderful. After years of prodding, Al Regnery finally convinced me to write *Men in Black*. Marji Ross, president and publisher, provided the opportunity and allowed me the freedom to write this book in my own way. Paula Decker's suggestions and attention to detail proved why she's the top editor in the business. She also pulled together all the loose ends to make the final product. And a special word for Harry

Crocker, Regnery's executive editor. He was instrumental in bringing this book to publication, from beginning to end. He's an exceptional talent. I am extremely proud of my association with Regnery.

I also want to thank Rush Limbaugh, Ed Meese, and Sean Hannity, all of whom enthusiastically agreed to endorse *Men in Black*. They've been important mentors and have had a profound influence on my life.

The directors of Landmark Legal Foundation have supported me in everything I do. More importantly, their guidance and wise judgment have made Landmark a preeminent legal foundation. I would be remiss in not acknowledging each of them for their efforts in defending individual liberty, the rule of law, and limited government: Lawrence Davenport, William Bradford Reynolds, Gary McDowell, Steve Matthews, John Richardson, and Ed Meese.

And thanks goes to Tim McCarthy, general manager at WABC, and Phil Boyce, program director. They had faith in my ability to host a radio program in the biggest market in America despite my limited broadcasting experience. It paid off. We're number one in talk radio!

Finally, I salute our founding fathers. Thanks to their vision and sacrifice, we are the freest, strongest, and most prosperous nation on the face of the earth. God bless America.

Notes

Foreword to the Paperback Edition

1. *Kelo* v. *City of New London*, 125 S.Ct. 2655 (2005).
2. U.S. Constitution, Amendment V.
3. *Kelo*, 125 S.Ct. 2655.
4. Ibid., 2685.
5. Sandra Day O'Connor, Remarks before American Academy of Appellate Lawyers, November 7, 2005. Available at www.appellateacademy.org.
6. Ruth Bader Ginsburg, "A Decent Respect to the Opinions of [Human]kind," The Value of a Comparative Perspective in Constitutional Adjudication, February 7, 2006. Available at http://www.supremecourtus.gov/publicinfo/speeches/sp_02-07b-06.html.

Preface: Men, Not Gods

1. David Pannick, "Supreme justice warts and all," *The Times*, March 16, 1993; Jules Loh, Associated Press, April 19, 1979; Fred Barbash, "Unveiling Ignited Great Debate; Some Founders Went Forward to Power, Others to Poverty," *Washington*

Post, September 17, 1987; Stephen Labaton, "Bankruptcy Is Better for Petitioners in America," *New York Times*, January 23, 1990; Michael Beebe and Dan Herbeck, "Laws for dealing with those failing to pay have long history," *Buffalo News*, October 12, 1997.

2. David J. Garrow, "Mental Decrepitude on the U.S. Supreme Court: The Historical Case for a 28th Amendment," 67 U. Chi. L. Rev. 995, 998–99 (Fall 2000).

3. Chris Mould, "Special Constitution Package: The original 13 states. South Carolina: A gentleman, a scholar and a madman," United Press International, August 25, 1987.

4. John M. Broder, "While Congress Is Away, Clinton Toys With Idea of an End Run," *New York Times*, November 24, 1997; Garrow, "Mental Decrepitude on the U.S. Supreme Court," 1000.

5. Richard Brookhiser, Book Review, "Duels, Deals and Down-and-Dirty Politics; Affairs of Honor—National Politics in the New Republic," *Los Angeles Times*, December 30, 2001.

6. Garrow, "Mental Decrepitude on the U.S. Supreme Court," 1002 (citations omitted).

7. Ibid., 1003–04.

8. Ibid., 1007.

9. William H. Rehnquist, *The Supreme Court* (Knopf: New York, 2001), 98.

10. *Morning Edition*, transcript of interview with Leon Friedman, NPR, January 3, 1994; Richard D. Friedman, "How to prevent justices from staying too long; Commentary; A committee of family members and colleagues is best suited to tell a Supreme Court member when it is finally time to step down," *Detroit News*, October 28, 2003.

11. Earl Raab, "With 2 Jews on court, official anti-Semitism ends," *Jewish Bulletin*, May 27, 1994.

12. Ruth Bader Ginsburg, "Justice, Guardian of Liberty," *Forward*, May 30, 2003. Available at www.forward.com/issues/2003/03.05.30/oped1.html.

13. Andrew L. Kaufman, *Cardozo* (Cambridge, MA: Harvard University Press, 1998), 480.

14. John Knox, *The Forgotten Memoir of John Knox* (Dennis J. Hutchinson and David J. Garrow, eds., Chicago: University of Chicago Press, 2000), 51.

15. Roger K. Newman, *Hugo Black: A Biography* (New York: Pantheon Books, 1994), 604.

16. Ibid., 597.

17. Ibid., 604.

18. Ibid., 620.

19. Jerry Schwartz, "Alger Hiss, Nixon Nemesis, Dead at 92," Associated Press, November 15, 1996; Sam Tanenhaus, *Whittaker Chambers* (New York: Random House, 1997), 232–33, 374–75.

20. Paul Craig Roberts and Lawrence M. Stratton, *The New Color Line: How Quotas and Privilege Destroy Democracy* (Washington, D.C.: Regnery, 1995), 38–43, 48–50.

21. Bruce Allen Murphy, *Wild Bill: The Legend and Life of William O. Douglas* (New York: Random House, 2003), 427–28.

22. Bill Kauffman, "The Ford Impeachment," *American Enterprise*, May 1, 1999.

23. Stephen Chapman, "Octogenarian justices are no asset to the court," *Chicago Tribune*, July 4, 1991.

24. Charles Lane, "Following Rehnquist," *Washington Post*, October 30, 2004.

25. David G. Savage, "In the Matter of Justice Thomas; Silent, Aloof and Frequently Dogmatic, Clarence Thomas' Judicial Persona Emerges," *Los Angeles Times*, October 9, 1994; "Best and Worst of the Century," *Washingtonian*, July 1999; Rehnquist, 198–99.

26. Kauffman, "The Ford Impeachment."

27. Jon Meacham, "Is Little Rock corrupting Washington? C'mon; political scandals before President Clinton," *Washington Monthly*, May 1994.

28. Chapman, "Octogenarian justices are no asset to the court."

29. Fred Bernstein, "Government Channels," *People*, September 27, 1982.

30. Richard Lacayo, "Marshall's Legacy; A Lawyer Who Changed America," *Time*, July 8, 1991.

31. Ibid.

32. Stuart Taylor, Jr., "Marshall Sounds Critical Note on Bicentennial," *New York Times*, May 7, 1987.

Chapter One: Radicals in Robes

1. Edwin Meese III, "How Congress Can Rein in the Courts," *Hoover Digest*, 1997 No. 4, adapted from IntellectualCapital.com, Volume 2, Issue 16, April 17, 1997, from an article entitled "The Judiciary vs. The Constitution?"

2. Alexander Hamilton said, "There is no liberty if the power of judging be not separated from the legislative and executive powers." Federalist 78, *Federalist Papers* (Clinton Rossiter, ed., New York: Penguin Books, 1961).

3. In Federalist 45, James Madison wrote, "the powers delegated by the proposed Constitution to the Federal Government are few and defined. Those which are to remain in the State governments are numerous and indefinite." Federalist 45, *Federalist Papers*.

4. John E. Thompson, "What's the Big Deal? The Unconstitutionality of God in the Pledge of Allegiance," 38 Harv. C.R.-C.L. L. Rev. 563, Summer 2003, citing John Hart Ely, *Democracy and Distrust: A Theory of Judicial Review* (1980), and Robert Bork, *The Tempting of America: The Usurpation of Law By Politics* (1999) 143–46.

5. Ibid., citing Bork, 165–66.

6. Ibid., citing Bork, 1–5, 143–46, 154–55, and Antonin Scalia, "Originalism: The Lesser Evil," 57 U. Cin. L. Rev. 849, 862–63 (1989)

7. *Dred Scott v. Sandford*, 60 U.S. 393 (1856).

8. James McPherson, *Battle Cry of Freedom* (New York: Ballantine Books, 1988), 170–71.

9. *Dred Scott*, 60 U.S. 420.

10. Abraham Lincoln's speech on Dred Scott, June 26, 1857. Available at www.teachingamericanhistory.org.

11. McPherson, 171.

12. *Dred Scott*, 60 U.S. 425–26.

13. Michael McConnell, "Symposium on Interpreting the Ninth Amendment: A Moral Realist Defense of Constitutional Democracy," 64 Chi.-Kent. L. Rev. 89, 101 (1988).

14. Ibid.

15. Ibid., citing, 60 U.S. 621 (Curtis, J., dissenting).

16. *Plessy v. Ferguson*, 163 U.S. 537, 539 (1896).

17. U.S. Constitutional Amendment XIV, § 1.

18. *Plessy*, 163 U.S. 551.

19. *Brown v. Board of Education*, 347 U.S. 483 (1954). The Supreme Court in *Brown* reached the right result but applied the wrong analysis. Rather than flatly rejecting *Plessy*'s faulty reasoning as a Fourteenth Amendment equal protection violation, the Court opened a Pandora's box of judicial activism moored in sociology and psycho-analysis.

20. *Korematsu v. United States*, 323 U.S. 214 (1944).

21. U.S. Constitutional Amendment V.

22. *Korematsu*, 323 U.S. 220.

23. Anthony Kennedy, Speech at the American Bar Association Annual Meeting, August 9, 2003. Available at www.supremecourtus.gov/publicinfo/speeches/sp_08-09-03.html.

24. Gina Holland, "Supreme Court Justice Applauds Judges for Bucking Tough Sentence Guidelines," Associated Press, March 17, 2004.

25. In 2004, the Supreme Court, in *Blakely v. Washington*, ruled that the state of Washington's sentencing guidelines were unconstitutional. *Blakely v. Washington*, 124 S.Ct. 2531 (2004). This decision sent shock waves throughout the federal criminal justice system because the question as to whether the *federal* sentencing guidelines were constitutional was not addressed. One federal appellate court, basing its decision on the Supreme Court's findings, ruled that the federal sentencing guidelines were unconstitutional. Another federal appellate court said the guidelines were constitutional. The *Washington Post* reported that "Defense attorneys [were] flooding U.S. districts courts with requests for new and reduced sentences." Dan Eggen and Jerry Markon, "High Court Decision Sows Confusion on Sentencing Rules," *Washington Post*, July 13, 2004. In an effort to end the confusion it had wrought,

the Supreme Court has stated that it would settle the issue of whether the federal sentencing guidelines are constitutional in its fall 2004 term. Associated Press, August 3, 2004.

26. Deborah L. Rhode, "A Tribute To Justice Thurgood Marshall: Letting the Law Catch Up," 44 Stan. L. Rev. 1259 (1992). Saundra Torry, "Change and Choice at the American Bar Association Convention," *Washington Post*, August 17, 1992. Former Independent Counsel Kenneth Starr cites this quote in his book, *First Among Equals* (xxvii). In a critique of Starr's book, Cass Sustein, a former clerk for Justice Marshall, doubts the veracity of such a statement by his former boss. However, two other independent sources (both former law clerks to Justice Marshall) provide confirmation that Justice Marshall made such a statement.

27. *Stenberg v. Carhart*, 530 U.S. 914 (2000).

28. Brookings Review, January 1, 2000, drawing from the Cardozo Lecture at the Association of the Bar of the City of New York given by Justice Ginsburg on February 11, 1999.

29. Mark R. Levin and Andrew P. Zappia, "Seek and Ye Shall Find—Ginsburg's Philosophy," *New Jersey Law Journal*, July 12, 1993.

30. *Lawrence v. Texas*, 123 S.Ct. 2472, 2481 (2003).

31. Ibid., at 2483, citing *P.G. & J. H. v. United Kingdom*, App. No. 00044787/98, P 56 (Eur. Ct. H.R., Sept. 25, 2001); *Modinos v. Cyprus*, 259 Eur. Ct. H. R. (1993); *Norris v. Ireland*, 142 Eur. Ct. H. R. (1988).

32. Justice Sandra Day O'Connor, Keynote Address Before the Ninety-Sixth Annual Meeting of the American Society of International Law, 96 Am. Soc'y Int'l L. Proc. 348, 350 (2002).

33. Ibid.

34. Sandra Day O'Connor, *The Majesty of the Law* (New York: Knopf, 2003).

35. Ibid., 234.

36. Ibid.

37. Hope Yen, "O'Connor Extols Role of International Law," Associated Press, October 27, 2004.

38. *Thompson v. Oklahoma*, 487 U.S. 815, 830 (1988).

Chapter Two: Judicial Review: The Counter-Revolution of 1803

1. "Thomas Jefferson's Reaction to *Marbury v. Madison*." Available at www.landmark-cases.org/marbury /jefferson.html.

2. "Delegates at Philadelphia must have known that the state constitutions were regarded as law by the state courts. When the Federal Convention assembled, the nature of a written constitution, emanating from an authority outside the government, had already been made manifest by several judicial decisions. In New Jersey,

as early as 1780, the court refused, in the case of *Holmes v. Walton*, to regard as valid an unconstitutional act of the legislature. Two years later a similar doctrine was laid down in Virginia, and in 1786, the Rhode Island court announced the same principle. Just as the convention was assembling at Philadelphia, the Superior Court of North Carolina asserted that the legislature could not by passing any act "repeal or alter the constitution, because if they could do this, they would at the same instant of time, destroy their own existence as a legislature, and dissolve the government thereby established." Andrew C. McLaughlin, *The Confederation and the Constitution, 1783–1789* (New York: Crowell-Collier Publishing Company, 1962), 169.

3. "The interpretation of the laws is the proper and peculiar province of the courts. A constitution, is, in fact, and must be regarded by the judges, as a fundamental law. It therefore belongs to them to ascertain its meaning, as well as the meaning of any particular act proceeding from the legislative body. If there should happen to be an irreconcilable variance between two, that which has the superior obligation and validity ought, of course, to be preferred; or, in other words, the constitution ought to be preferred to the statute, the intention of the people to the intention of their agents." Clinton Rossiter, ed., Federalist 78, *Federalist Papers* (New York: Penguin Books, 1961).

4. The Constitution of the Commonwealth of Virginia §7, June 12, 1776. The Avalon Project at the Yale University School of Law. Available at www.yale.edu/lawweb/avalon/states/va05.htm.

5. Articles of Confederation. *Documents Illustrative of the Formation of the Union of the American States* (Washington, D.C.: Government Printing Office, 1927), 27.

6. Variant texts of the Virginia plan presented by Edmund Randolph to the Federal Convention, May 29, 1787, *Documents Illustrative of the Formation of the Union of the American States*, 953.

7. Ibid., 955.

8. Debates in the Federal Convention of 1787 as reported by James Madison, *Documents Illustrative of the Formation of the Union of the American States*.

9. Ibid. Madison then inserted in his notes a verbatim account of the language of his amendment. "Every bill which shall have passed the two houses, shall, before it become law, be severally presented to the President of the United States, and to the judges of the supreme court for the revision of each. If, upon such revision, they shall approve of it, they shall respectively signify their approbation by signing it; but if, upon such revision, it shall appear improper to either, or both to be passed into a law, it shall be returned, with the objections against it, to that house, in which it shall have originated, who shall enter the objections at large on their journal, and proceed to reconsider the bill: but if, after such reconsideration, two thirds of that house, with either the President, or a majority of the judges shall object, or three fourths, where both shall object, shall agree to pass it, it shall, together with

the objections, be sent to the other house, by which it shall likewise be reconsidered; and, if approved by two thirds, or three fourths of the other house, as the case may be, it shall become a law."

10. Debates in the Federal Convention of 1787 as reported by James Madison, *Documents Illustrative of the Formation of the Union of the American States*.

11. *Documents Illustrative of the Formation of the Union of the American States*.

12. Madison's notes, *Documents Illustrative of the Formation of the Union of the American States*, 551.

13. Ibid.

14. "The judicial Power of the United States, shall be vested in one supreme Court, and in such inferior Courts as the Congress may from time to time ordain and establish. The Judges, both of the supreme and inferior Courts, shall hold their Offices during good Behaviour, and shall, at stated Times, receive for their Services a Compensation, which shall not be diminished during their Continuance in Office. The judicial Power shall extend to all Cases, in Law and Equity, arising under this Constitution, the Laws of the United States, and Treaties made, or which shall be made, under their Authority; to all Cases affecting Ambassadors, other public Ministers and Consuls; to all Cases of admiralty and maritime Jurisdiction; to Controversies to which the United States shall be a Party; to Controversies between two or more States; between Citizens of different States; between Citizens of the same State claiming Lands under Grants of different States." U.S. Constitution, Article III § 1.

"In all Cases affecting Ambassadors, other public Ministers and Consuls, and those in which a State shall be Party, the supreme Court shall have original Jurisdiction. In all the other Cases before mentioned, the supreme Court shall have appellate Jurisdiction, both as to Law and Fact, with such Exceptions, and under such Regulations as the Congress shall make." U.S. Constitution, Article III § 2.

"The Trial of all Crimes, except in Cases of Impeachment, shall be by Jury; and such Trial shall be held in the State where the said Crimes shall have been committed; but when not committed within any State, the Trial shall be at such Place or Places as the Congress may by Law have directed." U.S. Constitution, Article III §1 and §2.

15. Federalist 78.

16. Robert Yates, "Essay No. 11," *Anti-federalist Papers*, first published in the *New York Journal*, March 20, 1788. Available at www.constitution.org.

17. Ibid.

18. Ibid.

19. Robert Yates, "Brutus 15," *Anti-federalist Papers*. Available at www.constitution.org.

20. William E. Nelson, Marbury v. Madison, *The Origins and Legacy of Judicial Review* (Lawrence, KS: University Press of Kansas, 2000), 54.

21. It is somewhat ironic that the Judiciary Act of 1802 led to the *Stuart v. Laird* decision by the Marshall Court just a few days after the *Marbury v. Madison* decision

was handed down. *Stuart v. Laird* upheld the right of Congress to abolish the judgeships established under the 1801 act. This decision also implicitly upheld the right of the court to review acts of Congress. At the time, *Stuart* was considered a major retrenchment by the Marshall Court from the stance it had taken at the time of the *Marbury* decision. *Stuart v. Laird*, 5 U.S. 299 (1803).

22. William Peters, *A More Perfect Union* (New York: Crown Publishers, Inc., 1987), 55.
23. The Republican Party, as led by Jefferson at the time, is the forerunner of the modern day Democratic Party.
24. For a brief account of the presidential election of 1800 see www.archives.gov/exhibit_hall/ treasures_of_congress/page_7.html#.
25. William Marbury, Dennis Ramsay, Robert Townsend Hooe, and William Harper were the four named in *Marbury v. Madison*, 5 U.S. 137 (1803).
26. A writ of mandamus is an order from a court directing a party to a suit to perform a specific function. In *Marbury v. Madison*, Marbury asked the court to order Madison to deliver his commission to the federal bench, allowing Marbury to assume the office to which he had been nominated and confirmed.
27. Peters, 55.
28. Jack Shepherd, *The Adams Chronicles, Four Generations of Greatness* (Boston: Little, Brown and Company, 1975), 213.
29. The Jeffersonian Congress had moved aggressively to undo previous acts of the Federalist Congress. The previous Congress, in the waning days of President Adams's term, had passed the Judiciary Act of 1801, which added several federal judicial positions and significantly changed the structure of the federal judiciary. The Judiciary Act of 1802 repealed the 1801 act. "Congress also postponed the next term of the Supreme Court until 1803 so that the Court could not rule on the constitutionality of the 1802 act [the Judiciary Act of 1802] before the act went into effect." Nelson, 69.
30. Page Smith, *The Constitution, A Documentary and Narrative History* (New York: William Morrow and Company, Inc., 1978), 318.
31. *Marbury v. Madison*, 5 U.S. 137 (1803).
32. Ibid.
33. Ibid., 178–79.
34. Letter from Thomas Jefferson to Abigail Adams, 1804. Available at etext.lib.virginia.edu/jefferson/quotations/jeff1030.htm.
35. Letter from Thomas Jefferson to William C. Jarvis, 1820. Available as cited above.

Chapter Three: In the Court We Trust?

1. Ronald Reagan, Radio Address to the Nation, September 18, 1982, reprinted in *The Quotable Ronald Reagan* (Peter Hannaford, ed., Washington, D.C.: Regnery, 1998), 247.

2. U.S. Constitutional Amendment I.

3. *Santa Fe Independent School District v. Doe*, 530 U.S. 290, 318 (2000).

4. This is the letter in which Jefferson introduced the phrase "wall of separation between Church & State," but in a context, as we'll see, that has been misappropriated by judges.

5. *Everson v. Board of Ed. of Ewing*, 330 U.S. 1, 8–10 (1947).

6. See Edwin Scott Gaustad, *A Religious History of America* (1990), 67–68, Timothy L. Hall, "Roger Williams and the Foundations of Religious Liberty," 71 B.U.L. Rev. 455, 464 (May 1991).

7. Thomas Jefferson, *Notes on Virginia*, in *The Life and Selected Writings of Thomas Jefferson* (Adrienne Koch & William Peden, eds., Modern Library, 1993), 173, 252–253.

8. Michael Novak, *On Two Wings: Humble faith and common sense at the American founding* (San Francisco: Encounter Books, 2002), 52.

9. Daniel L. Dreisbach, *Thomas Jefferson and the Wall of Separation Between Church and State* (New York: New York University Press, 2002), 32–33.

10. Ibid.

11. Ibid., 33.

12. During the Constitutional Convention, Madison opposed a Bill of Rights. He was concerned, like most others at the Convention, that by listing certain rights, it might be misconstrued as leaving unprotected, from the federal government, those rights not listed. George Mason, also a delegate to the Constitutional Convention from Virginia, had authored the Virginia Declaration of Rights in 1776. He insisted on the adoption of a federal Bill of Rights. It was voted down. For this reason, among others, Mason voted against the Constitution. Madison later supported amending the Constitution to include most of the rights protected in the Virginia Declaration of Rights, and as the primary author of the Bill of Rights, Madison borrowed liberally from Mason's writings. For the quote, see: *Wallace v. Jaffree*, 472 U.S. 38, 95 (1985) (Rehnquist J. dissenting, citing J. Elliot, *Debates on the Federal Constitution* 659 (1891), 730).

13. Novak, 33.

14. Joseph Loconte, "Faith and the founding: the influence of religion on the politics of James Madison," *Journal of Church and State*, September 22, 2003, 7.

15. Vincent Phillip Muñoz, "Establishing Free Exercise," *First Things*, December 2003, 14, 18.

16. Ibid.

17. Ibid.

18. Joseph Loconte, "James Madison and Religious Liberty," Heritage Foundation Reports, Executive Memorandum, No. 729, March 16, 2001.

19. *Wallace v. Jaffree*, 472 U.S. 38, 100-01 (1985) (Rehnquist J. dissenting, citing 1 Annals of Cong 914 (1789)).

20. Ibid., 102–03.
21. Ibid., 103.
22. *Everson v. Board of Ed. of Ewing*, 330 U.S. 1 (1947).
23. Although the Supreme Court first mentioned Jefferson's metaphor in 1879, in the case *Reynolds v. United States*, in which the Court upheld a law banning polygamy, it didn't become constitutional doctrine until *Everson*.
24. Dreisbach, 1–2.
25. Ibid., 21–22. Michael Knox Beran, "Behind Jefferson's Wall," *City Journal*, Spring 2003, 68–79.
26. Dreisbach, 57–58.
27. *Everson v. Board of Ed. of Ewing*, 330 U.S. 1, 3 (1947).
28. Ibid., 16.
29. Ibid.
30. Ibid., 18.
31. Roger K. Newman, *Hugo Black, A Biography* (New York: Pantheon Books, 1994).
32. Gerald T. Dunne, *Hugo Black and the Judicial Revolution* (New York: Simon & Shuster, 1977), 269, quoting Hugo Black, Jr., *My Father* (New York: Random House, 1975), 104.
33. Bruce Fein, "Religious Season, Consideration of State Influence; Scrutiny of government's assistance to religions should focus on the furthermore [sic] of predominant secular purposes," *The Recorder*, December 27, 1993.
34. *Wallace v. Jaffree*, 472 U.S. 38, 92 (1985).
35. Robert Chanin, FOX *Special Report With Brit Hume*, February 19, 2002.
36. Rev. Barry Lynn, "Court Upholds Vouchers; Cleveland tuition program OK'd in 5–4 decision," *Cleveland Plain Dealer*, June 28, 2002.
37. Ralph Neas, "Bully Pulpit," *Richmond Times Dispatch*, February 15, 2004.
38. *Wallace v. Jaffree*, 472 U.S. 38, 107.
39. Ibid., 107.
40. Ibid., 110–111.
41. *Zelman v. Simmons-Harris*, 536 U.S. 639 (2002).
42. Ibid., 662.
43. Ibid., 686.
44. *Locke v. Davey*, 124 S.Ct. 1307 (2004). The scholarship was open to students graduating in the top 15% of their class or achieving a score of 1200 or better on the Scholastic Aptitude Test or a 27 or better on the American College Test. The student's family income had to be "less than 135% of the State's median." Each student had to enroll at least half time in an eligible postsecondary institution in Washington.
45. Ibid., 1311.
46. *Engel v. Vitale*, 370 U.S. 421 (1962). See the discussion in David Limbaugh's *Persecution* (Washington, D.C.: Regnery, 2003), 18–20.

47. *Lee v. Weisman*, 505 U.S. 577 (1992).

48. Ibid., 93.

49. Vincent Phillip Muñoz, testimony before the Senate Judiciary Committee, June 8, 2004.

50. *Elk Grove Unified School District v. Newdow*, 124 S. Ct. 2301 (2004).

51. Ibid., 2306.

52. Tony Mauro, "The Custody Dispute Behind the Pledge of Allegiance Case; Court could duck issue by finding father's unsettled status voids standing," *New Jersey Law Journal*, November 10, 2003.

53. Howard Fineman, "One Nation, Under... Who?" *Newsweek*, July 8, 2002, 20.

54. Ibid.

55. Mauro, "The Custody Dispute Behind the Pledge of Allegiance Case."

56. *Newdow v. United States Cong.*, 328 F.3d 466, 483 (9th Cir. 2002).

57. *Newdow v. United States Cong.*, 292 F.3d 597, 607 (9th Cir. 2002).

58. Ibid., 602.

59. Mauro, "The Custody Dispute Behind the Pledge of Allegiance Case."

60. Ibid.

61. *Newdow v. United States Cong.*, 313 F.3d 500, 502–03 (9th Cir. 2002).

62. Maura Dolan, "They Pray for Judicial Restraint; Advisors to a volatile atheist hope he is up to the delicate task of arguing his Pledge of Allegiance case before the Supreme Court," *Los Angeles Times*, March 23, 2004.

63. *Elk Grove Unified School District v. Newdow*, 124 S. Ct. 2301, 2316 (2004).

64. Ibid., 2320.

65. Ibid., 2321.

66. Ibid., 2301.

67. Ibid., 2328.

68. On August 19, 2004, the U.S. Court of Appeals for the Third Circuit struck down a law that required schoolchildren to either sing the national anthem or recite the Pledge of Allegiance. Associated Press, "Judge: Pa.'s Pledge law violates First Amendment," August 20, 2004. We have now reached the point at which judges are striking down laws that embrace the very traditions our nation is founded upon.

69. Available at www.aclu.org/ReligiousLiberty/ReligiousLibertylist.cfm?c=38.

Chapter Four: Death by Privacy

1. Ronald Reagan, "Abortion and the Conscience of the Nation," *National Review Online*, June 10, 2004, originally appearing in the *Human Life Review*, Spring 1983.

2. *Poe v. Ullman*, 367 U.S.497 (1961). The first legal mention of a "right to privacy" was in an article in the *Harvard Law Review* in 1890, written by Louis Brandeis and Samuel Warren, but it was about a different issue entirely: protecting people from

an intrusive press. See Gary McDowell, "Private Lives, Perverted Law," *New Jersey Law Journal*, June 20, 1991.

3. Melvin L. Wulf, "On the origins of privacy; constitutional practice," *The Nation*, May 27, 1991.

4. *Poe*, 367 U.S. 539.

5. Wulf, "On the origins of privacy; constitutional practice." Emphasis added.

6. Tamar Lewin, "The Bork Hearings; Bork is Assailed Over Remarks on Contraceptive Ruling," *New York Times*, September 19, 1987.

7. *Griswold v. Connecticut*, 381 U.S. 479 (1965).

8. Ibid., 484.

9. Webster's New World Dictionary (third edition, 1991).

10. *Griswold*, 381 U.S. 485.

11. Ibid., 508.

12. Ibid., 509.

13. Ibid., 510.

14. *Eisenstadt v. Baird*, 405 U.S. 438 (1972).

15. Ibid., 453.

16. Ibid.

17. Ibid.

18. *Roe v. Wade*, 410 U.S. 113, 118 (1972).

19. David Gergen, *Eyewitness to Power: the essence of leadership: Nixon to Clinton* (New York: Simon & Schuster, 2000), 20.

20. Transcript, "Justice Harry Blackmun's newly released papers," National Public Radio, March 8, 2004.

21. Ibid.

22. Aaron Epstein, "Abortion Decision is his Legacy; Blackmun Defended Individuals' Rights," *Detroit Free Press*, April 7, 1994.

23. Bob Woodward and Scott Armstrong, *The Brethren* (New York: Avon Books, 1981), 214.

24. David G. Savage, "The Nation; Papers of Roe-Wade Author to Be Released," *Los Angeles Times*, February 29, 2004.

25. Woodward and Armstrong, 215.

26. Lyle Denniston, "Blackmun, author of Roe vs Wade, dies; Retired justice, 90, saw 1973 abortion ruling as women's rights victory," *Baltimore Sun*, March 5, 1999.

27. Woodward and Armstrong, 272–73.

28. Ibid.,196.

29. *Roe v. Wade*, 410 U.S. 113, 116 (1972).

30. Ibid., 152–53. (internal citations omitted).

31. Ibid., 162.

32. Ibid., 159.
33. *Stenberg v. Carhart*, 530 U.S. 914 (2000).
34. Ibid., 930.
35. Savage, "The Nation; Papers of Roe-Wade Author to Be Released."
36. Chris Bull, "Balance of justice: cultural advances, openly gay clerks, and specula-tion about the sexual orientation of one of their own have substantially changed the way the Supreme Court justices weigh civil rights," *The Advocate*, March 4, 2003.
37. *Callins v. Collins*, 510 U.S. 1141, 1145–1146 (1994).
38. Responding pointedly to Blackmun's pronouncement, Justice Scalia stated: "Justice Blackmun begins his statement by describing with poignancy the death of a con-victed murderer by lethal injection. He chooses, as the case in which to make that statement, one of the less brutal of the murders that regularly come before us, the murder of a man ripped by a bullet suddenly and unexpectedly, with no opportunity to prepare himself and his affairs, and left to bleed to death on the floor of a tavern. The death-by-injection which Justice Blackmun describes looks pretty desirable next to that. It looks even better next to some of the other cases currently before us, which Justice Blackmun did not select as the vehicle for his announcement that the death penalty is always unconstitutional, for example, the case of the 11-year old girl raped by four men and then killed by stuffing her panties down her throat. How enviable a quiet death by lethal injection compared to that!" Ibid., 1143.
39. Paul Sullivan, "Retired Justice Blackmun Dies," *Boston Herald*, March 5, 1999.
40. *Planned Parenthood v. Casey*, 505 U.S. 833, 923 (1992).
41. *Planned Parenthood v. Casey*, 505 U.S. 833 (1992).
42. Fred Barbash, "Blackmun's Papers Shine Light Into Court; Justice's Trove Opened by Library of Congress," *Washington Post*, March 5, 2004.
43. Pennsylvania had enacted the Abortion Control Act, which required informed con-sent, a twenty-four-hour waiting period, spousal notification for adult women, and parental consent for minors. There was a provision for minors to seek consent from a judge when parental consent was impracticable. In *Casey*, the Supreme Court created a new test for future legislative abortion limits: the undue burden test. It found that only the spousal notification provision failed this test.
44. *Casey*, 505 U.S. at 850–51.
45. Ibid., 851.
46. *Lawrence v. Texas*, 123 S. Ct. 2472, 2489 (2003).
47. Ibid.
48. Ibid., 2475.

Chapter Five: Justices in the Bedroom

1. Lawrence v. Texas, 539 U.S. 558, 602 (2003).
2. Nancy Dillon and Michael Saul, "Say 'nay' to gay nups," *New York Daily News*, March 15, 2004.
3. Lambda Legal Defense and Education Fund, Freedom to Marry/Marriage Project Brochure, available at www.lambdalegal.org.
4. *Bowers v. Hardwick*, 478 U.S. 186 (1986).
5. *Lawrence v. Texas*, 539 U.S. 558 (2003).
6. *Romer v. Evans*, 517 U.S. 620 (1996).
7. William F. Buckley Jr. "Bedroom Rights: Should Kerry be denied communion?" *National Review Online*, May 4, 2004. Available at www.nationalreviewonline.com.
8. Stuart Taylor, Jr., "Case on Rights for Homosexuals Will be Heard by Supreme Court," *New York Times*, November 5, 1985.
9. Ibid. Al Kamen, "High Court to Review Rights of States to Regulate Adults' Sexual Activities; Constitutional Issue Addressed for First Time in Sodomy Case," *Washington Post*, November 5, 1985; Stuart Taylor, Jr., "High Court, 5–4, Says States Have the Right to Outlaw Private Homosexual Acts; Division is Bitter," *New York Times*, July 1, 1986. "Powell Wavered on Sodomy Ruling," *Chicago Tribune*, July 14, 1986.
10. *Bowers v. Hardwick*, 478 U.S. 186, 191 (1986).
11. Ibid.
12. Ibid., 191–92.
13. Ibid., 193–94.
14. Ibid., 194.
15. Ibid., 195.
16. Ibid., 195–96.
17. Ibid., 216.
18. Ibid., 196.
19. Ned Zeman and Michael Meyer, "No 'Special Rights' for Gays," *Newsweek*, November 23, 1992.
20. Editorial, "The Case for the Colorado Boycott," *New York Times*, December 21, 1992.
21. Al Knight, "Romer's political instincts don't live up to their billing," *Denver Post*, October 30, 1994.
22. *Romer v. Evans*, 517 U.S. 620 (1996).
23. Kennedy was President Ronald Reagan's third choice for his seat on the Court, following the 58–42 Senate vote against Robert Bork and Douglas Ginsburg's withdrawal.
24. *Romer v. Evans*, 517 U.S. 620, 631 (1996).
25. Ibid., 632.

26. Ibid., 636, citing *Bowers v. Hardwick*, 478 U.S. 186 (1986).

27. Ibid., 641.

28. Ibid., 653.

29. *Lawrence v. Texas*, 538 U.S. 918 (2003).

30. Charles Lane, "Justices Overturn Texas Sodomy Ban; Ruling is Landmark Victory for Gay Rights," *Washington Post*, June 27, 2003.

31. Paul Duggan, "Texas Sodomy Arrest Opens Legal Battle for Gay Activists," *Washington Post*, November 29, 1998.

32. *Lawrence v. Texas*, 2003 U.S. TRANS LEXIS 30 (U.S. TRANS, 2003). A transcript that identifies which justice is speaking is available on the Internet at www.oyez.org/oyez/resource/case/1542/argument/transcript). The full text of the poem, written by an Oxford student in 1680, is, "I do not love thee, Dr. Fell, The reason why I cannot tell; But this alone I know full well, I do not love thee, Dr. Fell." (Michael Kirkland, "Court hears challenge to Texas sodomy ban," United Press International, March 26, 2003.)

33. Ibid.

34. Associated Press, April 20, 2003.

35. "Senate Republican Caucus chair Rick Santorum is a bigot," *Capital Times* (Madison, WI) April 25, 2003.

36. *New Republic*, May 5, 2003.

37. *Lawrence v. Texas*, 123 S. Ct. 2472, 2475 (2003).

38. Ibid., 2494.

39. Ibid., 2480.

40. Ibid., 2481.

41. Ibid., 2484.

42. Ibid.

43. Ibid., 2495.

44. Ibid., 2498.

45. Lambda Legal Defense Fund, "A New Era for Gay Americans," June 26, 2003, available at www.lambdalegal.org.

46. Transcript of Susan Sommer, Lambda Legal Supervising Attorney, discussing *Lawrence v. Texas*, June 26, 2003. Available at www.lambdalegal.org.

47. *Goodridge v. Dept. of Pub. Health*, 14 Mass. L. Rep. 591 (Mass. Super. Ct. 2002).

48. *Goodridge v. Dept. of Pub. Health*, 440 Mass. 309, 312 (Mass. 2003).

49. Ibid., 343.

50. Ibid.

51. Ibid., 344.

52. Opinions of the Justices to the Senate, 440 Mass. 1201, 1202 (Mass. 2004).

53. Ibid., 1207–08.

54. Ken Maguire, "Marriage-license applications given to same-sex couples in Massachusetts," Associated Press, May 17, 2004.

55. U.S. Constitution, Article IV, § 1.

56. 28 USC § 1738(C) (2004).

57. Matthew Spaulding, "A Defining Moment: Marriage, the Courts, and the Constitution," Heritage Foundation Reports, Backgrounder No. 1759, May 17, 2004.

58. Kelly Wiese, "Missouri Voters Approve Gay Marriage Ban," Associated Press Online, August 24, 2004.

59. Frank J. Murray, "Despite Constitution, states choose marital laws they want," *Washington Times*, December 10, 1996.

60. U.S. Constitution, Article III, § 2.

61. Maggie Gallagher, "An Ambiguous Amendment," *National Review Online*, March 29, 2004.

62. Associated Press, "Bush expresses support for constitutional amendment," February 24, 2004.

63. Ibid.

64. Facts on File World News Digest, "Senate Blocks Amendment Barring Same-Sex Marriages; Republicans Divided," July 15, 2004.

65. Marriage has never been exclusively a state matter. As columnist Maggie Gallagher wrote:

    Why is monogamy both the legal and social norm in America? For one reason only: Between 1862 and 1887, Congress repeatedly passed laws designed to stamp out polygamy in U.S. territory. The lengths to which Congress went strike us now as extreme. But without decisive federal intervention, America today would have polygamy in some states and not in others.

    In 1862, Congress passed the Morrill Act criminalizing bigamy. Under that law, no married person could "marry any other person, whether single or married, in a Territory of the United States," under penalty of a $500 fine or five years in prison. In 1874, responding to the difficulty of getting convictions in regions where people supported polygamy, Congress passed the Poland Act, transferring plural marriage cases from Mormon-controlled probate courts to the federal system. In 1882, Congress passed the Edmunds Act, which vacated the government in the Utah territory, created a five-man commission to oversee elections, and forbade any polygamist, past or present, to vote. By 1887, half the prison population in Utah territory were people charged with polygamy. That year, Congress passed the Edmunds-Tucker Act, which, partly to facilitate polygamy convictions, allowed wives to testify against husbands in court. By 1890, the Church of the Latter Day Saints threw in the towel, advising its members "to refrain from contracting any marriages forbidden by the law of the land." Maggie Gallagher, "Latter Day Federalists," *Weekly Standard*, March 29, 2004.

66. Helen Dewar, "Ban on Gay Marriage Fails," *Washington Post*, July 15, 2004.

67. Mary Fitzgerald and Alan Cooperman, "Marriage Protection Act Passes," *Washington Post*, July 23, 2004.

68. Steven Dinan, "House targets marriage validation," *Washington Times*, July 23, 2004.

69. Ibid.

Chapter Six: Endorsing Racism

1. Fred Barbash, "Justice Douglas' Memoirs," *Washington Post*, September 11, 1980. Justice William O. Douglas attributes this quote to Justice Thurgood Marshall in his memoirs, *The Court Years, 1939–1975; The Autobiography of William O. Douglas.*

2. The History of Affirmative Action Policies, Americans for Fair Chance, August 7, 2003. Available at www.inmotionmagazine.com/aahist.html.

3. Richard Nixon, *RN: The Memoirs of Richard Nixon* (New York: Grosset & Dunlap, 1978), 437. Available at www.policyalmanac.org.

4. *Regents of the University of California v. Bakke*, 438 U.S. 265 (1978).

5. Ibid., 274.

6. Ibid.

7. Ibid., 276.

8. Ibid., 277.

9. *Strauder v. West Virginia*, 100 U.S. 303, 308 (1880).

10. *Yick Wo v. Hopkins*, 118 U.S. 356 (1886).

11. *Truax v. Raich*, 239 U.S. 33, 41 (1915).

12. *Korematsu v. United States*, 323 U.S. 216 (1944).

13. *Hernandez v. Texas*, 347 U.S. 475 (1954).

14. *Bakke* at 293, citing *McDonald v. Santa Fe Trail Transportation Co.*, 427 U.S. 273, 296 (1976).

15. The Court tells us that "strict scrutiny" differs from a "rational basis" examination in that in order to pass constitutional muster under the "rational basis" test, a law need only be "rationally related" to a "legitimate" government interest.

16. *Bakke*, 307.

17. Ibid., 310.

18. Ibid., 311.

19. Ibid., 315.

20. Ibid., 318.

21. *Grutter v. Bollinger*, 539 U.S. 306, 328 (2003).

22. *Gratz v. Bollinger*, 539 U.S. 244 (2003).

23. *Grutter v. Bollinger*, 539 U.S., 333.

24. Ibid., 325.

25. Ibid.

26. Ibid.

27. Ibid., 326.
28. Ibid., 330.
29. Ibid., 333.
30. Ibid.
31. Ibid., 338, citing *Bakke* at 317.
32. Ibid., 341. Internal citations omitted.
33. Ibid.
34. Ibid., 342.
35. Brian T. Fitzpatrick, "The Diversity Lie," 27 Harv. J.L. & Pub. Policy 385 (2003).
36. Daniel Golden, "Some Backers of Racial Preference Take Stand Beyond Diversity: Society Wins With Integrated Elite," *Wall Street Journal*, June 14, 2003.
37. U.S. Census Bureau, "Census Bureau Projects Tripling of Hispanic and Asian Populations in 50 Years; Non-Hispanic Whites May Drop To Half of Total Population," press release, March 18, 2004.
38. Mary Wiltenburg and Amanda Paulson, "All in the (mixed-race) family: a US trend," *Christian Science Monitor*, August 28, 2003.
39. *Grutter v. Bollinger*, 539 U.S. at 385.
40. Ibid., 355.
41. Ibid., 351.
42. *Gratz v. Bollinger*, 539 U.S. 244 (2003).
43. Ibid., 272.
44. Ibid., 255.
45. Ward Connerly, "Murder at the Supreme Court," *National Review Online*, June 26, 2003.

Chapter Seven: Citizenship Up for Grabs

1. *Plyler v. Doe*, 457 U.S. 202, 242 (1982).
2. U.S. Constitution Article 1, § 8.
3. Don Collins, "Illegal Immigration is Ravaging Arizona," *Pittsburgh Tribune-Review*, June 22, 2004. Available at pittsburghlive.com/x/tribune-review/opinion/columnists/guests/print_199848.html.
4. Yilu Zhao, "Wave of Pupils Lacking English Strains Schools," *New York Times*, August 5, 2002.
5. Ibid.
6. Stephen Dinan, "States pay $7.4 billion to educate illegals; Report notes drain on U.S. children," *Washington Times*, August 21, 2003.
7. Ibid.
8. Jerry Seper, "Report ties health care struggles to immigration; Increase in uninsured aliens seen straining hospital budgets," *Washington Times*, February 26, 2004.

9. Immigration Laws 1700–1800, "Colonial Period: Legal Authority over Immigration." Available at oriole.umd.edu.

10. Ibid.

11. Ibid.

12. Immigration and naturalization are the two main classifications of law in this regard. Immigration refers to emigrants from other countries entering the United States. Naturalization concerns the process by which immigrants become citizens of the United States.

13. U.S. Constitution Amendment I, § 8

14. Joseph Story, *Commentaries on the Constitution of the United States*, "Power Over Naturalization and Bankruptcy," § 1098.

15. The term "Alien and Sedition Acts" is commonly used as shorthand for three acts of Congress: the Naturalization Act of 1798, the Aliens Act of 1798, and the Alien Enemy Act of 1798.

16. Ibid.

17. Immigration Act of 1875.

18. Ibid. Coolies were bonded workers from China, India, and other nations in Asia.

19. Naturalization Act of 1855.

20. 8 U.S.C. § 1101 (2000).

21. 8 U.S.C. § 1103 (2000).

22. U.S. Constitution Amendment V. The Fifth Amendment delineated the limitations on the federal government's power over individuals. In addition to requiring that no person can be deprived of "life, liberty, or property" without due process of law, it provides for the use of a grand jury to indict someone and prohibits double jeopardy and self-incrimination. The Fourteenth Amendment imposes similar restrictions on the authority of state governments.

23. U.S. Constitution Amendment XIV. The Fourteenth Amendment, in particular, was written to ensure that state governments did not treat individuals, or groups of individuals, unequally under the law, or that individuals or groups were not treated differently solely because of their race or ethnic heritage. It was not written to guarantee identical treatment for everyone everywhere, nor to provide for equal outcomes under the law for everyone.

24. *Graham v. Richardson*, 403 U.S. 365 (1971).

25. The *Graham* decision also cited other cases in which the premise of no distinction between benefits or privileges and rights should be made. These cases include *Sherbert v. Verner*, 374 U.S. 398 (1963), *Shapiro v. Thompson*, 394 U.S. 627 (1969), *Goldberg v. Kelly*, 397 U.S. 254 (1970), and *Bell v. Burson*, 402 U.S. 535 (1971).

26. *Heim v. McCall*, 239 U.S. 175, 188 (1915).

27. Ibid., 191.

28. *Ohio ex rel. v. Clarke Deckebach Auditor*, 274 U.S. 392 (1927).

29. Ibid., 395.

30. Ibid., 397.

31. Ibid.

32. Ibid., 367.

33. *Graham v. Richardson*, 403 U.S. 367.

34. Ibid.

35. Ibid., 368.

36. Ibid., 376.

37. Ibid., 372.

38. 1866 Civil Rights Act, 14 Stat. 27–30, Section 1. "Be it enacted by the Senate and House of Representatives of the United States of America in Congress assembled, That all persons born in the United States and not subject to any foreign power, excluding Indians not taxed, are hereby declared to be citizens of the United States; and such citizens, of every race and color, without regard to any previous condition of slavery or involuntary servitude, except as a punishment for crime whereof the party shall have been duly convicted, shall have the same right, in every State and Territory in the United States, to make and enforce contracts, to sue, be parties, and give evidence, to inherit, purchase, lease, sell, hold, and convey real and personal property, and to full and equal benefit of all laws and proceedings for the security of person and property, as is enjoyed by white citizens, and shall be subject to like punishment, pains, and penalties, and to none other, any law, statute, ordinance, regulation, or custom, to the contrary notwithstanding,"

39. *Hampton v. Mow Sun Wong*, 426 U.S. 88 (1976).

40. In 1971, the Post Office, which was a federal agency, was semi-privatized and became the U.S. Postal Service.

41. In 1979, the federal department of Health, Education, and Welfare was reorganized into two agencies, the Department of Education and the Department of Health and Human Services.

42. *Hampton v. Mow Sun Wong*, 426 U.S. at 102-03.

43. Ibid., 106.

44. *Sugarman v. Dougall*, 413 U.S. 634 (1973).

45. Ibid., 637. The four employees were among approximately 450 employees who actually worked for private sector nonprofit organizations that received funding through a federal agency, the United States Office of Economic Opportunity. In 1970, federal funding for those organizations was stopped and the nonprofits absorbed by a New York City agency, the Manpower Career and Development Agency (MCDA). When the jobs were moved under the city, the state's civil service requirements became applicable and the noncitizen employees were dismissed.

46. Ibid.

47. Ibid., 639–40.

48. Ibid., 651.

49. *Plyler v. Doe*, 457 U.S. 202 (1982).

50. Ibid., 205.
51. Ibid., 210.
52. Ibid., 220.
53. Ibid., 221.
54. Ibid., 222.
55. Ibid., 229.
56. Ibid., 242–43.
57. *In Re Griffiths*, 413 U.S. 717 (1973).
58. *Nyquist v. Mauclet*, 432 U.S. 1 (1977).

Chapter Eight: Al Qaeda Gets a Lawyer

1. Ronald Reagan, Remarks at a meeting with members of the American Business Conference, The White House, April 15, 1986. *The Quotable Ronald Reagan* (Washington, D.C.: Regnery, 1998).
2. An illegal or unlawful combatant, who is not protected by the laws of war, is an individual waging war who does not comply with any of the following require- ments, according to the Second Hague Convention of 1899 and the Third Geneva Convention: (1) In uniform: Wear distinctive clothing making them recognizable as soldiers from a distance; (2) Openly bearing arms: Carrying guns or small arms and not concealing them; (3) Under officers: Obedient to a chain of command ending in a political leader or government; (4) Fighting according to the laws of war: Not committing atrocities or crimes, not deliberately attacking civilians or engaging in terrorism. 6 U.S.T. 3516 (1949).
3. Remarks by Alberto R. Gonzales, counsel to the president, before the American Bar Association Standing Committee on Law and National Security, February 24, 2004.
4. William J. Haynes II, general counsel to the Department of Defense, "Enemy Combatants." Available at www.cfr.org/publication.php?id=5312, citing *Ex Parte Quirin*, 317 U.S. 37 (1942), *Colepaugh v. Looney*, 235 F.2d. 429, 432 (10th Circuit 1956), *In re Territo*, 156 F.2d. 142, 145 (9th Circuit 1946), *Hamdi v. Rumsfeld*, 296 F.3d 278, 281, 283 (4th Circuit 2002). This decision was subsequently modified by the Supreme Court in *Hamdi v. Rumsfeld*, 542 U.S. ___, 124 S.Ct. 2633 (2004).
5. *Rasul v. Bush*, 542 U.S. ___, 124 S.Ct. 2686 (2004), Brief for the Respondent President George W. Bush, 5–6.
6. Ibid. Brief for the Respondent George W. Bush, 6.
7. Ibid.
8. Ibid., 7.
9. Ibid.
10. Ibid.
11. Ibid.

12. *Rasul v. Bush*, 542 U.S. ___, 124 S.Ct. 2686, 2004 U.S. LEXIS 4760 at *1 (2004). The Supreme Court also decided the case *Rumsfeld v. Padilla*, 542 U.S. ___, 124 S.Ct. 2711 (2004). *Padilla* differed from *Rasul* and *Hamdi* in that it dealt with a case in which a U.S. citizen was apprehended on U.S. soil and alleged to be actively planning terrorist activities.

13. *Hamdi v. Rumsfeld*, 542 U.S. ___, 124 S.Ct. 2633, 2004 U.S. LEXIS 4761 at *1 (2004). It's important to note that before the Supreme Court heard the case, the Fourth Circuit ruled that while Hamdi could seek judicial review of his detention, he was not entitled to challenge the government's evidence. It was enough that a legally valid basis for his detention was provided to the court. *Hamdi v. Rumsfeld*, 296 F.3d 278 (4th Circuit 2002).

14. Ibid., *6.

15. Ibid., *10.

16. Ibid., *8–*9.

17. Ibid., *6.

18. Congress has the power to declare war. U.S. Constitution, Article I, § 8. However, the Constitution provides no guidance about the form of such a declaration. There are no required phrases or terms. On September 18, 2001, Congress passed a joint resolution authorizing the president "to use all necessary and appropriate force against those nations, organizations, or persons he determines planned, authorized, committed, or aided the terrorist attacks that occurred on September 11, 2001, or harbored such organizations or persons, in order to prevent any future acts of international terrorism against the United States by such nations, organizations, or persons." Pub. L. No 107–40, § 2(a), 115 Stat. 224 (2001). This suffices as congressional authorization for war.

19. *Hamdi*, 2004 U.S. LEXIS 4761, *20.

20. Ibid., *21.

21. Ibid., *26.

22. Ibid., *46. Hamdi, was in fact, permitted to file a writ of habeas corpus and did so. The government, however, argued that he did not have a right to be represented by counsel; it feared that Hamdi would cease to be a source for wartime intelligence.

23. Ibid., *104, citing *Chicago & Southern Air Lines, Inc. v. Waterman S.S. Corp.*, 333 U.S. 103, 111 (1948).

24. Ibid., *127.

25. In October 2004, Hamdi was returned to Saudi Arabia, required to renounce his American citizenship, and required to notify Saudi officials if he became aware of any terrorist activities. Associated Press, "Hamdi Returns to Saudi Arabia," October 11, 2004.

26. *Rasul*, 2004 U.S. LEXIS 4760, *1.

27. Ibid., *9.

28. Ibid., *1.

29. *Johnson v. Eisentrager*, 339 U.S. 763 (1950).

30. Robert Alt, "Dangerous Decision," *National Review Online*, June 29, 2004, citing *Eisentrager*, 339 U.S., 779.

31. *Eisentrager*, 339 U.S., 766–67.

32. Ibid., 765.

33. Ibid., 768.

34. Ibid., 778.

35. Ibid., 771–72.

36. *Rasul*, 2004 LEXIS 4760, *18-*19.

37. Ibid., *13–*14 (citing 28 U.S.C. § 2241 (2004)).

38. *Rasul*, 2004 LEXIS 4760, *23.

39. The federal judicial system includes district courts, appellate courts, and the Supreme Court. Each district and appellate court is limited in that it can only hear cases or controversies that arise from the court's physical territory. For example, the Ninth Circuit Court of Appeals, located in the western part of the United States, cannot hear a case that was originally brought in federal court in the Eastern District of Virginia.

40. *Rasul*, 2004 LEXIS 4760, *23.

41. Ibid., *56.

42. Andrew C. McCarthy, "A Mixed Bag," *National Review Online*, June 30, 2004.

43. U.S. Constitution, Article I, § 9, Cl. 2.

44. Craig Smith, "Political Communication." Available at www.csulb.edu.

45. Ibid.

46. *Ex Parte Merryman*, 17 F. Cas. 144 (1861).

47. Smith, "Political Communication." My view is that one branch of the federal government does not have the authority to assume constitutional power from or cede it to another branch. Their powers are derived from the Constitution, not from their own actions. Therefore, with or without congressional approval, Lincoln did not have the authority to suspend the writ of habeas corpus, an exclusively congressional function.

48. The two are Yaser Esam Hamdi, who was captured in Afghanistan, and Jose Padilla, who was allegedly planning a terrorist attack in the United States.

49. Executive Order No. 9066 (1942).

50. Associated Press, "Terror Suspects Told of Right to Use U.S. Courts," July 12, 2004.

51. Literally within a few months of the Supreme Court's *Rasul* decision, two federal district courts conferred additional rights on illegal combatants. Judge Colleen Kollar-Kotelly, a Clinton appointee, ruled that these detainees have a right to a taxpayer-financed attorney to help them file habeas petitions, and to unmonitored consultations with their attorney. *Odah v. United States*, No. 02-828 (D.D.C. Octo-

ber 20, 2004). Judge James Robertson, another Clinton appointee, ruled that Osama bin Laden's former driver, Salim Ahmed Hamdan, was entitled to a hearing in which the judge would determine whether the executive branch properly designated Hamdan an illegal combatant or whether he should be entitled to more lenient treatment as a prisoner of war. *Hamdan v. Rumsfeld*, No. 04-1519 (D.D.C. Nov. 8, 2004). Both opinions are available at www.dcd.uscourts.gov/district-court-2004.html.

Chapter Nine: Socialism from the Bench

1. Milton Friedman, *Capitalism and Freedom* (Chicago: University of Chicago Press, 1962.)
2. U.S. Constitution, Article I, § 8.
3. Articles of Confederation, Article II.
4. U.S. Constitution, Amendment IX.
5. Steven G. Calabresi, "A Government of Limited and Enumerated Powers: In Defense of *United States v. Lopez*," 94 Mich. L. Rev. 752, 770 (1995).
6. *Gibbons v. Ogden*, 22 U.S.1 (1824).
7. Ibid., 194.
8. *U.S. v. Lopez*, 514 U.S. 549, 599 (1995).
9. *Railroad Retirement Bd. v. Alton R. Co.*, 295 U.S. 330 (1935).
10. Ibid., 374.
11. *A.L.A. Schechter Poultry Corp. v. United States*, 295 U.S. 495, 548 (1935).
12. Ibid., 543.
13. Ibid.
14. Ibid., 546.
15. Ibid.
16. *Carter v. Carter Coal Co.*, 298 U.S. 238 (1936).
17. Ibid., 238.
18. Ibid., 308.
19. Franklin Delano Roosevelt press conference, May 31, 1935. Available at academic.brooklyn.cuny.edu.
20. *U.S. v. Lopez*, 514 U.S. 549, 555 (1995) (citing NLRB v. Jones & Laughlin Steel Corp., 301 U.S., 37).
21. *Wickard v. Filburn*, 317 U.S. 111 (1942).
22. Ibid., 113–15.
23. Ibid., 111.
24. Ibid., 128.
25. Richard A. Epstein, "Constitutional Faith and the Commerce Clause," 71 Notre Dame L. Rev. 167, 172–73 (1996).

26. *Maryland v. Wirtz*, 392 U.S. 183 (1968).

27. Ibid., 194.

28. Ibid., 195.

29. Epstein, "Constitutional Faith and the Commerce Clause," 187.

30. *Perez v. United States*, 402 U.S. 146 (1971).

31. Ibid., 157.

32. Michael W. McConnell, "Federalism: Evaluating the Founder's Design," 54 U. Chi. L. Rev. 1484, 1494 (1987). McConnell has recently been confirmed by the Senate and now sits on the Tenth U.S. Circuit Court of Appeals.

33. *United States v. Lopez*, 514 U.S. 549 (1995).

34. Ibid., 567.

35. *U.S. v. Lopez*, 514 U.S. 549, 619–20. Internal citations omitted.

36. *U.S. v. Morrison*, 529 U.S. 598 (2000).

37. Ibid., 613.

38. Ibid.

39. Chris Edwards, "Downsizing the Federal Government," Cato Policy Analysis No. 515, June 2, 2004, 1.

40. Bill Steigerwald, "Milton Friedman bemoans a 50 percent socialist U.S.A.," *Pittsburgh Tribune Review*, April 8, 2001.

41. Clyde Wayne Crews, Jr., "Ten Thousand Commandments: An Annual Snapshot of the Federal Regulatory State," Cato Paper, June 28, 2003, 1.

42. Ibid., 9.

43. Ibid., 2. U.S. GDP was estimated at nearly $10.5 trillion for 2002.

44. Ibid., 6.

Chapter Ten: Silencing Political Debate

1. George Washington, "Address to officers of the Army," March 15, 1783. Appears in John Bartlett's *Familiar Quotations* (Boston: Little, Brown and Company, 1980).

2. *McConnell v. FEC*, 124 S.Ct. 619 (2003).

3. *Texas v. Johnson*, 491 U.S. 397 (1989).

4. *Hill v. Colorado*, 530 U.S. 703 (2000).

5. *Tinker v. Des Moines Indep. Com. School Dist.*, 393 U.S. 503 (1969).

6. *Santa Fe Indep. School Dist. v. Doe*, 530 U.S. 290 (2000).

7. U.S. Constitution, Amendment I.

8. *Mills v. Alabama*, 384 U.S. 214, 218 (1966).

9. 145 Cong. Rec. S12585, October 14, 1999.

10. Ibid., S12586.

11. Ibid.

12. 2 U.S.C. 431 (2002).

13. U.S. Constitution, Amendment I.
14. *Buckley v. Valeo*, 424 U.S. 1 (1976).
15. Ibid., 16.
16. Ibid., 20.
17. *McConnell v. FEC*, 124 S.Ct. 619 (2003).
18. Prior to the Court's ruling in *McConnell*, soft money was not subject to federal campaign finance regulation. For example, the Democratic Party expended "soft money" when it conducted "get out the vote" drives. Such activities are now illegal.
19. Campaign Legal Center. Available at www.campaignlegalcenter.org.
20. Adam Nagourney, "McCain-Feingold School Finds Many Bewildered," *New York Times*, February 19, 2003.
21. Ibid.
22. *McConnell v. FEC*, 124 S.Ct 619, 661 (2003).
23. Steve Chabot, Hearing Statement of Steve Chabot, "Constitutional Issues Raised By Recent Campaign Finance Legislation Restricting Free Speech," June 12, 2001.
24. "A Campaign Finance Triumph," *New York Times*, December 11, 2003.
25. "John Kerry for President," *New York Times*, October 17, 2004.
26. "Upheld," *Washington Post*, December 11, 2003.
27. *McConnell v. FEC*, 124 S.Ct. at 706.
28. Laura Blumefeld, "Soros's Deep Pockets vs. Bush," *Washington Post*, November 11, 2003.
29. "Soros, George and Susan W., Contributions to 527 Committees," Center for Public Integrity, August 17, 2004. Available at membership.publicintegrity.org.
30. "Lewis, Peter B., Contributions to 527 Committees," Center for Public Integrity, August 17, 2004. Available at www.publicintegrity.org.
31. OpenSecrets.org, "527 Committee Activity, Top 50 Organizations," December 2, 2004. Available at www.opensecrets.org.
32. Jan Withold Baran and Barbara Van Gelder, "Sentencing Guidelines Impose Tough New Criminal Penalties," *Election Law News*, March 2003.
33. *Lorillard Tobacco Co. v. Reilly*, 533 U.S. 525 (2001).
34. Ibid., 565.
35. Ibid.
36. Ibid., 566.
37. Let me further clarify my position. I don't have a problem with tobacco advertising per se. My problem is the logic and consistency of the Supreme Court.
38. *Ashcroft v. Free Speech Coalition*, 535 U.S. 234 (2002).
39. Ibid., 250. Internal citations omitted.
40. Ibid., 245.
41. *Texas v. Johnson*, 491 U.S. 397 (1989).
42. Ibid., 419.

43. George W. Bush, "President Signs Campaign Finance Reform Act," March 27, 2002. Available at www.whitehouse.gov.

Chapter Eleven: The Court Counts the Ballots

1. Donald Lambro, "Democrats won't knock Jackson," *Washington Times*, December 13, 2000.
2. "If the returns for any office reflect that a candidate was defeated or eliminated by one-half of a percent or less of the votes cast for such office, that a candidate for retention to a judicial office was retained or not retained by one-half of a percent or less of the votes cast on the question of retention, or that a measure appearing on the ballot was approved or rejected by one-half of a percent or less of the votes cast on such measure, the board responsible for certifying the results of the vote on such race or measure shall order a recount of the votes cast with respect to such office or measure. A recount need not be ordered with respect to the returns for any office, however, if the candidate or candidates defeated or eliminated from contention for such office by one-half of a percent or less of the votes cast for such office request in writing that a recount not be made. Each canvassing board responsible for conducting a recount shall examine the counters on the machines or the tabulation of the ballots cast in each precinct in which the office or issue appeared on the ballot and determine whether the returns correctly reflect the votes cast. If there is a discrepancy between the returns and the counters of the machines or the tabulation of the ballots cast, the counters of such machines or the tabulation of the ballots cast shall be presumed correct and such votes shall be canvassed accordingly." Fla. Stat. § 102.141(4) (2000).
3. "Any candidate whose name appeared on the ballot, any political committee that supports or opposes an issue which appeared on the ballot, or any political party whose candidates' names appeared on the ballot may file a written request with the county canvassing board for a manual recount. The written request shall contain a statement of the reason the manual recount is being requested." Fla. Stat. § 102.166(4)(a) (2000). "Such request must be filed with the canvassing board prior to the time the canvassing board certifies the results for the office being protested or within 72 hours after midnight of the date the election was held, whichever occurs later." Fla. Stat. §102.166(4)(b) (2000).
4. Fla. Stat. § 102.166(6) (2000).
5. Fla. Stat. § 102.166(7)(a) (2000).
6. Fla. Stat. § 102.166(4)(b) (2000).
7. Fla. Stat. § 102.112(1) (2000).
8. 3 U.S.C. 5 (2000). The citizens of the United States do not directly choose their president and vice president (so much for the Democrats' mantra that Gore won

the majority of the votes cast). The president is chosen by the electoral college, which is comprised of electors (equal to the number of senators and representatives from each state) chosen by the state legislatures. U.S. Constitution, Article II, § 1, Cl. 1–4. If no candidate for president receives a majority of the electoral college (half plus one, or 270 votes), the U.S. House of Representatives then votes by state delegations from among the top three candidates for whom the electoral college voted. U.S. Constitution, Amendment XII. If no candidate for vice president receives a majority of the electoral college, the Senate chooses one (by a vote of the individual senators). Ibid. The electoral college is important because it makes candidates consider smaller states in order to achieve the necessary 270 electoral votes. For example, in 2000, smaller states such as Minnesota and Wisconsin received significant attention from Gore and Bush. If there wasn't an electoral college, candidates would only focus on large population areas such as New York or Los Angeles. Less populated regions, such as the Midwest, could be ignored. Congress sets the date a presidential election will be held around the country (in 2000 that date was November 7) as well as the date the electoral college members will meet (in 2000 that date was December 18). See U.S. Constitution Article II., § 1. Cl. 1–4; 3 U.S.C 7 (2000); and U.S. Constitution Article II.

9. 3 U.S.C. 11, 12 (2004).
10. U.S. Constitution, Article II.
11. Tony Sutin, "Presidential Election Law," Jurist Legal Intelligence. Available at jurist.law.pitt.edu/election/electiontime.htm.
12. Fla. Stat. § 102.141(4) (2000).
13. Sutin, "Presidential Election Law."
14. "How we got here: A timeline of the Florida recount," CNN.com, December 13, 2000. Available at www.cnn.com/2000/ALLPOLITICS/stories/12/13/got.here/index.html. Complicating the issue of tabulating Florida's ballots was the fact that several counties used paper punch card ballots. Voters used a stylus to punch out squares next to candidates' names to cast their votes. Due to the age of some of the equipment used by several counties, as well as poorly conceived designs for some ballots and voter mistakes, a small percentage of ballots could not be read by tabulating machines. In addition, some voters chose not to vote for one or more offices (including president) on the ballot, while casting votes for other offices. The small percentage of votes that were thus "spoiled" in Florida in 2000 was not unusual when compared with past Florida elections or with elections in other states. The recount regulations required by Florida's election laws enumerated specific procedures for both manual and machine recounts to minimize the number of uncounted ballots.
15. Fla. Stat. § 102.166.(4)(a) (2000).
16. Fla. Stat. § 102.166(5) (2000).
17. "How we got here: A timeline of the Florida recount."

18. Ibid.
19. *Touchston v. McDermott*, 234 F.3d 1133 (11th Circuit, 2000); *Palm Beach County Canvassing Bd. v. Harris*, 772 So. 2d 1220 (Fla. 2000); *Siegel v. LePore*, 120 F. Supp. 2d 1041 (D. Fla. 2000).
20. Fla. Stat. § 102.111 (2000).
21. Fla. Stat. § 102.112 (2000).
22. Jackie Hallifax, "Deadline Looms As Recount Continues," Associated Press Online, November 13, 2000.
23. Fla. Stat. § 102.111 (2000).
24. "How we got here: A timeline of the Florida recount."
25. Palm Beach County Canvassing Bd. v. Harris, 772 So. 2d 1220, 1227 (Fla. 2000).
26. "Judge finds Harris acted with discretion in rejecting manual recounts," CNN.com, November 17, 2000. Available at www.archives.cnn.com/2000/LAW/11/17/harris.discretion.ruling.02.pol/. McDermott v. Harris, No. 00-2700, unpublished order at 2 (Fla. 2d Cir. Ct. Nov. 17, 2000).
27. *Palm Beach County Canvassing Bd. v. Harris*, 772 So. 2d 1220, 1227 (Fla. 2000).
28. *Touchston v. McDermott*, 234 F.3d 1130 (11th Cir. 2000).
29. Ibid., 1132.
30. *Palm Beach County Canvassing Bd. v. Harris*, 772 So. 2d 1220, 1240 (Fla. 2000).
31. Linda Greenhouse, "Counting the Vote: The Supreme Court; U.S. Supreme Court to Hear Florida Recount Case," *New York Times*, November 25, 2000.
32. Rick Bragg and Lynette Holloway, "Counting the Vote: The Recount; Tempers Flaring Under Pressure," *New York Times*, November 26, 2000.
33. Transcript, "Political Headlines," Fox Special Report with Brit Hume, November 29, 2000; Bill Sammon, *At Any Cost: How Al Gore Tried to Steal the Election* (Washington, D.C.: Regnery, 2001), 164–65.
34. Sammon, 164–65.
35. Todd J. Gillman, "Palm Beach struggles to reconcile vote discrepancies; County delay raises concerns," *Dallas Morning News*, November 29, 2000.
36. Jay Weaver, "Gore Readying New Venture in State Court Suit; Will Claim Recount Invalid Without Dade," *Miami Herald*, November 25, 2000.
37. "Jeb Bush Certifies Florida Win," Associated Press Online, November 27, 2000.
38. Scott Shepard, "Don't count me out, Gore says: He insists Bush win not final," *Atlanta Journal-Constitution*, November 28, 2000.
39. David Barstow, "Contesting the Vote: The Florida Legislature; Lawmakers Move Closer to Special Florida Session for Naming Bush Electors," *New York Times*, December 1, 2000.
40. Steve Lash, "Election 2000; High drama lands in high court; In historic session on nation's future, jurists break custom while grilling lawyers for Gore and Bush," *Houston Chronicle*, December 2, 2000.

41. Mark Z. Barabak and Richard A. Serrano, "Decision 2000/America Waits; Rulings Narrow Gore's Options," *Los Angeles Times*, December 5, 2000.

42. *Gore v. Harris*, 772 So. 2d 1243, 1247 (S. Ct. Fla. 2000).

43. John Pacenti, Brian E. Crowley, and George Bennett, "Can Hand Counts Offset Bush's 930-Vote Lead?" *Palm Beach Post*, November 19, 2000.

44. *Gore v. Harris*, 772 So. 2d 1243, 1247 (S. Ct. Fla. 2000).

45. Ibid., 1262.

46. Ibid., 1273.

47. Ibid., 1263–64.

48. Ibid., 1269.

49. *Bush v. Gore*, 531 U.S. 1046 (2000).

50. "How we got here: A timeline of the Florida recount."

51. *Bush v. Gore*, 531 U.S. 98, 109 (2000). Federal law contains a "safe harbor" provision, which provides that a state's selection of electors "shall be conclusive, and shall govern in the counting of electoral votes" provided the electors were chosen under laws that were "enacted prior to the day fixed for the appointment of the electors." 3 U.S.C. § 5 (2000).

52. *Bush v. Gore*, 531 U.S. 98, 104-05 (2000), citing *Harper v. Virginia Bd. of Elections*, 383 U.S. 663, 665 (1966).

53. *Bush v. Gore*, 531 U.S. 109.

54. Al Gore, "Campaign 2000: Vice President Gore Delivers Remarks," December 13, 2000. Available at www.cnn.com/ELECTION/2000/transcripts/121300/t651213.html.

55. U.S. Constitution, Article II, § 1, Clause 2.

56. *Bush v. Gore*, 531 U.S. 111.

57. Mark R. Levin, "What We have Wrought," *National Review Online*, December 14, 2000. Available at www.nationalreview.com/comment/comment121400g.shtml.

58. Sandy McClure and Peter Eichenbaum, "Democrats Plan to Replace Him on Ballot, GOP objects to opponents' maneuvering to retain control of U.S. Senate," *Asbury Park Press*, October 1, 2002.

59. *New Jersey Democratic Party v. Samson*, 175 N.J. 178, 814 A.2d 1028, 1036 (2002), cert. denied sub nom. *Forrester v. N.J. Democratic Party, Inc.*, 537 U.S. 1083 (2002).

60. *Southwest Voter Registration Education Project v. Shelly*, 344 F.3d 914, 917 (9th Cir. 2003).

61. Ibid.

62. Scott Wyman, "Potential For Election Nightmare Still Looms; Concerns Mount on Whether All Eligible Voters Will Get Chance," *Sun-Sentinel*, October 23, 2004; Anne Gearan, "Lawyers prepare for another deadlock, more recounts or a trip to the Supreme Court," Associated Press, September 20, 2004; Kim Cobb and Patty Reinert, "An army of lawyers stands by for Nov. 2," *Houston Chronicle*, October 17, 2004; George Bennett, "Judge Rules Against Voting Paper Trail," *Palm Beach Post*,

October 26, 2004; David B. Caruso, "Republicans Sue to Stop Prisoners from Voting," Associated Press, November 1, 2004.

63. U.S. Constitution, Article II.

64. David Barstow, "Contesting the Vote: The Florida Legislature; Lawmakers Move Closer to Special Florida Session for Naming Bush Electors," *New York Times*, December 1, 2000.

65. "Jeb Bush Certifies Florida Win," Associated Press Online, November 27, 2000. An interesting question would have arisen if the legislature had intervened, selected the Democratic slate of electors, and then ordered Jeb Bush to rescind his earlier certification. Technically, he could ignore the direction of the legislature claiming that federal law gave him the sole authority to certify electors, regardless of how they were selected by the legislature. I suppose the legislature could then send its own certification to the federal government, and the ballot challenge procedures in Congress would kick in. The legislature could then impeach Jeb Bush, if it chose, to punish him for failing to follow their directions. The question this poses, though, is that, even though the legislature is the only body authorized by the Constitution to select presidential electors, could the executive of a state ignore the will of the legislature by certifying a slate of electors in contravention of the will of the legislature?

66. Any challenge to electors in Congress must be approved by a majority of both houses of Congress (meeting separately). 3 U.S.C. 15 (2000). The Republicans had a majority in the House of Representatives of 221 to 212 (with two independents). The Senate was split 50–50 with the vice president (Al Gore) giving the Democrats a voting majority. So a challenge to Florida's slate of Republican electors would not have succeeded.

67. "It shall be the duty of the executive of each State, as soon as practicable after the conclusion of the appointment of the electors in such State by the final ascertainment, under and in pursuance of the laws of such State providing for such ascertainment, to communicate by registered mail under the seal of the State to the Archivist of the United States a certificate of such ascertainment of the electors appointed, setting forth the names of such electors and the canvass or other ascertainment under the laws of such State of the number of votes given or cast for each person for whose appointment any and all votes have been given or cast..." 3 U.S.C. 6 (2000).

68. 3 U.S.C. 15 (2000).

69. U.S. Constitution, Amendment XII.

70. U.S. Constitution, Article II § 1, cl. 2.

71. Fla. Stat. §§ 102.141, 102.151 (2000).

72. Fla. Stat. § 102.166 (2000).

73. Fla. Stat. § 102.111 (2000).

74. 3 U.S.C. 6 (2000).

75. 3 U.S.C. 11 (2000).
76. Judge N. Sanders Sauls was the rare exception where a judge limited his role in the controversy to that which was contemplated by the legislature. Activist judges will never limit their roles when the opportunity to shape public policy arises.

Chapter Twelve: Liberals Stack the Bench

1. George W. Bush, "Remarks by the President During Federal Judicial Appointees Announcement," May 9, 2001. Available at www.whitehouse.gov.
2. George W. Bush, Presidential debate, Boston, Massachusetts, October 3, 2000.
3. Press Release, March 22, 2001, "Leahy, Schumer: Bush Move to Curb ABA Review Will Hurt Federal Bench."
4. "Congress and the Court," *Boston Globe*, April 22, 2001.
5. Bruce Ackerman, "Foil Bush's Maneuvers for Packing the Court," *Los Angles Times*, April 26, 2001.
6. Indeed, despite Democrats' statements to the contrary, the use of the filibuster to block judicial nominees is unprecedented. Democrats rely on the case of Supreme Court Justice Abe Fortas's unsuccessful attempt to be confirmed as chief justice. However, as pointed out by Senator John Cornyn of Texas, Fortas's confirmation vote was delayed because his opponents wanted "adequate time to debate and expose serious problems with his nomination." Moreover, "Fortas wasn't denied confirmation due to a filibuster; he was denied confirmation due to the opposition of a bipartisan majority of senators." John Cornyn, "Falsities on the Senate Floor," *National Review Online*, November 13, 2003.
7. Memorandum to Senator Edward Kennedy, dated April 17, 2002. See Appendix.
8. Memorandum to Senator Edward Kennedy, dated June 4, 2002. See Appendix. Kate Michelman announced that she would be leaving her position as president of NARAL Pro-Choice America as of April 24, 2004.
9. People for the American Way website. Available at www.pfaw.org.
10. NARAL Pro-Choice America website. Available at www.prochoiceamerica.org.
11. Memorandum to Senator Edward Kennedy, dated June 4, 2002. See Appendix.
12. "Who is Priscilla Owen?" May 14, 2003. Available at www.whitehouse.gov.
13. Memorandum to Senator Dick Durbin, dated November 7, 2001. See Appendix.
14. Alliance For Justice, "Preliminary Report Opposing Professor Michael W. McConnell's Nomination to the U.S. Court of Appeals for the Tenth Circuit," September 18, 2002. Available at www.allianceforjustice.org.
15. Byron York, "Catholics Need Not Apply?" *National Review Online*, July 30, 2003. Available at www.nationalreviewonline.com.
16. Memorandum to Senator Dick Durbin, dated June 3, 2002. See Appendix.
17. Memorandum to Senator Dick Durbin, dated November 6, 2001. See Appendix.

18. "Members Meeting with Leader Daschle," Memorandum, Jan. 30, 2003. See Appendix.
19. "Talking Points on Estrada for Caucus," Memorandum. See Appendix.
20. U.S. Department of Justice, Office of Legal Policy, "Miguel Estrada, Biography." Available at www.doj.gov.
21. U.S. Constitution, Article II, § 2.
22. Clinton Rossiter, ed., Federalist No. 66, *Federalist Papers* (New York: Penguin Books, 1961).
23. John O. McGinnis, "The President, the Senate, the Constitution, and the Confirmation Process," 71 Tex. L. Rev. 633, 636 (1993).
24. Ibid., 654. Internal citations omitted.
25. Michael J. Gerhardt, "Toward a Comprehensive Understanding of the Federal Appointments Process," 21 Harv. J.L. & Pub. Policy 467, 479 (Spring 1998).
26. Senator John Cornyn, "Our Broken Judicial Confirmation Process and the Need for Filibuster Reform," 27 Harv. J.L. & Pub. Policy 181, 196 (Fall 2003).
27. Evans v. Stephens, ___ F.3d. ____ (11th Circuit, 2004), 2004 U.S. App. LEXIS 21354, 6.
28. Ibid.
29. Ibid.
30. Byron York, "Will the GOP 'Go Nuclear' Over Judges?" *National Review Online*, May 8, 2003. Available at www.nationalreview.com.
31. President George W. Bush, "President Calls for Judicial Reform," May 9, 2003. Available at www.whitehouse.gov.
32. President George W. Bush, "President Calls for Action on Judicial Nominees," August 1, 2003. Available at www.whitehouse.gov.
33. Ibid.

Chapter Thirteen: Restoring the Constitution

1. Frédéric Bastiat, The Law, 1850.
2. U.S. Constitution, Article III, § 1.
3. U.S. Constitution, Article II, § 2.
4. U.S. Constitution, Article II, § 4.
5. Franklin Roosevelt, "Fireside Chat on Reorganization of the Judiciary," March 9, 1937.
6. Gregory A. Caldeira, "FDR's Court Packing Plan in the Court of Public Opinion." Paper prepared for delivery at the 1999 Annual Meeting of the American Political Science Association, August 15, 1999. Available at pswebsbs.ohio-state.edu.
7. "Garner, John Nance," biography. Available at www.rra.dst.tx.us. Prior to the court packing proposal, Garner had been Roosevelt's primary liaison with Congress. The

vice president was thought by many observers to be the second most powerful leader in Washington, behind only FDR himself.

8. Letter from Chief Justice Hughes to Senator Burton K. Wheeler, March 22, 1937.

9. The "Four Horsemen," as the justices were known, were James McReynolds, Willis Van Devanter, Pierce Butler, and George Sutherland. Justice Owen Roberts and Chief Justice Charles Evans Hughes frequently voted with the four to form narrow majorities against New Deal legislation on constitutional grounds.

10. "Members of the Supreme Court of the United States." Available at www.supreme-courtus.gov/about/members.pdf.

11. U.S. Constitution, Article IV, § 4.

12. John Pickering, judge of the U.S. District Court for New Hampshire; removed from office March 12, 1804. Samuel Chase, associate justice of the Supreme Court; acquitted March 1, 1805. James H. Peck, judge of the U.S. District Court for Missouri; acquitted January 31, 1831. West H. Humphreys, judge of the U.S. District Court for the middle, eastern, and western districts of Tennessee; removed from office June 26, 1862. Charles Swayne, judge of the U.S. District Court for the northern district of Florida; acquitted February 27, 1905. Robert W. Archbald, associate judge, U.S. Commerce Court; removed January 13, 1913. George W. English, judge of the U.S. District Court for the eastern district of Illinois; resigned November 4, 1926; proceedings dismissed. Harold Louderback, judge of the U.S. District Court for the northern district of California; acquitted May 24, 1933. Halsted L. Ritter, judge of the U.S. District Court for the southern district of Florida; removed from office April 17, 1936. Harry E. Claiborne, judge of the U.S. District Court for the district of Nevada; removed from office October 9, 1986. Alcee L. Hastings, judge of the U.S. District Court for the southern district of Florida; removed from office October 20, 1988. Walter L. Nixon, judge of the U.S. District Court for Mississippi; removed from office November 3, 1989. Available at www.infoplease.com/ipa/A0194049.html.

13. William Rehnquist, *Grand Inquests* (New York: William Morrow & Co., 1992), 76. At the time and up until the late nineteenth century, in addition to sitting on the Supreme Court, justices were expected to travel judicial circuits around the country and preside over civil and criminal trials in conjunction with lower court judges.

14. Ibid. The Sedition Act, enacted in 1798, made it illegal to make derogatory remarks against the president or Congress.

15. Ibid., 22–23.

16. Ibid., 59.

17. Ibid.

18. Ibid.

19. Ibid., 60.

20. Ibid., 77.

21. Ibid., 104. On only two of the articles was there even a majority vote in favor of conviction, and on none was there the two-thirds majority required for conviction.

22. Ibid., 114.

23. Raoul Berger, *Impeachment: The Constitutional Problems* (Cambridge, MA: Harvard University Press, 1973), 53.

24. 28 U.S.C. 372 (1980).

25. Ibid. The Judicial Conference of the United States was created by an act of Congress in 1922 (it was originally called the Conference of Senior Circuit Judges) to be the principal policy-making body for the federal judiciary. In 1948, the name was changed to the Judicial Conference of the United States. In 1957, federal district judges were added to the conference.

26. Ibid.

27. 28 U.S.C 372 (2004).

28. Judges, judicial committees, or the judicial conference under the statute have full subpoena power for the purposes of investigating a complaint against a judge.

29. 28 U.S.C. 372 (1980).

30. *Reno v. American Arab Anti-Discrimination Committee*, 525 U.S. 471 (1999). Congress also has limited judicial review in the 1996 Prison Litigation Reform Act, in which the scope of the judiciary's authority was severely restricted in the nature of the relief it could grant in altering prison conditions. Also, in the Antiterrorism and Effective Death Penalty Act, Congress restricted the number of habeas corpus petitions inmates can make to federal courts. Such limitations, however, would have to be included in each piece of legislation Congress passes. Another example is when the House of Representatives voted 233–194 in July 2004 for the Marriage Protection Act, a measure that would limit the Court's jurisdiction in determining the constitutionality of the Defense of Marriage Act.

31. 42 U.S.C. 1997 (2004).

32. 22 U.S.C. 22 (2004).

33. Mary Fitzgerald and Alan Cooperman, "Marriage Protection Act Passes," *Washington Post*, July 23, 2004.

34. U.S. Constitution, Article I, § 5. "Each House shall be the Judge of the Elections, Returns and Qualifications of its own Member..."

35. *Powell v. McCormack*, 395 U.S. 486 (1996).

36. Ibid., 490.

37. Ibid., 549.

38. I would suggest three-year intervals between terms and filling unexpired judicial terms by the same laws and customs that pertain to filling unexpired terms in the Senate or other fixed term offices. In other words, should a justice die, be removed, or leave office voluntarily at any point in the term, his or her successor would serve until the original term expires. This would ensure that the staggering of the terms

of office would be preserved regardless of how many vacancies occur during any single presidential term or Congress.

39. "'The magic number in the Senate is 60, not 50,' Senator Charles E. Schumer, the New York Democrat who sits on the Judiciary Committee, said in an interview. Mr. Schumer added, 'If the president nominates people who are not part of the mainstream but who are far off, who will try to make law, not interpret it, and who will be way over to the ideological extreme, the controversy over judges will be alive.'" Sheryl Gay Stolberg, "Despite G.O.P. Gain, Fight Over Judges Remains," *New York Times*, November 5, 2004.

40. Linda Greenhouse, "Life at the Court Proceeds, but with Sadness and Uncertainty," *New York Times*, November 7, 2004 .

41. Ibid. See also Charles Lane, "Following Rehnquist," *Washington Post*, October 30, 2004.

42. Lane, "Following Rehnquist."

43. Neal A. Lewis, "Clinton Pulls a Fast One," *New York Times*, December 31, 2000.

44. Greenhouse, "Life at the Court Proceeds, but with Sadness and Uncertainty."

45. Thomas Jefferson. Available at www.quotedb.com.

INDEX